Value Creation 4.0

Marketing Products in the 21st Century

Value Creation 4.0

Marketing Products in the 21st Century

Gábor REKETTYE

With global case contributions by

Xiaoliang **Fan**, S. **Gayathri**, Shirshendu **Ganguli**, Rajashekharaiah **Jagadeesh**, Rita **Lukács**, Ismaila Ola **Ogundega**, Blessing **Okpala**, Árpád **Papp-Váry**, Ganes M. **Pandya**, Nilay J. **Shah**, Ratan **Taparia**, Tanya **Tewari**, Vasanthi Reena **Williams**, Bo **Yang**, Ahmet Murat **Yetkin**

TRANSNATIONAL PRESS LONDON

2019

Value Creation 4.0 - Marketing Products in the 21st Century
By Gábor REKETTYE

First Published in 2019 by TRANSNATIONAL PRESS LONDON in the United Kingdom, 12 Ridgeway Gardens, London, N6 5XR, UK.
www.tplondon.com

Transnational Press London® and the logo and its affiliated brands are registered trademarks.

Requests for permission to reproduce material from this work should be sent to:
sales@tplondon.com

Paperback (Colour)
ISBN: 978-1-912997-21-3
Paperback (B&W)
ISBN: 978-1-912997-24-4
Hardcover (Colour)
ISBN: 978-1-912997-25-1

Cover Design: Gizem Çakır
Cover image: Thanks to Andre Benz (andre-benz-LEikIOMSxfs-unsplash at unsplash.com)

www.tplondon.com

SUMMARY CONTENT

CONTENT

ABOUT THE AUTHOR

Gábor Rekettye is a Professor Emeritus at the Faculty of Business & Economics, Pécs University, and he is a honorary professor at Szeged University. He received his master's degree at the Budapest University of Economics, and his PhD at the Hungarian Academy of Sciences, both in economics. Dr Rekettye is the author of several textbooks, which are taught at different Universities in Hungary. In addition, he has written over 300 publications in Hungary and abroad. His latest book co-authored by Professor Jonathan Liu about pricing was published last year in London.

In his carrier he was working in the industry, in foreign trade and for five year he has served as commercial counsellor of Hungary in Tokyo, Japan. Between 1993 and 1996, he was the Dean of the Business School at the University of Pécs. For 16 years, between 1993 and 2009 he was heading the Marketing Department of the School. He has served as Chairman of the Hungary Japan Economic Club, as chair of the Hungarian Association of Marketing Educators, as chairperson of the Editorial Board of the Hungarian Journal of Marketing & Management.

Gábor Rekettye received the highest scientific title in Hungary, 'The Doctor of the Hungarian Academy of Sciences' in 2003. In 2005, he was elected to Chairman of the Committee of Marketing Science at the Hungarian Academy of Sciences. He was decorated by the President of Hungary with the Hungarian Order of Merit Officers Cross in 2013.

CASE CONTRIBUTORS

Mrs Xiaoliang Fan, PhD student at the Faculty of Business and Economics, University of Pécs, Master of Business Administration from the University of Science and Technology of China (USTC), worked at Huishang Bank in China for 14 years.

Dr S. Gayathri holds a Ph.D in Corporate Governance from The University of Madras, India. Her teaching and research interests include Strategic Management, Innovation, Sustainability and CSR. She is currently associated with Vels Institute of Science, Technology and Advanced Studies, Chennai.

Dr Shirshendu Ganguli is a Professor of Marketing with more than 18 years of corporate and academic experience. He has many publications in international and national journals, magazines and books (book chapters and cases). He handles marketing and research methodology related courses. He is affiliated with T A Pai Management Institute, Manipal, India.

Dr Rajashekharaiah Jagadeesh is working as Professor of Operations Management at SDM IMD, Mysore, India, where he teaches subjects like Quality Management, Technology Management and Innovation, Supply Chain Management, and Quantitative Techniques. He has served as an Adjunct Faculty at Fox Business School, Temple University, Philadelphia, USA.

Dr Rita Lukács is an Assistant Professor of the Institute of Tourism and Marketing at Budapest Metropolitan University. Rita has more than 10 years' experience in Corporate Social Responsibility (CSR) as a researcher and as a consultant, with a special focus on CSR communication.

Dr Ismaila Ola Ogundega holds a PhD and MBA from the Cardiff Metropolitan University, UK. He also holds a BSc degree in Electrical Engineering from the University of Lagos, Nigeria. He is experienced in telecoms, business, project management and lecturing.

Dr Blessing Okpala is a PhD graduate in Business and Management from Cardiff Metropolitan University Wales United Kingdom. Her thesis focused on the operational performance of the UK retail industry: statistical analysis of operational KPIs and their impacts on profitability. She also holds an MBA in International Business and B.Sc in Parasitology. She is a positive and result-oriented individual constantly seeking ways to proffer solutions to real world problems. She has interest in technology, statistical analysis, business development and management.

Dr Árpád Papp-Váry (PhD) is professor and Dean at the Budapest Metropolitan University, His teaching and research areas are country branding, city branding, personal branding, sports branding and branded entertainment. Árpád is the author of four books and several hundred publications, most of which are available online at www.papp-vary.hu.

Dr Ganes M. Pandya enjoys teaching and learning at T A Pai Management Institute. Manipal – India. He has more than two decades of academic experience and handles Decision Science courses.

Mr Nilay J. Shah is a Postgraduate Student at T A Pai Management Institute Manipal – India. Prior to his post-graduation, Mr.Shah was Project Management Officer at Tata Consultancy Services for three years.

Mr Ratan Taparia works at Helios – Bangalore, India as Marketing Manager and is passionate about creating innovative strategies for Marketing. He is an alumni of T A Pai Management Institute, Manipal – India and worked in domains of sales, marketing and product development for Titan Company Limited.

Ms Tanya Tewari is a Postgraduate Student at T A Pai Management Institute, Manipal – India. Prior to his post-graduation, Ms. Tewari was Business Development Associate at Cognizant Technology solutions for 3 years.

Prof Vasanthi Reena Williams, specializes in Strategic Management, Human Resource Management and Marketing Management and has several papers published to her credit. Her experience spans 26 years as an academic and administrator at various institutions. She is presently heading the Vidya Vikas Post Graduate Department of Commerce, affiliated to the University of Mysore.

Mr Bo Yang is a PhD student at the Faculty of Business and Economics, University of Pécs, Master of Business Administration from the University of Science and Technology of China (USTC).

Mr Ahmet Murat Yetkin has been studying for his PhD at the University of Pécs in Hungary since 2015. He graduated from the University of Warsaw with a Master's degree in Economics. He has project management, business development, and digital sales experience gained from working for IBM in Slovakia for nearly four years, and having completed IBM Global Sales School and IBM Software Top Gun trainings.

ACKNOWLEDGEMENTS

An author coming from a Central and Eastern European (CEE) country had to learn a lot to catch up with the level of those Western European and North American academics that were born into an already working and effective system of marketing practice and science. I was very fortunate in the process of closing up to their way of thinking. In 1989 when the big transformation from communism to market system took place in the CEE countries, I just returned home from a five-year practical work experience in an extraordinary capitalist country, Japan. I joined my University and very soon was invited by the consortium of the best American Universities to visit them and see what and how they teach. These visits had a deep impact on my thinking. Only a few of my colleagues can boast of having worked with and learned from professors, like Michael E. Porter, Benson P. Shapiro, W. Earl Sasser, Thomas R. Piper or John Quelch at Harvard Business School; Philip Kotler, Sidney J. Levy, Lakshman Krishnamurthi, Dipak C. Jain at Kellogg Graduate School of Management.

Then in 1994, I was teaching one semester /three months at Ohio University School of Business where I had the possibility to work together with Professor John R. Schermerhorn, Jr. and Professor Ashok Gupta, the latter one contributed with two chapters to my book published in Hungary under the title "Value Creation in Marketing", and this cooperation led to a joint research project.

The next great influence on my thinking came from Middlesex University London, where I spent one month and started a co-operation between our Universities, which continues to this day. Here I worked together with Professor Abby Ghobadian and Professor Jonathan Liu. We have had many joint publications, and Jonathan is my co-author of the book "Pricing – The New Frontier" published in 2018.

I also want to acknowledge how much I learned from my colleagues here at the Institute of Marketing and Tourism at the University of Pécs and the Faculty of Business Administration of the University of Szeged, where I have been teaching for ten years. My academic friends from the Netherlands, Finland, Croatia, and Poland also influenced my thinking, and indirectly contributed to the birth of this book.

I also want to thank Ms. Ágnes Oláh for her help in preparing the English text of the book.

Finally, thanks to Professor Ibrahim Sirkeci, the publications editor and his staff at Transnational Press London for their work on publishing this book.

Special thanks go to the National Excellence in Higher Education

Programme in Hungary, since the underlying research has been conducted as part of this programme (reference number of the contract: 20765-3/2018/FEKUTSTRAT).

PREFACE

The primary aim of a preface is to explain the title, the objectives and the concept of books. If it is written by the author himself, it will inevitably become subjective to a certain degree. I think that it is good for the reader since it helps to understand better the aims and the thoughts of the author.

Well, let us start at the beginning. My book entitled 'Value Creation in Marketing' was published in the middle of my career in 1997 by KJK the most famous Hungarian publisher in economics and law. When I first held the book in my hands, I felt overjoyed. It made me remember the student years I spent at the Karl Marx University of Economics in Budapest. At that time when I came across the books written by my renowned professors and published by KJK, I could not help but think – and I was not the only one – WOW, that is amazing to have a book published by KJK. Although I had already had a few books published by other publishers, I still felt very proud that I managed to get there myself, even if somewhat later, as I missed out 17 years from my teaching and research career while I was practising the profession.

The book became a success partly because, as many local academics claimed, it introduced the concept of value creation to the marketing profession in Hungary, and partly because the two editions of the book have made it the most cited marketing work in the country.

Nowadays, I no longer get overexcited about the publication of any of my new books, but I felt pleased when Professor Veres (the editor of the marketing series of Akadémiai Kiadó) asked me to rewrite this topic after 20 years. I did it in 2018. The market of the Hungarian books is somewhat limited since less than 15 million people understand this language in the world. That is why it is understandable that every ambitious academic endeavours to appear with their work on the large English language market. That is the reason why I was happy when Professor Sirkeci from Transnational Press London offered me the possibility to publish the book in English. It is my second book published in the United Kingdom, after the book Pricing – The New Frontier.

So, why Value Creation 4.0? Well, there is a subjective and an objective reason for this. The subjective one is that it is my fourth book dealing with value creation. The objective one is that we are living in the age of the fourth industrial revolution ('Industry 4.0'). The cyber age of Industry 4.0 represents radical changes in many industrial sectors, in value creation and customers' value judgements. With this title, I wanted to draw attention to the situation which poses new challenges and risks for the whole of humanity.

The book takes an essentially practice-oriented approach. It does so even at the expense of theory. Researchers usually like to read deep theories, which appeared in scientific journals. The book intends to highlight the importance of the topic, define its conceptual framework and present its practical applications. The book is therefore primarily recommended for practitioners – product, brand and line managers, and so on. The topics of the book together with the supporting exhibits and cases – which also include international dimensions – provide information for them that can help increase their competitiveness.

The book can also be very handy in higher education. Whole courses can be built on it, as the book comprises 4 parts and 14 chapters which can provide the basis for lectures. Each part is illustrated with cases, and some of the more than 30 exhibits could be used for the efficient processing of the material and for further reflection.

I am convinced that the book is easy to read and was published in a format and design that meet the visual expectations of the modern reader, and as such can help the work of both the managers reading the book and the students learning from it. The illustrations and photos can facilitate understanding and processing the contents.

Gábor Rekettye

London

INTRODUCTION

Marketing represents two things: a business philosophy and a set of instruments. Marketing-oriented business philosophy is nothing other than the ability, which puts the consumers, the users, collectively known as the customers, in the centre of attention. Any organization using this approach is seeking to make its supply meet customers' needs as much as possible, and create products that represent the highest possible "value" to them. The marketing approach requires companies, which used to be preoccupied with their internal affairs, were inward-looking and production- or product-oriented to change radically and reach outward, and take into consideration the needs of the environment and the customers.

Creating value for the customers, "reaching outward" requires a proper set of instruments. This is the other important aspect of applying marketing in businesses. There is interdependence between the philosophy and the set of instruments; the direction of operation of these instruments is determined by the market-oriented way of thinking, but putting it into practice requires the existence of the instruments. However, it must be emphasized that the customer-oriented philosophy is the determinant of the two. The marketing approach of a big company is not necessarily better just because its managing director talks about how consumer-oriented the company is in the brochures prepared by the marketing department while the employees dealing with customers are rude, and the quality of the company's products cannot match the competition than the approach of a small business which may not have a marketing department yet, but the owner of which makes every effort to meet his/her customers' needs.

Marketing contributes to creating value in two ways:

- it attempts to identify *what is considered valuable* by the customers using market research tools;

- it actively participates in its field in creating, communicating and delivering this value, to the customers.

PART I: VALUE

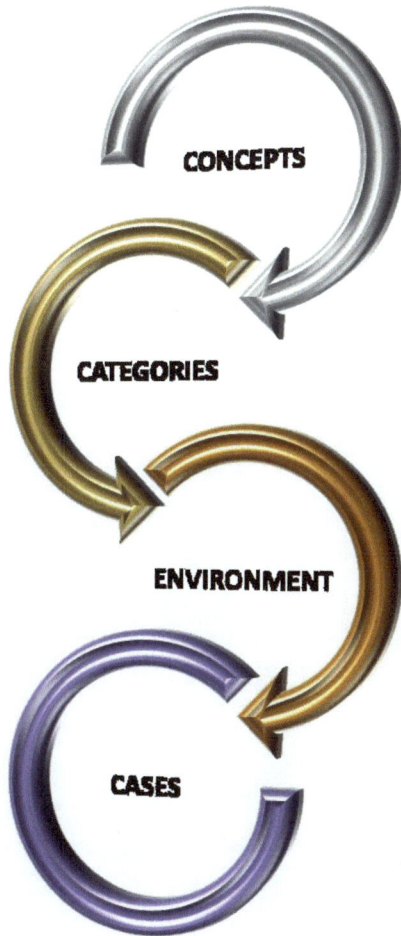

CONCEPTS

CATEGORIES

ENVIRONMENT

CASES

CHAPTER 1

MARKETING INTERPRETATION OF THE VALUE CONCEPT

For customers to accept a product or service which satisfies their needs, the product or service must represent *value* for them. (Chikán – Demeter, 1999). It is difficult to define and even more difficult to quantify what constitutes *value* for the customers. The concept tries to capture the place a specific product occupies in the customers' value systems. Based on their previous experience, information and assumptions people develop a so-called 'value expectation' and seek to make the best buy within the limits of their financial resources, the far from perfect information available to them and their room to manoeuvre, in other words, to maximize the value obtainable. If a product reaches or exceeds this value expectation the customer is satisfied, and the company can expect a rebuy.

Customer value and customer satisfaction are also dependent on the price or on the other costs incurred during the purchase and the use of the product.

Consumers are interested in obtaining the highest possible value at the lowest possible cost. (Microeconomics calls reservation price the highest amount customers are willing to pay for a product.) Companies, on the other hand, work towards bringing the price as close to the customer value as possible and create as big a gap, i.e., a margin, between the price and costs of production as possible.

1.1. THE PERCEIVED VALUE

It is important to note that when we talk about customer value in marketing, we always mean the so-called *perceived value*. This distinction is also important within the company because technical professionals think in terms of functions and performances that can be measured and described by different parameters, while marketing professionals always focus on the customers and their perceptions.

Figure 1.1. Factors influencing perceived value

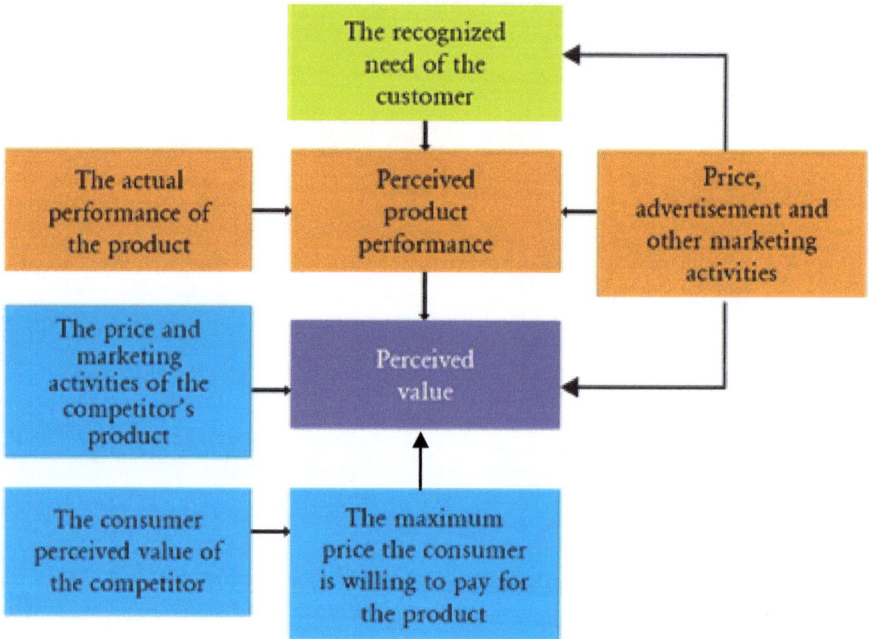

Figure 1.1. presents the factors that influence perceived value. First, it is important to find out which of the benefits offered by the product are recognized and considered necessary by the consumers. There are two factors which determine how and to what extent the potential performance of a product becomes accepted value: the company's marketing activity, and the way the competing (substitute) products are marketed, including the related marketing efforts by the competitor companies. From a practical point of view, the two main questions concern how it is possible to get to know the main components of perceived value, and how to measure the influence thereof. There is a consensus in the marketing literature that *perceived value can be defined as the trade-off between the benefits offered to the customer by the product or service and the costs (monetary and non-monetary) incurred by the customer (Figure 1.2.).*

Today's value-conscious consumers cannot be persuaded by the best products or the lowest prices alone. Their decisions are most often driven by the thorough assessment of the benefits gained and the costs resulting from the purchase and the use of the product.

Figure 1.2. Definition of perceived value

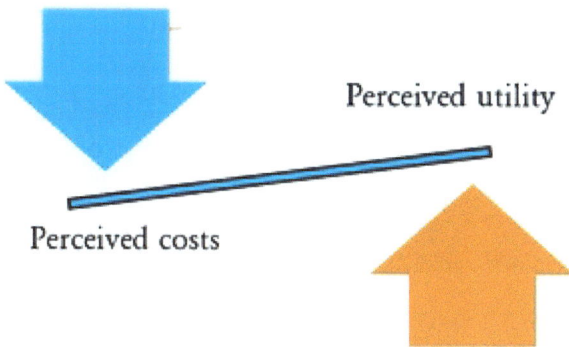

1.2. THE ELEMENTS OF VALUE

Based on the literature and our empirical research the two sides – the value offered to the consumers and the costs incurred by them – can be defined as presented in Figure 1.3.

Figure 1.3. The anatomy of customer value

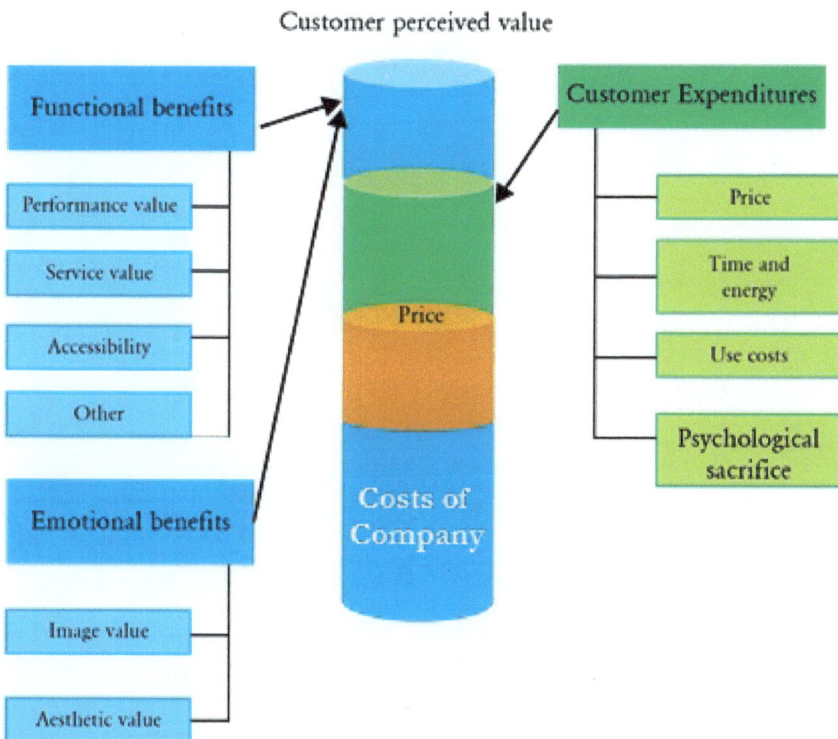

Customer perceived value

Functional benefits

Performance value

Service value

Accessibility

Other

Emotional benefits

Image value

Aesthetic value

Costs of Company

Price

Customer Expenditures

Price

Time and energy

Use costs

Psychological sacrifice

The value offered to customers is, in fact, the *benefit* of the product or the service, or in a broader sense its *quality*. Quality is one of the most often used terms in the management literature, yet its definition is far from evident. Using a marketing approach for defining the quality of products and services requires that the expectations of the customers are taken as the starting point.

The problem is that customer expectation varies by product categories and by customer groups. Nevertheless, we believe that expected benefits can be classified into two main categories: Functional and Emotional benefits.

The share of these two elements varies in the different product categories.

EXHIBIT 1.1. THE 30 ELEMENTS OF VALUE ACCORDING TO BAIN & CO.

Given company practices usually focus only on one side of the equation illustrated in figure 2, namely on the costs and even more restrictively on the *price*, Bain & Company Inc. tried in 2015 to develop a general classification system for the different elements of value. Their results were published in the Harvard Business Review (Almquist et al., 2015). According to their study, the elements of value are nothing but the extension of Maslow's hierarchy of needs when people are viewed as consumers (see next figure[1]).

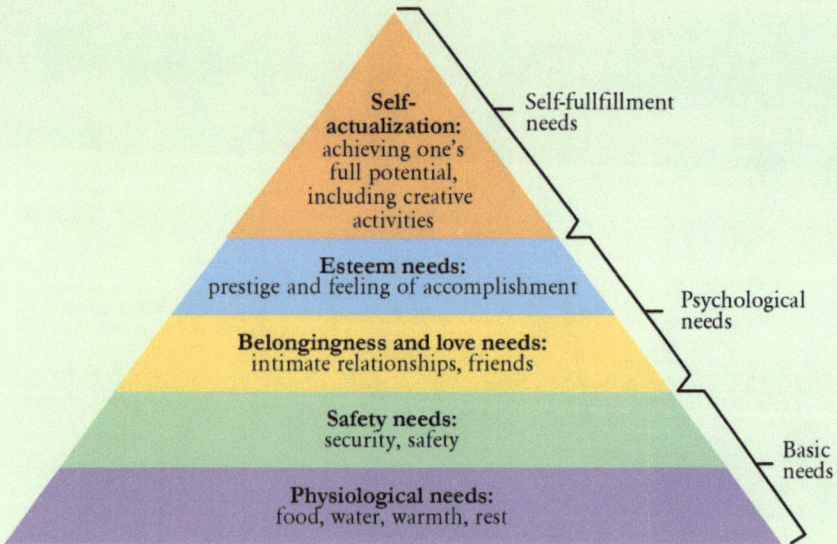

The company conducted quantitative and qualitative research for a decade including popular "laddering" interviews to find preference motives, which led

---

[1] Source: Maslow's Hierarchy of Needs, By Saul McLeod, updated 2018 (https://www.simplypsychology.org/maslow.html)

the researchers to identify 30 elements of value. In addition to the functional-emotional division, they introduced the life-changing and social impact value categories (See next figure).

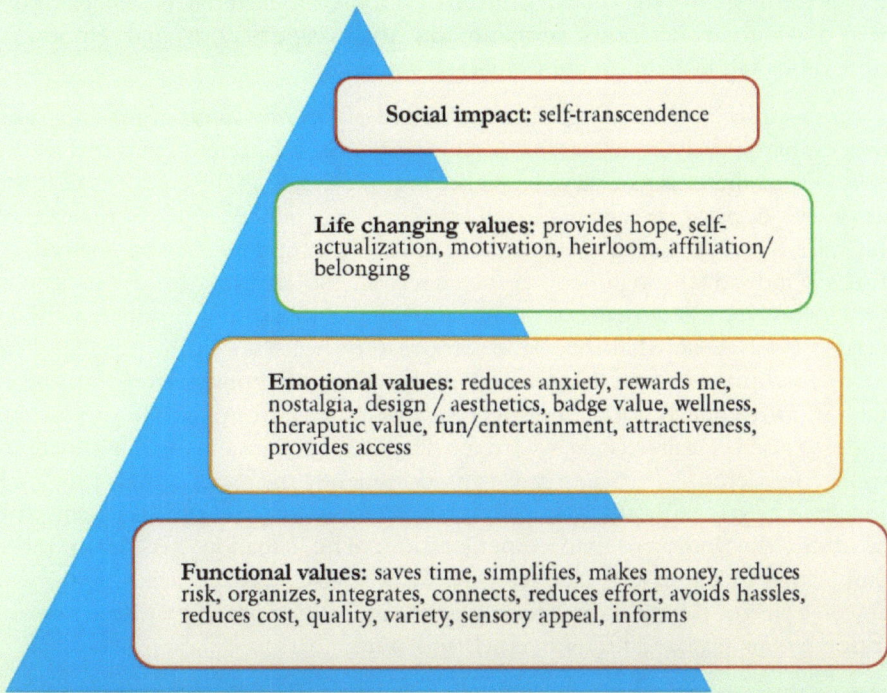

Social impact: self-transcendence

Life changing values: provides hope, self-actualization, motivation, heirloom, affiliation/belonging

Emotional values: reduces anxiety, rewards me, nostalgia, design / aesthetics, badge value, wellness, theraputic value, fun/entertainment, attractiveness, provides access

Functional values: saves time, simplifies, makes money, reduces risk, organizes, integrates, connects, reduces effort, avoids hassles, reduces cost, quality, variety, sensory appeal, informs

The study also concludes that the elements listed above are not equally important. The customers' opinion is primarily influenced by the **quality** in almost all sectors; the other elements have a varying degree of importance depending on the industry. For instance, the order of importance of the first five elements is the following:

• In the case of food and drinks: quality, sensory appeal, variety, design/aesthetics, therapeutic value;

• In the case of retail sale of clothing: quality, variety, hassle avoidance, design/aesthetics, time saving;

• In the case of smartphones: quality, effort reduction, variety, organizes, connects;

• In the case of retail banking: quality, access, heirloom, hassle avoidance, anxiety reduction.

Feelings and emotions always play and will continue to play an important role in how customers evaluate products. As Bagozzi et al. (1999, 202) said: "Emotions are ubiquitous throughout marketing" — and will always be, we may add.

It is true even if today the rapid development of digitalization allows customers to get detailed information about the operation and performance of a given product and, as a result, make more rational decisions. It can nevertheless be concluded that in the case of consumer goods, for example, customers most often base their decisions primarily on their expectations and emotional impressions rather than on the functional value.

It must also be emphasized that the nature of *first time buying* of products and services, particularly in the case of consumer goods, is different from that of the rebuy. From the point of view of marketing, the essential difference is that the customer's decision to rebuy is based on actual experiences, while in the case of first-time buy it is based on expectations and perceptions. When customers, primarily individual consumers, make a decision about buying for the first time, they do not have any real experience about how to use the product, so their decision is based on what they have seen, read or heard about the product. The rate of first-time buy and rebuy varies in the different product categories: most sales of convenience goods are the result of repeated buys, while the sale of shopping and specialty goods, where the period of rebuy is so long that the rebuy can be considered as first-time buy, is predominantly the result of first-time buy. First-time buy is particularly important in the case of new products: this will constitute the basis of market penetration. The situation gets even more complicated in the case of services. There is a vast literature available on this subject. Some of the most outstanding works in international literature are books written by Grönroos (2007), Lovelock and Wirtz (2011).

ATTRACTIVENESS

The factors influencing first-time buying are different from those of rebuy. *First-time buying* is determined mainly by *the value perceived/assumed before consumption or use*. The value recognized before purchase is called "attractiveness" by Nilson (1992).

Consequently, one of the main tasks of product policy (or we could call it *value management*) is to make the product attractive and so incite customers to try and buy the product.

During the rebuy, customers primarily base their decision on their experiences gained from the actual use of the product or the reflection of these in their memory. Nowadays, this experience is not restricted to potential buyers; it also includes the experiences of those who shared them on social media. *How successfully the product satisfies the needs of the customers* proves to be more important in this situation than attractiveness. Also, this is determined by the quality (in its broad sense) and the functional benefits of the product/service. The experiences of actual use naturally have an impact on attractiveness in an indirect way, through the experiences of others and word-of-mouth advertising, and can stimulate or hold back first-time buying.

HIGH-QUALITY NEED SATISFACTION

The practices used by countries with highly developed markets prove that those products can become truly successful which not only satisfy the needs of the customers but which do it at an extremely high-quality level.

Nilson (1992) talks downright about *over-satisfaction*, while a survey conducted in the UK in 1989 by the Nielsen research institute proved that the ten most successful products of groceries had been on the market for 42 years on average (for over 70 years by now). The secret of their success lies in their commitment to value management and the continuous improvement of their products. These products are listed here:

Persil detergents,

Nescafé coffees,

Whiskas cat food,

Ariel detergents,

Andrex toilet paper,

Coca-Cola soft drinks,

PG Tips tea,

Pedigree Chum dog food,

Heinz beans and

Flora margarine.

The photo shows an old Swedish Persil enamel advertising sign

Although customers are faced with new products every day on the market, most of the rebuys are generated by products in the maturity phase of their life cycle, which supports the importance of rebuy. Other researchers (Shapiro, Kotler) emphasize the importance of customer retention and provide evidence that acquiring new customers is always more costly for a company than to retain the existing ones by continuously developing their products and improving customer service. Product development in the marketing literature usually means the development of new products. The literature refers to this with the acronym

NPD (new product development). Well, without undermining the importance of NPD, we cannot but emphasize the need for developing the already existing products. We can call it OPD (old product development). In addition to *attractiveness* and *high-quality need satisfaction,* the literature has lately added the notion of *customer experience (*CX) to the key factors of success. Although the literature refers to this term all the time, it is very difficult to define it.

CUSTOMER EXPERIENCE According to Forrester marketing research company based in Cambridge in the United States, customer experience reflects the quality of the *interactions* with the company and is composed of three things. From the product's point of view, it means that it should be:

USEFUL - i.e., it should deliver value for the customer,

USABLE - i.e., it should be easy to find and engage with the value, and

ENJOYABLE - i.e., the customer should enjoy using the product and should be emotionally attached to it.

Interaction means any two-way relationship between the customers and the company. "When customers navigate your Web site, call into your contact centre, when they talk to one of your employees, use your products, respond to your emails, that's when they're making judgments about whether or not you meet their needs, are easy to do business with, and are enjoyable to do business with. This is what customer experience is - says Harley Manning, research director of Forrester. (Source: https://www.usertesting.com/blog/2016/03/09/ what-is-cx/)

Positive customer experience leads to increased customer loyalty and contributes to sales growth. In the columns of Harvard Business Review, P. Kriss reported about a study conducted among American companies whose turnover exceeded one billion dollars. Researchers concluded that in transaction-based businesses customers who had positive customer experience spent 140% more on the company's products than those who had poor customer experience. Similarly, in subscription-based businesses customers who gained bad experiences terminated the relationship with the company within a year, while those with positive experiences remained loyal for at least six years (Kriss, 2014).

Apple is one of the best examples of how to create a positive customer experience. Data presented in Figure 1.4. illustrate the rate of loyalty of Americans who wanted to buy new smartphones in 2017.

Figure 1.4. Loyalty rate to smartphones in the US in 2017 expressed in %

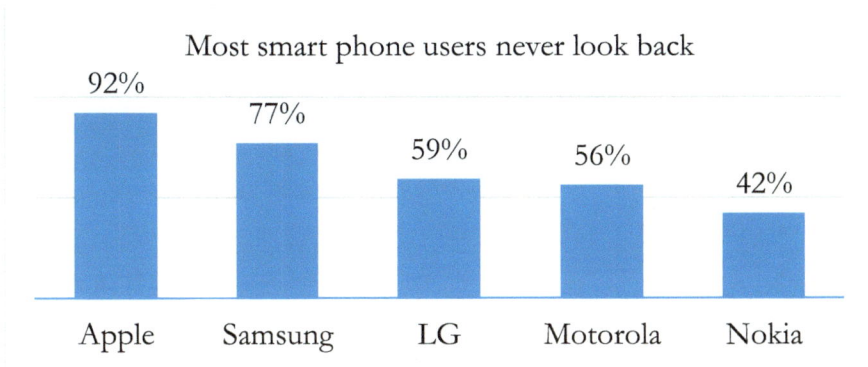

Most smart phone users never look back

| Apple | Samsung | LG | Motorola | Nokia |
| 92% | 77% | 59% | 56% | 42% |

Source: April 2017 survey of 1,000 US smartphone owners that are likely to upgrade in the next 12 months. Share that intend to replace their current phone with another from the same vendor. Morgan Stanley via media reports

To summarize the above, it can be concluded that the task of product and value management is to try to maximize the value perceived and accepted by the customers (Figure 1.5.).

Figure 1.5. Maximizing value

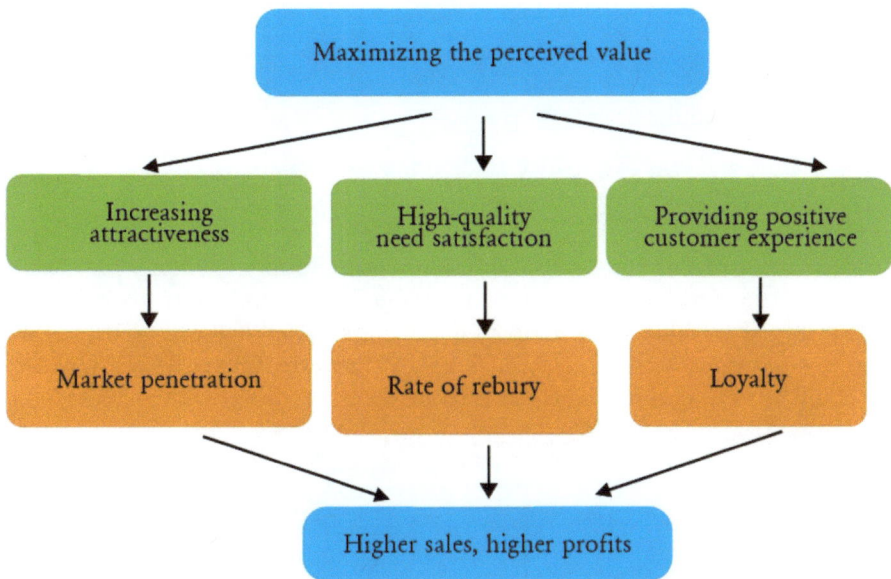

Maximizing the perceived value

Increasing attractiveness → Market penetration

High-quality need satisfaction → Rate of rebury

Providing positive customer experience → Loyalty

Higher sales, higher profits

The motives and circumstances of purchasing industrial products are different (Törőcsik, 1996). In reporting the findings of his research conducted in the information technology and communication industries, Lapierre (2000) classified the drivers of benefit and sacrifice perceived by the customers as follows:

❖ Benefits linked to products

    ➤ Alternative solution to the given problem

    ➤ Product quality

    ➤ Product customization

❖ Benefits linked to services

    ➤ Responsiveness

    ➤ Flexibility

    ➤ Reliability

    ➤ Technical competence

❖ Benefits linked to the relationship with the seller

    ➤ Image of the seller company

    ➤ Confidence in the salesperson

    ➤ Solidarity of the seller to the buyer

Cost structure:

❖ Attachment to the product and the service

    ➤ The price

❖ Attachment to the relationship

    ➤ Time and energy sacrifice

    ➤ Conflict management

He concluded that the value offered by information technology products is more than the product itself, more than the service and more than just the relationship. The value is made up of the different combinations of these three sources – product, service, and relationship (Lapierre, 2000). This conclusion can easily be extended to the whole B2B market.

CHAPTER 2

CLASSIFICATION OF VALUE-EMBODYING PRODUCTS AND SERVICES

The product dimensions presented in the previous chapter can explain why companies need to develop different marketing strategies for their different product groups. In this part we review the classification most often used by the marketing literature. Products can primarily be grouped into two large categories:

Consumer goods – Products and services purchased by people in order to satisfy their personal needs.

Industrial goods – Products purchased for the production of other products or for ensuring the functioning of the business.

This distinction of products is essentially based on the differing objectives of customers and purchasers, as well as the differing buying behaviour of customers, rather than on the different product characteristics. Individual consumers enjoy a fairly high level of freedom in their buying decisions, especially when spending their so-called discretionary income. When deciding 'whether to buy or not' or 'what to buy', customers can freely choose from goods which are very distant from each other from the point of view of need satisfaction. Their decisions include both rational and emotional elements. By contrast, industrial or organizational customers have much more limited freedom in making decisions due to functional constraints, and they usually use more rational methods when choosing from these limited options. (When purchasing raw materials, a textile company can decide from what source they want to buy the cotton, but only the cotton and nothing else.) Several authors treat the market *of institutions and public entities* as a separate category due to their different buying (purchasing) motives. Contrary to company purchases, their main motive is not further production or direct gain from use.

> The question 'what can be a product?' is answered in a broader sense: Anything is considered a product that can be marketed. Beside goods and services, places, concepts, people, events, organizations, information, ideas, etc.

Such a place is the town of Pécs (located in Hungary) for example, which won the title of European Capital of Culture in 2010. This event was accompanied by significant marketing work (before, during and after). That's another matter that the success of the event was diminished somewhat by the global financial crisis which started in 2008.

Source: http://www.ep-webeditors.eu/2010/05/pecs-the-cultural-capital-of-europe-2010-and-more/

The 'consumer goods - industrial goods' distinction may contain overlaps. Fuel oil, electricity, flour, desks, etc. sold to households or individuals are considered to be consumer goods, but if companies purchase the same goods, they are referred to as industrial goods. Despite these overlaps, this classification has its own merits because even the same type of products may require the use of different marketing tools, including different product and pricing policies depending on whether they are sold to the consumers or organizations. The packaging, the presentation, the price can vary; the distribution channels are necessarily different, as are the most effective market influencing tools. Let us consider, for example, cars: individual buyers will buy *one* car, companies may purchase several. The conditions of the so-called fleet-sale, therefore, will be very different.

Similarly to tangible goods, services can also be classified according to whether they target general consumers or non-general consumers. This way we can distinguish between *consumer services and non-consumer, industrial services.*

Consumer goods

- Products purchased by the final consumer for personal consumption.

Convenience goods

- Consumer goods which are purchased regularly by the customers with not much comparison or energy.

Shopping goods

- Customers make comparisons about the quality, the functions, the form and the price of competing products during the purchase decision.

Specialty goods

- Products having unique features and strong band awareness, a large group of customers are willing to make special efforts for their purchase.

2.1. CONSUMER GOODS

The marketing literature has, for a very long time (Copeland 1923), classified consumer goods according to typical consumer behaviour, especially the time and energy put into the purchase. The three-way categorization of consumer goods (convenience goods, shopping goods, and specialty goods) is generally accepted.

Convenience goods

The main features of *convenience goods* include that (1) consumers possess sufficient information about them before their purchase, and (2) they are purchased with little effort or time sacrifice. Consumers believe that the additional sacrifice of comparing the prices and quality of these goods is not worthwhile, and they are willing to purchase the readily available product.. For most customers. this category of goods includes vegetables, cheaper spices, basic cosmetics, bulbs, batteries, etc. The unit price of convenience goods is typically low; they are not subject to changes in fashion, do not weigh much and are purchased frequently. The literature uses two expressions for these products: FMCG - Fast Moving Consumer Goods and FMPG - Fast Moving Packed Goods.

These goods are not too important for the customers, so they are easily substituted. The right course of action for the producer is to distribute these products as widely as possible. Since retailers market several competing products and typically keep small amounts of each in stock, the producer has no choice but to advertise its products himself and sell them through wholesale.

Convenience goods can be categorized further. Within this category, McCarthy and Perreault (1987) distinguish between

- staple goods, which are purchased often and routinely, without too much

deliberation,

- impulse goods, which are purchased without planning to satisfy a sudden need triggered by on-site influences, and

- emergency products, which are bought urgently in situations of crisis. (e.g., a sudden rainfall - umbrella, a blizzard – snow chains, unexpected guests – ice cubes, a car broken down by the road - trailer, etc.) In such situations, the price is obviously not the most decisive factor.

In a hypermarket (e.g. in Interspar as above) tens of thousands of brands are displayed at the same time. It is not easy to stand out among them. That is why the use of distinctive packaging is important, as is the place where the product is placed within the shop.

Shopping goods

Before purchasing shopping goods, customers usually go through the decision-making process which was described in the previous chapter. They typically gather information via the Internet, visit several shops and compare the prices, the quality and the other characteristics of the product because they believe that the time and effort put into this process will be recouped by acquiring the best product. The distribution channel in the case of these products can be shorter. Retailers will order larger quantities and will be willing to take part in advertising the products. Brand awareness is essential, however, the reputation of the shop where the customer makes the purchase can often be just as important. This category of products includes, for example, less expensive outer garments, cheaper household appliances, and consumer electronics.

Specialty goods

With regard to specialty goods, customers are characterized by strong brand preferences and a higher degree of loyalty. This also means that during the decision journey many customers immediately drop into the 'loyalty loop'. The customers already know the product, the given brand represents a high value to them and they are not willing to substitute the given brand with a different one as in the case of the other two groups of products. They are ready to invest a considerable amount of money, time and energy into buying the preferred brand. Being aware of this consumer behaviour the manufacturers of specialty goods do not need to distribute their products broadly, it is sufficient to distribute them in one or a limited number of places. They can establish a direct connection with the retailer and can share the costs of advertising the products. These products include passenger cars, professional consumer electronics, and many other branded goods.

Table 2.1. Marketing of consumer goods

Marketing considerations	Convenience goods	Shopping goods	Specialty goods
Customer behaviour	Frequent purchases with little planning, low effort, few comparisons	Less frequent purchases, more planning and comparison (price, quality, design)	Strong brand preference, loyalty, low price sensitivity few comparisons, high purchase effort
Price	Low	Higher	High
Distribution	Widespread, the comfort of the place is pivotal	Fewer shops, selective distribution	Exclusive distribution, one or only a few shops in a market
Promotion	Mass communication typically by producers	Advertising and direct sales by both the producer and the trader	Precisely targeted by both the producer and the middleman
Examples	Toothpaste, newspapers, detergents	Household appliances, TV-s, furniture, clothing	Luxury products, such as Rolex watches, china products

In addition to the previously presented categories, consumer goods can also be classified according to durability: durable, semi-durable and non-durable/daily consumer goods.

> The three-way categorization of consumer goods presented above is closely related to how much the customer is „affected by" or involved in the purchase of the given product. With regard to the category of "involvement", most researchers agree that the level of "commitment" perceived by the consumer is composed of two main parts: a durable (enduring involvement, EI) and a situational (situational involvement, SI) component. These categories of involvement can be associated with the categorization of consumer goods. In the case of convenience goods, both the EI and the SI are low, while shopping goods are characterized by mostly SI and specialty goods by EI.

2.2. CLASSIFICATION OF INDUSTRIAL GOODS

There are several known ways to classify non-consumer goods. The grouping criteria used for the classification presented here are based on the roles the product plays in the production and operating processes of the buyer and its relationship with them. Because it determines (1) how important the product is for the buyer, (2) how the buyer company finances the purchase of the product, and (3) how the costs of the purchase are accounted for; and furthermore, what behaviour the buyer shows during the purchase of the product as a result. According to the marketing literature, three typical buying behaviours can be distinguished during the purchase of industrial products:

- *new-task buying*, the purpose of which is to satisfy a new need recognized in the company,

- *straight rebuy*, the routine repetition of former purchases, and

- *modified rebuy*, which includes the review of previous purchases to a certain degree.

The classification of industrial goods includes three main categories:

• MATERIALS AND PARTS. Goods directly used during the manufacturing of the products (or the operation of the company), the value of which immediately and completely enters the manufacturer's products or services. Their purchase price can be recognized as a direct cost element of products (services).

• CAPITAL ITEMS. Goods directly linked to the buyer's production (operating) processes, but the purchase value of which does not directly and immediately enter the manufactured products or services, only over the long-term and in small parts. Their purchase, in general, cannot be recognized as a cost; they are rather considered as investment type resources and are depreciated over the years.

• SUPPLIES AND SERVICES. Goods only indirectly linked with the manufacturing-operating processes, which are used in the preparation, facilitation and improvement of the manufacturing process, but the purchase value of which does not directly enter the manufactured products or services. They are generally recognized as general cost.

Table 2.2. Characteristics of industrial buying processes

The type of process Characteristics	New-task buying	Modified rebuy	Straight rebuy
The time requirement	big	medium	little
Number of influencing factors	high	medium	low
Are the suppliers rated?	yes	sometimes	no
The amount of necessary information	big	medium	small

2.3. CLASSIFICATION OF SERVICES

In the developed economies the service sector makes by far the largest contribution to the gross domestic product, and the amount of money spent on purchasing services represents an ever-increasing share in consumer spending.

The share of the services sector in the production of the GDP is dependent from the level of development of the given country. For example according to the CIA Factbook estimation, it accounted in 2017 to 80.4% in the UK, to 80.2% in the USA, to 70.7% in the European Union, to 64.7% in Hungary and to 57.4% in Poland. .

Source: https://www.cia.gov/library/publications/the-world-factbook/fields/ 2012. html, retrieved in 25.11.2018

That is why the marketing literature felt the need decades ago to classify the services, similarly to tangible goods, into homogenous categories from marketing point of view. However, a generally accepted classification of services has still not yet been developed as in the case of tangible goods. There is, however, a general consensus on the characteristics of services which affect marketing activities. They are presented in the following figures and tables.

Figure 2.1. The characteristics of services

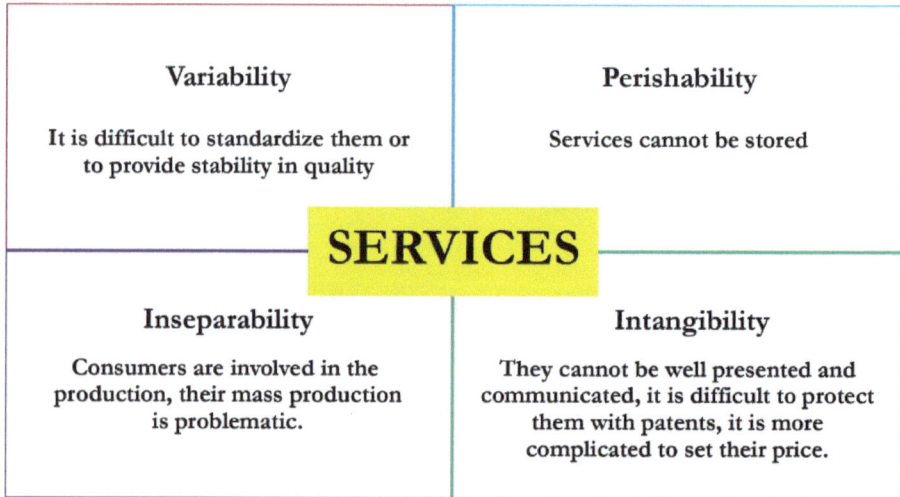

Variability	Perishability
It is difficult to standardize them or to provide stability in quality	Services cannot be stored
SERVICES	
Inseparability	Intangibility
Consumers are involved in the production, their mass production is problematic.	They cannot be well presented and communicated, it is difficult to protect them with patents, it is more complicated to set their price.

There are different classifications of services known from the literature, but most of them classify services primarily according to operational efficiency. Let us present two marketing focused classifications. Pride and Ferrel [1989, 747 p.] classify services as presented in Figure 2.2.

According to Lovelock [1992], answering the following questions may help us understand and classify services:

• What is the nature of the service?

• What kind of relationship exists between the service provider and the customers?

• To what extent can service providers benefit from their own value judgments and "customize" their services?

• What is the nature of the demand and the supply for the service?

• How are the services delivered to the customers?

The classification scheme used by Lovelock is presented in Table 2.3.

Figure 2.2. The classification of services according to Pride and Ferrer

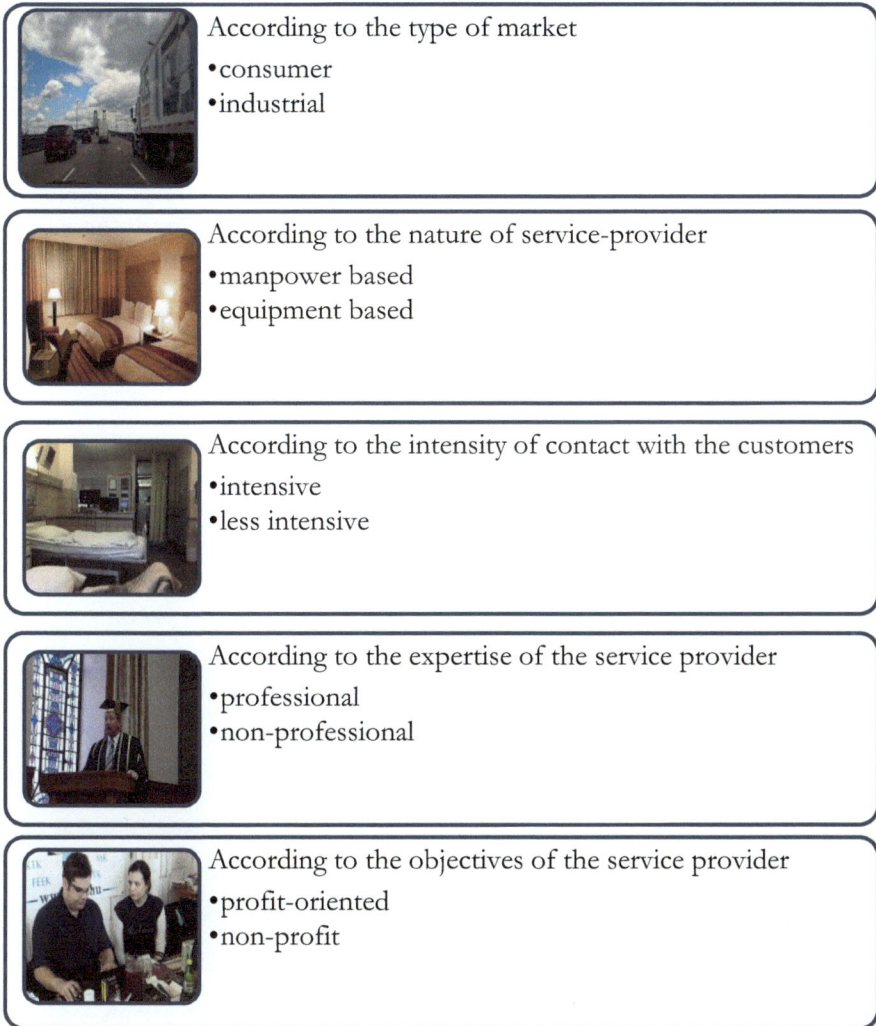

According to the type of market
•consumer
•industrial

According to the nature of service-provider
•manpower based
•equipment based

According to the intensity of contact with the customers
•intensive
•less intensive

According to the expertise of the service provider
•professional
•non-professional

According to the objectives of the service provider
•profit-oriented
•non-profit

Table 2.3. Characteristics of services according to Lovelock

The nature of the service		
Type of service	Who or what is it directed at?	Examples
Tangible actions	Directed at the human body	Passenger transportation Health care Restaurant Haircutting
	Directed at a product, or other physical object	Freight transportation Repair, maintenance Laundry and dry cleaning Lawn care
Intangible actions	Directed at the human mind	Education Radio, television Theatre Museum
	Directed at intangibles	Banking services Legal counselling Accounting Insurance
Relationship between the service provider and the customers		
Continuous delivery of service	Membership	Insurance Telephone subscription College, university Automobile club
	No formal relationship	Radio station Police Public motorway
Non-continious delivery of service/discrete transaction	Membership	Long distance calls Season ticket to the theatre Rail pass
	No formal relationship	Postal services Public transport Movie theatre Toll motorway
Customizing the service and utilizing the service provider's own value judgements		
Service provider can benefit greatly from their own judgements in satisfying customer needs	The service can be customized to a great extent	Legal services Health care Architecture Taxi services Plumbing Education (individual)
	The service can be customized to only a minor extent	Education (big classes) Preventive healthcare

Table 2.3. Characteristics of services according to Lovelock (continued)

Service providers personnel can benefit from their own judgements to a small extent in satisfying customer needs	The service can be customized to a great extent	**Telephone** **Hotels** **Good restaurant** **Retail banking**
	The service can be customized to only a minor extent	Public transport Routine repairs Fast food restaurant Cinema
The nature of supply and demand in service industries		
Peak demand can usually be satisfied without any particular delay	The fluctuation in demand is high	Electricity Gas supply Telephone Health care Police, fire brigade
	The fluctuation in demand is not high	Insurance Legal services Banking services Cleaning
Demand in peak times exceeds capacity	The fluctuation in demand is high	Accounting, tax return Passenger transport Hotel Restaurant Theatre
	The fluctuation in demand is low	Any services similar to the above, where capacity is insufficient
Getting the service to the customer		
Customer goes to the service provider	The service is available only on one site	Theatre Hairdresser
	The service is available on multiple sites	Bus service Fast food restaurant
The service provider goes to the customer	The service is available only on one site	Gardening Taxi
	The service is available on multiple sites	Mail delivery Local repair by automobile club
The customer and the service provider operate at a distance from each other	The service is available only on one site	Credit card Local TV station
	The service is available on multiple sites	Mass communication Telephone

CHAPTER 3

VALUE CREATION IN THE 21ST CENTURY, THE INTERNATIONAL ENVIRONMENT

Professionals and researchers dealing with the economy, particularly business life, agree that it is a big mistake at the end of the second decade of the 21st century to restrict the validity of thoughts and theories to only one country, no matter how big or small it may be. The changes started at the end of the previous millennium gradually turning the world into a "global village" have accelerated in the first two decades of the new millennium and consider that any kind of act of narrowing is extremely short-sighted and deeply provincial.

The term global village was coined by Marshall McLuhan, who - based on his research of the media - predicted as early as in 1962 that the whole world would be interlinked electronically. Oxford University Press published this book in 1989, after his death.

Those who do not recognize the increasing interdependence of the markets and the national economies and do not address the effects of international trends are clearly in a dead-end street.

The research institutions focusing on the future of the world have identified and envisaged several megatrends which will affect the whole world. According to our research, the following six of these trends will have the biggest impact on

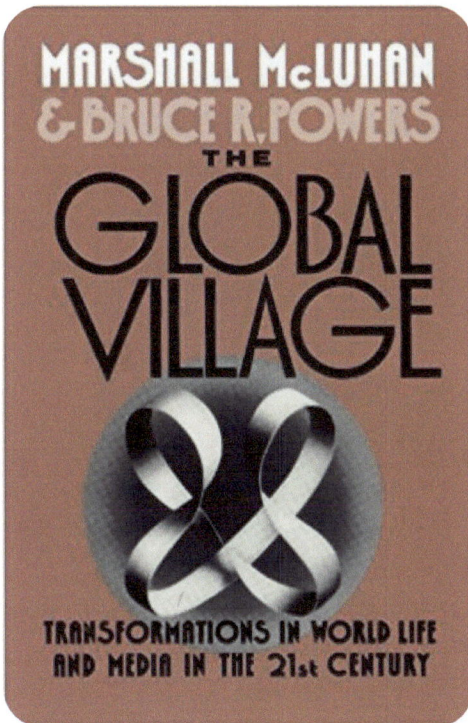

43

marketing (Figure 3.1.).

3.1. GLOBAL MEGATRENDS

Figure 3.1. Global megatrends which shape the future (Rekettye, Rekettye Jr. 2013)

Global climate change
- Sustainable development, environment-friendly products
- Beginning of climate migration

Aftershocks of the crisis
- Price sensitivity - changed consumer habits
- Rising share of discount shops and private brands

Power shift in world economy
- Economic power shifts from west to east and south
- Immense new markets are developing in the emerging countries

Demographic trends
- Aging population in the west, overpopulation and urbanization in the east
- Strengthening role of women in the economy and in the consumption

Proliferation
- Proliferation of new products and brands
- Appearance and expansion of new channels and media

Industrial development
- Rapid development in IT
- The fourth industrial revolution - SMACT

EXHIBIT 3.1. DIFFERENT ASSESSMENT OF THE IMPORTANCE OF MEGATRENDS: INDIA VS HUNGARY

In his doctoral dissertation in 2016, Rekettye Jr. examined how, in the opinion leaders' evaluation, these megatrends influenced the business environment in a given country, among others in India and Hungary, and how these megatrends were prioritized. We will present from this survey the order of importance of these trends in India and Hungary (see the following figure).

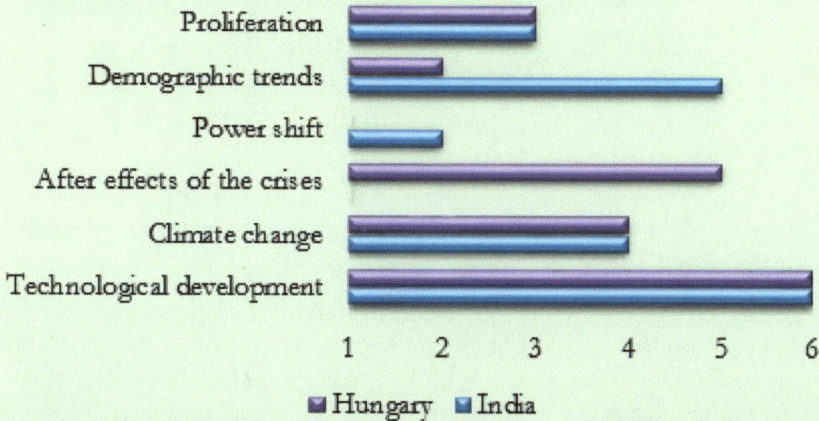

Note: 6 = most important, 1 = least important

Source: G. Rekettye Jr. (2017)

As can be seen in the table, there was an agreement among the stakeholders in both countries that technological development would have the biggest impact on the business environment. They also agreed on the role of climate change and proliferation. There was, however, a significant difference in the way they assessed the aftershocks of the crisis and the demographic trends. It was presumed that the crisis was still strongly present in Hungary in 2016 as opposed to India. The shift in power seemed so distant in both countries that its importance was rated quite low. It is an unfortunate fact that Hungarians gave very little attention to international changes or the prevalent demographic problems.

Each global megatrend affected the value creation function of companies:

Global warming, for example, has impelled companies to design and sell eco-friendly products. A good example is Toyota, which was the first car manufacturer that launched a hybrid car, the Prius in 1997, the biggest merit of which was that it promoted a more environmentally behaviour among drivers. Almost all car manufacturers followed the example of Toyota.

The 2009 model of Toyota Prius

Source: By IFCAR - A feltöltő saját munkája, Közkincs, https://commons.wikimedia.org/w/index.php?curid=17760529"

According to a global survey conducted by Nielsen in 2015, 66% of people are willing to pay more for products and services which are environmentally friendly. It showed a 16% increase compared to the year before (Nielsen, 2015).

- After the *financial crisis,* the value preferences of people changed. For many, brand, quality and comfort were replaced by low prices. Manufacturers and traders both had to respond because those who were not able to respond quickly could easily go out of business.

- Not only did preferences change but buying habits too. The well-known retail chains in the US (e.g., Sears, Radio Shack, J.C. Penny, Macy's, Abercrombie & Fitch) were forced to close more than three and a half thousand stores in 2017 because their turnover and liquidity dropped too low (Source: Loeb, 2017). At the same time, Aldi increased the number of its shops to 1,600 in the US (Peterson, 2017) and Lidl was planning to open stores in the United States in 2017. These two German discount chains distribute mainly private brands, and their price levels are nearly half of that of traditional American shops.

The photo shows JCPenny's store located in the Aventura shopping centre in Florida

CC BY-SA 3.0, https://commons.wikimedia.org/w/index.php?curid=593445

It must also be noted that the poor business performance of "brick and mortar" retail was not only the result of the after-effects of the crisis, especially not in the US, but was due to the rise in online sales driven by the development of technology. Derek Thomson, in an article published in The Atlantic on April 10, 2017, wrote that while in the third quarter of 2010 only 2.4% of total shopping was done online, this figure increased to 20% by the third quarter of 2016. The journalist mentioned another interesting trend: the significantly growing wages of the past few years in the United States resulted in people dining out more often, making restaurants boom, which also added to the misery of food retailers.

- *Power shift* means that economic power started to move rapidly from west to east and south. China and India, the two most populated countries in the developing world, are experiencing rapid growth which, according to most predictions, will lead to the emergence of *a strong middle class, whose demand will be the driving force of the global economy*. Companies wishing to exploit this new opportunity are already lagging . The value expectations of the local consumers are clearly different, mainly due to their different cultural background and income situation, from those of the consumers in the west. Companies targeting these markets must redesign their business models based on customer value. Even McDonalds was forced to redesign almost everything, from the products to the advertisements (including the chairs used in the restaurants).

Photo:

McDonald's, Old Mahabalipuram Road, Chennai, India

Source: Ajayy99 at English Wikipedia, CC BY-SA 3.0, https://commons.wikimedia.org/w/index.php?curid=57996109

- The *demographic trends* forecast the risks of aging of the population in the European region. According to the calculation of the World Bank, the so-called "old age dependency ratio", which measures the number of those aged above 65 as a share of the working population (aged between

14-65) reached 30.5% in Europe in 2017 (*https://data.worldbank.org/ indicator/SP.POP.DPND.OL*) and is predicted to increase to 52% by 2050. (European Commission, 2014, p. 22.) This change also requires serious moves on the part of sellers. The value expectations and buying habits of the aging consumers differ greatly from those of the young ones.

Spiegel and Statista concluded that the age structure of the world population changed from the pyramid shape typical of the 1950s to a bell shape in 2015 and will develop into "skyscraper shape" by 2100.

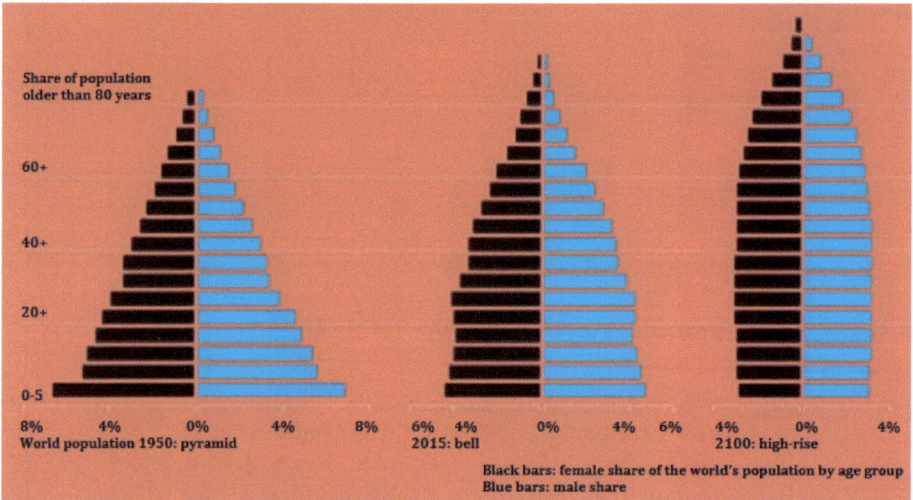

Source: United Nations Population Division

- Many areas of the markets are characterized by *proliferation* in the new millenium. Let us quote the words of Alex Myers, the marketing director of Carlsberg beer manufacturer. "We can see the proliferation of everything, consumers, consumer segments, the media, and brands. Beer brewers used to have a strong presence in the middle of the market. Going even further back in time, we can see that each town had its own brand of beer. Nowadays, we experience the polarization of brands: upward and downward. The risk is to stay in the middle.

I can see big opportunities upmarket: where variety and experience delivered to customers can yield higher profits.

A few products by Carlsberg targeting the upper segment of the market.

It seems as if beer was part of the entertainment or the chocolate industry, new varieties and new tastes must be offered at high prices. Downmarket is an entirely different story. Here you should rely on fewer brands and larger volumes and must make sure that you can offer them in a cost-efficient way. Serving the market requires us to be present in both areas" (Court et al., 2007).

3.2. THE FACTOR HAVING THE MOST INFLUENCE ON THE BUSINESS ENVIRONMENT IN THE FUTURE: TECHNICAL DEVELOPMENT

Looking at the table presenting the megatrends (Figure 3.1), the expression the Fourth Industrial Revolution was used to characterize the technological development. This compound expression is actually the title of the book by *Klaus Schwab (see his photo below!)*, the founder and executive chairman of the World Economic Forum, which was published in 2016. According to him the technical development of the world has entered a phase which can easily be called a revolution, and this is a change (development) which could transform earlier trends and redefine our whole life. Moreover, it can have a profound effect on the creation of customer value, on the motivating factors behind it, on its methods of implementation, its results, and impacts.

Let us examine the evolution of production in the past two-three centuries.

Figure 3.2. The industrial revolutions

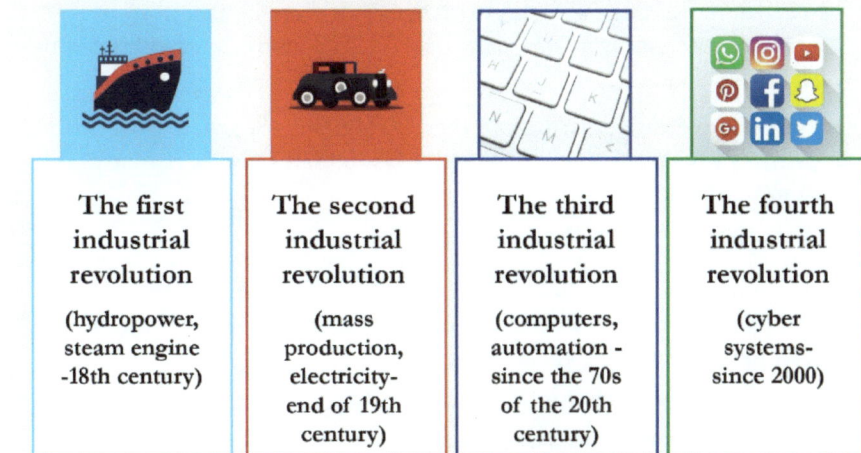

The first industrial revolution	The second industrial revolution	The third industrial revolution	The fourth industrial revolution
(hydropower, steam engine -18th century)	(mass production, electricity- end of 19th century)	(computers, automation - since the 70s of the 20th century)	(cyber systems- since 2000)

The consequences of the fourth industrial revolution are unforeseeable today. What concerns us from value creation point of view are the following two aspects:

- how will this new world, often referred to as 'cyber age', change people's value expectations and preferences, and

- how can production systems change and react to the changing needs of customers in this new world?

First, let us see what kind of changes we are dealing with. The research team of the Sogeti research institute, VINTlabs (Vision,- Inspiration – Navigation – Trends) in 2013 wrote that the building blocks of the "smarter world", like social media, smart phones, analytical abilities, cloud technology hand in hand with the internet of things, can create coherent and synergic systems, which allow us to make our things smarter and to create smarter things (SMACT, Figure 3.3.). Source: (https://www.sogeti.com/why-us/leading-innovation/)

A few statistical data to help clarify the figure 3.3:

The Internet of things:

According to Statista, more than 23 billion devices have been connected since 2008 and they estimate its number to 75 billion by 2025 (https://www.statista. com/statistics/471264/iot-number-of-connected-devices-worldwide/).

- The so-called ambient intelligence emerged in 2002,

- The first driverless car appeared in 2012,

- IPV6 appeared in 2011.

Mobile (smart) phones:

- In 2018, more than 2.5 billion smartphones were in use (https://www.statista.com/statistics/330695/number-of-smartphone-users-worldwide/).

- Until the middle of 2018 more than 200 billion apps were downloaded (https://www.statista.com/statistics/330695/number-of-smartphone-users-worldwide/).

Social media:

- The number of Facebook users in the third quarter of 2018 exceeded 2.5 billion, https://www.statista.com/statistics/264810/number-of-monthly-active-facebook-users-worldwide/

- The number of active Twitter users was around 326 million in 2018 (https://zephoria.com/twitter-statistics-top-ten/)

- Facebook generates 4 new petabytes of data per day

- There are 500 million Tweets sent each day. That's 6,000 Tweets every second (https://www.brandwatch.com/blog/amazing-social-media-statistics-and-facts/#section-10)

Analytics:

- Our current output of data is roughly 2.5 quintillion bytes a day. (https://www.iflscience.com/technology/how-much-data-does-the-world-generate-every-minute/

- 2005- Madoop

- 2011- Watson

Cloud:

- Amazon EC2 – 2007

- IBM Message Site – 2013 (handles one million messages per second)

- Microsoft Skydrive

Each operation can be broken down into three types of relationship:

- human-to-machine (H2M),

- machine to machine (M2M) and

- machine to human (M2H).

Figure 3.3. The components of SMACT

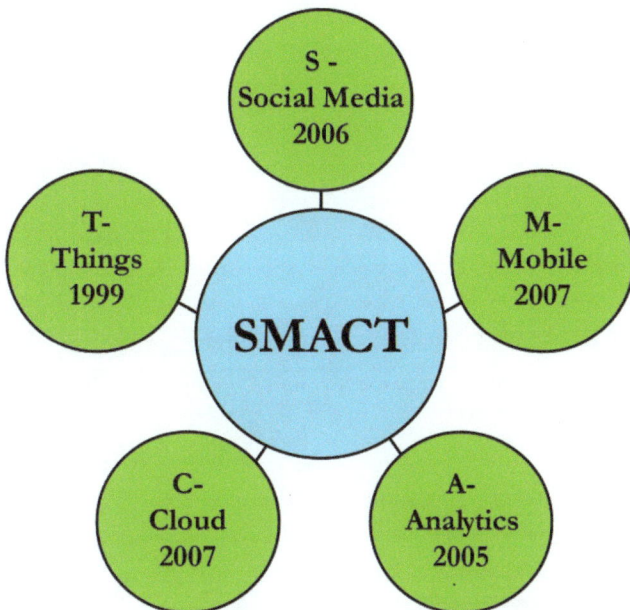

Note: The Gartner research institute created and used the abbreviation SMAC in their research entitled Nexus of Forces, to which VINTlabs added the T, the Internet of Things.

These operations can be simple, complex or continuous process chains. "SMACT is the process of automation, which will affect our lives to an increasing extent" (Bloem, et al., 2014, p. 3.).

In view of these global developments, the big think tanks are active in preparing for almost every industry. In the next exhibit, some thoughts are presented about the future of the automotive industry – as seen by the experts of PriceWaterhouseCompany.

EXHIBIT 3.2. "EASCY" – FIVE TRENDS THAT ARE DRIVING THE TRANSFORMATION OF THE AUTOMOTIVE INDUSTRY

According to the PwC experts the future of the automotive industry can be described with five letters, EASCY (*electrified, autonomous, shared, connected and yearly updated*). Let us see their explanations and predictions!

Electrified The transition to emissions-free individual mobility would hardly be possible without the electrification of the drive train. First, there is the issue of local components – the fact that cars now only emit very low levels of harmful substances, dust, and noise. It also seems that going "emissions-free" will be a global initiative: The idea is that the electricity used to charge the vehicles will come from renewable sources to ensure CO^2-neutral mobility.

Prediction: Over **55 %** of all new car sales could be fully electrified by 2030.

Autonomous The rapid progress made in areas such as artificial intelligence, machine learning, and deep neural networks makes it possible to achieve what until recently seemed utopian – namely the development of autonomous vehicles, which require no human intervention even in complex traffic situations. It will completely redefine the use of individual mobility platforms. New application scenarios are emerging that would have been unthinkable just a few years ago.

Prediction: **40 %** of the mileage driven in Europe could be covered by autonomous vehicles in 2030.

Shared For several years, many big cities have offered car-sharing facilities. While these are currently often run as pilot projects or citizen initiatives, sharing concepts will become economically viable with the introduction of autonomous vehicles. It will no longer be necessary to search for a shared vehicle in the surrounding area: instead, it will be possible to order vehicles to wherever the user happens to be via a convenient "on demand" service.

Prediction: Autonomous vehicles will have a strong positive impact on sharing concepts.

Connected

The fourth "eascy" dimension is the networking of cars with the outside world – summarised by the concept of the Connected Car. This term actually represents two concepts at once. On the one hand, it applies to Car2Car and Car2X communication, which is the networking of the car with other cars or with the transport infrastructure (such as traffic lights). On the other hand, the term also covers the networking of vehicle occupants with the outside world. In the future, they will be able to communicate, work, surf the internet or access multi-media services during the journey.

Prediction: Maintenance and repair costs will drop, and lower accident rates will mean that cars will be able to travel many more miles. Personal mileage in Europe could rise by 23% by 2030 to 5.88 trillion kilometres. Forecasts predict an increase of 24% in the US and 183% in China.

Yearly updated

The development topics of electrified, autonomous, connected and shared will lead to a clear increase in the rate of innovation within the automotive industry. Model cycles of five to eight years, which have always been common in this sector, could soon be a thing of the past. Instead, the range of models will be updated annually in order to integrate the latest hardware and software developments. As customers will naturally not want to buy a new vehicle every year due to the high purchase costs, the short innovation cycles will enter the market primarily through regular upgrades of shared vehicles.

Prediction: Future vehicles will be used far more intensively and will therefore be replaced sooner.

Source: Excerpts from the study written by PwC experts Kuhnert F., Stürmer C. and Koster A. Five trends transforming the Automotive Industry, Published by PricewaterhouseCoopers in 2018 https://www.pwc. com/gx/en/industries/automotive/publications/eascy.html

EXHIBIT 3.3. TOYOTA INVEST INTO TECHNOLOGICAL STARTUPS

In contrast to venture capital funds, Toyota Ventures itself will determine the most important research fields. They are planning to invest in the fields of artificial intelligence, robotics, autonomous mobility solutions, as well as data and cloud technology.

The international research institute of Toyota founded a venture capital subsidiary under the name of Toyota AI Ventures. This investment which cost 100 million dollars to the company will be used in the first round by the institute to finance the start-up of Intuition Robotics (Israel), Slamcore (United Kingdom) and Nauto (Silicon Valley). The new company is planning to make investments in the fields of artificial intelligence, robotics, autonomous mobility, data and cloud technology. (Note: AI in the name of the company obviously refers to the abbreviation of artificial intelligence. Source: Kreatív online, July 20th, 2017.)

The fourth industrial revolution became the central theme of the World Economic Forum in Davos in 2016 with the title "Mastering the Fourth Industrial Revolution". The Forum addressed the different positive and negative aspects of the fourth industrial revolution. Because, as Schwab said, "There has never been a time of greater promise or peril".

The opportunities lie in, what has already been described by the theory of SMACT, that today the building blocks of a more ideal life constitute an integrated system.

John Moavenzadeh examined a different aspect of this topic in his keynote speech delivered at the DHL Global Engineering & Manufacturing Summit held in Amsterdam (2015). He concluded that the fourth industrial revolution would completely transform the *global production system*.

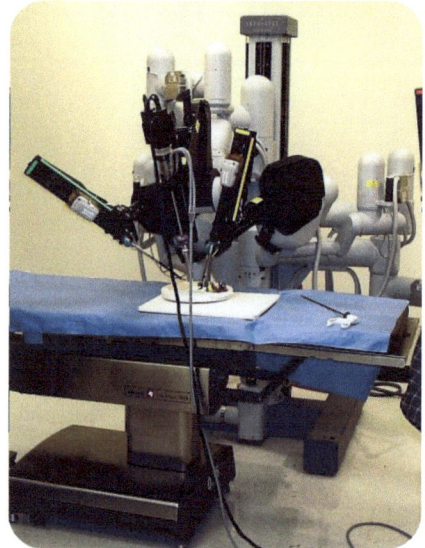

A robot capable of performing laparoscopic surgery

Photo: Nimur at the English language Wikipedia, CC BY-SA 3.0, https://commons.wikimedia.org/ w/index.php?curid=3158337

EXHIBIT 3.4. FLEX: 4.0 WILL FUNDAMENTALLY CHANGE THE FORMS OF PRODUCTION AND CONSUMPTION

According to Francois Barbier, the president of the global company Flex (former Flextronics), 4.0 will fundamentally change the forms of production and consumption as the fourth industrial revolution has brought radical changes in five areas:

- *Provides a 360-degree perspective.* The virtual world makes it possible to have a prior simulation of products and product lines. FLEX uses augmented reality to allow a Chinese engineer to consult with an American partner in a live view without the need to change location.

- *3D printing* makes it possible to produce something from one piece only instead of six pieces as was done earlier, saving time and material.

- *Automated production.* Already 50% of companies are using robot technology. The new generation of robots can be used much more easily and are capable of performing very complex human tasks.

- *Intelligent factories in the cloud.* In addition to robotics, the use of cloud computing also constitutes an advantage. Smart sensors can convert data into units of measurement and can communicate with other machines. IoT (Internet of Things) enables us to receive the right information at the right time to make the right decision. All this allows us to satisfy the real needs of customers in a better and more cost-effective way.

- *Robots on the rise - smart manufacturing needs human managers.* Many people are concerned about jobs. Well, artificial intelligence and robots need to be programmed and managed. According to Forrester Research, close to 15 million new jobs will be created over the next decade in the U.S. alone. But there will be job losses too.

Source: Fransois Barbier, 5 trends for the future of manufacturing, WEF (June 22nd, 2017) https://www.weforum.org/agenda/2017/06/what-s-going-on-with-manufacturing-b013f435-1746-4bce-ac75-05c642652d42

The evolving cyber-physical system combines communication, information technology, data, physical elements and a range of basic technologies, such as:

- reception systems (receptors),

- the infrastructure for internet communication (IP),

- intelligent parallel processing (CPU),

- the participants of mechanical activities,

- "big data" and its acquisition,

- automated operation and management systems,

- advanced robotics, and

- 3D and 4D printing.

All this will fundamentally change the business model of the industry. A survey conducted among corporate strategic managers in 2015, for example, revealed that

- 88% of experts in the automobile industry thought that by 2030 at least one large automobile manufacturing would generate more turnover from the sale of data and services than from the sale of cars and spare parts;

- 92% of bank professionals agreed that the so-called "distributed ledger" technology would undermine our whole financial system by 2030. (see next exhibit)

EXHIBIT 3.5. HOW THE NEW TECHNOLOGY CAN TRANSFORM THE FINANCIAL MARKET

A new technology has emerged stirring up the stagnant waters of financial markets. This new technology is called DLT, distributed ledger technology. Let us examine what exactly it involves and why it is so crucial for central banks, including the European Central Bank.

The distributed ledger technology registers the transaction of assets, financial or other. At present, banks conduct their transactions, operations involving the transfer of ownership of money or other financial assets, via centralized systems usually operated by central banks. Banks keep records of these transactions in local databases, which are updated when the transactions have been completed in the central system.

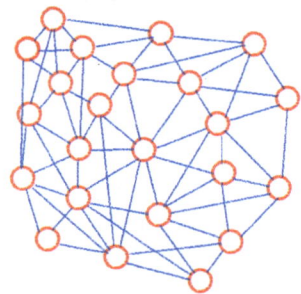

The distributed ledger is a transactional database, which can be shared across the network of several computers and is not stored in a central location. All participants within the network can read the information and can add information according to their access rights.

The most common form of DLT is the **blockchain**. The name comes from the fact that the transactions are aggregated into groups, i.e. blocks, which are attached to each other in chronological order to create a chain. The whole chain is protected by complicated mathematical algorithms, which ensure the integrity and security of the data. The chain then forms the comprehensive register of all the transactions entered in the database.

Since the algorithms ensure the security of the data, and the actors connected to the network are informed about any changes in the register, the technology decreases the risk of transactional fraud.

Besides, it also increases efficiency, because the keeping of records can be automated which potentially eliminates the likelihood of human error and simplifies the otherwise very complicated processes.

Some go so far as to boldly saying that by eliminating the intermediaries, DLT could fundamentally change the ways financial markets operate. For example, it will enable the performance of payment transactions between banks without the involvement of a third party or having to go through a payment system. Moreover, some predict that even payment between private persons, which today are made through the account holder banks of the participants in the transaction, can be performed entirely 'bank free", because natural persons will be able to directly connect to the shared database.

Source: https://www.ecb.europa.eu/explainers/tell-me-more/html/distributed_ledger_ techno-logy. hu. html (April 19th, 2017)

- The majority of institutional investors and finance managers agree that most financial transactions and even corporate documents will be administered in the blockchain system by 2025.

"The technology likely to have the biggest impact on the next few decades has arrived. And it's not social media. It's not big data. It's not robotics. It's not even AI (artificial intelligence). You'll be surprised to learn that it's the underlying technology of digital currencies like Bitcoin. It's called **Blockchain**."

Don Tapscott, *The author of the book Blockchain Revolution.*

Source: https://www.linkedin.com/pulse/blockchain-technology-wikipedia-non-technical-ankur-chugh

All in all, we can say that IT (information technology) will be integrated with OT (operational technology), which will lead to a shift in paradigm through the communication of M2M (machine to machine). The internet-based cyber-physical system developed this way will create favourable changes in value creation (Figure 3.4.).

Figure 3.4. The merger of IT and OT

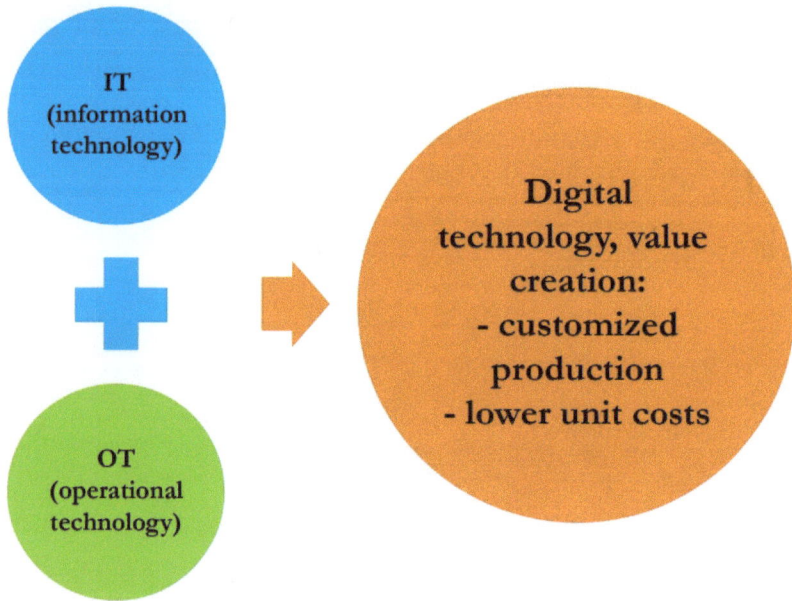

EXHIBIT 3.6. HOW BITCOIN WORKS?

Blessing C. Okpala

Cryptocurrency works based on the theory of solving encryption algorithms to form unique hashes that are limited in number (DeVries, 2016). It works in combination with a network of computers that authenticate transactions, thereby allowing users to exchange hashes as if they are exchanging physical currency. However, there is a limited quantity of bitcoin that can ever be produced to avoid excessive circulation. According to Wan and Hoblitzell (2014), bitcoin works when bitcoin users secure access to their balance via a password known as a private key. Afterwards, transactions are authenticated by a network of users called miners that present their computing power in exchange for an opportunity to obtain more bitcoins. It is noteworthy that anybody with a public key can transfer money to a Bitcoin address, however, only a signature generated by the private key can release money from it.

A step-by-step Illustration of How Bitcoin Works

Step 1: User (X) installs a Bitcoin wallet on a mobile phone or computer to generate a Bitcoin address (Bitcoin, 2009-2019). The Bitcoin wallet is required for storing Bitcoin, and multiple wallets can be created when needed. Once installation of the wallet is complete, the user is then assigned a public key (username) and a private key (password or signature). Public keys and private keys comprise of a set of letters and numbers. The private key is a user's identity and access to Bitcoin on the blockchain and should always be kept safe. User (Y) requires the public key to send money to user (X). Being a set of letters and numbers, the sender does not need the receiver's name or email address to send bitcoin. The private key or signature stops the transaction from being altered once accomplished (Naware, 2016).

Step 2: The Bitcoin address is then communicated from user (X) to another user (Y) that requires it. A user can have several Bitcoin addresses but only a unique address can be used for each transaction.

Step 3: The unique address for the transaction is then generated by the Bitcoin websites and software the moment a user makes a payment request or creates an invoice (Bitcoin Wiki, 2018).

Step 4: The Bitcoin transactions are then assembled together and stored in blocks that are connected to each other in chains. This is the reason it is referred to as a blockchain.

Step 5: With the Bitcoin address, user (X) can be paid by user (Y) or vice versa. Bitcoins can be transferred or signed over from one address to the other even when a user has multiple addresses.

Step 6: Bitcoin then processes and verifies payments using public key (username) cryptography, peer-to-peer networking, and proof-of-work (Bitcoin Wiki, 2018).

Step 7: The payment transaction is then shared to the network and on the blockchain to prevent the used bitcoins from being spent twice. Note that a public key is written on every transaction in the block while a user's private key is designated on his/her Bitcoin.

Step 8: All the transactions are broadcast between users and confirmed within 10 minutes by the network via a Bitcoin mining process (Naware, 2016). Mining is a process that identifies the "proof of work", verifies transactions and lists them on the ledger of previous Bitcoin transactions (Cocco and Marchesi, 2016).

References:

Bitcoin (2009-2019), How does Bitcoin work? This is a question often surrounded byconfusion, so here's a quick explanation! Accessed online [https://bitcoin.org/en/how-it-works], Access date [24/01/2019].

Bitcoin Wiki (2018), Address, Accessed online [https://en.bitcoin.it/wiki/Address#A_Bitcoin_ address_ is_ a_single-use_token], Access date [23/01/2019].

Bitcoin Wiki (2018), How does Bitcoin work? Accessed online [https://en.bitcoin.it/wiki/

Main_Page], Access date [24/01/2019].

Cocco, L. and Marchesi, M. (2016), Modeling and Simulation of the Economics of Mining in the Bitcoin Market, PLoS ONE 11(10): e0164603. https://doi.org/10.1371/journal.pone.0164603

DeVries, P. D. (2016), An Analysis of Cryptocurrency, Bitcoin, and the Future, International Journal of Business Management and Commerce, Vol. 1, No. 2, pp.1-9.

Naware, A. M. (2016), Bitcoins, Its Advantages and Security Threats, International Journal of Advanced Research in Computer Engineering & Technology (IJARCET), Vol. 5, Iss. 6, pp.1732-1735.

Wan, T. and Hoblitzell, M. (2014), Bitcoin: Fact. Fiction. Future. Deloitte University Press.

3.3. OUTLOOK: VALUE ADDED ON THE INTERNATIONAL STAGE

Value added represents the net value created as the difference between the output and all the costs incurred during the production (material, energy, wages, cost of capital needed, etc.). It is the fundamental goal of every business entity, economic sector and country to produce the highest possible value added. *Value added, therefore, is not the same as customer value.* There is, however, a strong correlation between the two, because the highest value added can obviously be created by those who manufacture products and services that represent value for the customers, and as a result, these products can be sold at a price which is much higher than their production costs.

As a consequence of the global changes presented earlier in this chapter, the extent of interconnection and technical development is so great that the different stages of product manufacturing can take place in geographically distant locations. The value chains and, looking at strictly the route of the product from the production of the raw material to the final consumption, even the so-called *supply chains* are becoming more and more international and global. So local companies operating in developing countries can simply *join one of these global supply chains instead of building their own.* There is concern that the "good stages" of the supply chain remain in the advanced countries, while the "bad jobs" are taken over by developing countries (Baldwin et al., 2014). This concern is closely related to the intellectual concept infamously known as the "smiling curve". The concept of the smiling curve was created by Stan Shih, the founder of Acer back at the beginning of the 1990s (Figure 3.5.).

The largest part of the value added is kept by the company (typically headquartered in advanced countries) controlling the beginning and the end of the supply chain. The cost analysis of Apple's first smartphone can serve as a good example for this (Figure 3.6.). Looking at this cost analysis, we can see that the assembly of the product in China created only 6.54 dollars' worth of value added, while the total cost of the parent company amounted to 330.62 dollars compared to the price of 600 dollars. It represents a 45% profit margin.

Figure 3.5. The smiling curve in the 21st century (the curve got its name from its shape resembling a smile), edited on the basis of Baldwin et al., (2014, 2)

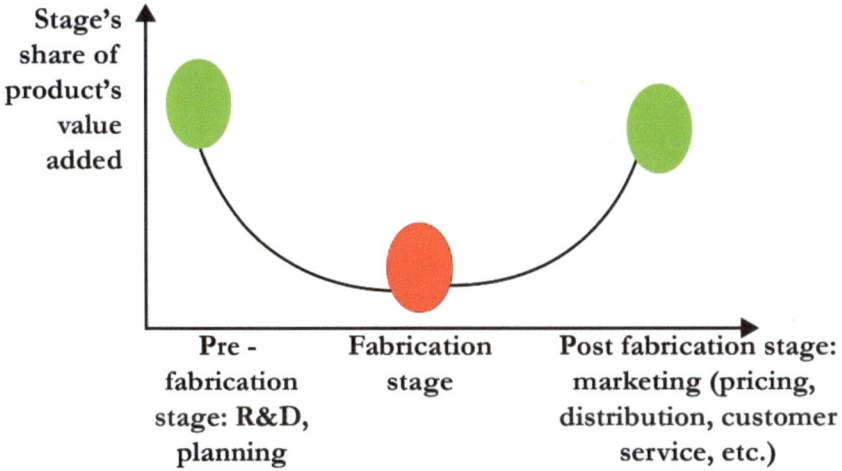

Figure 3.6. Cost analysis of the iPhone 4

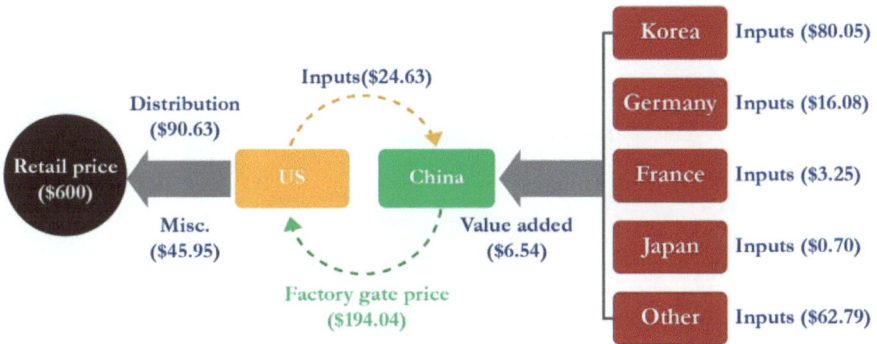

Source Deloitte University Press | DUPress.com

Note: It's not a coincidence that shortly after the launch of the product, Steve Jobs (the CEO of the company at the time, now deceased) decided to decrease the price by 200 dollars offending large masses of customers who bought the product early. And it is not a coincidence either that Apple was the most valuable brand in 2017 according to the ranking by Forbes with a value of 170 billion dollars, preceding Google and Microsoft, etc. (https://www.forbes.com/ powerful-brands/list/#tab:rank)

Fernandez-Stark (2011) and others studied the smiling curve of the apparel/clothing industry in several developing countries and wanted to come up with a recipe for how a manufacturing company could work itself up to the stages of the value chain which generate more value added.

Figure 3.7. The smiling curve in the apparel/clothing industry

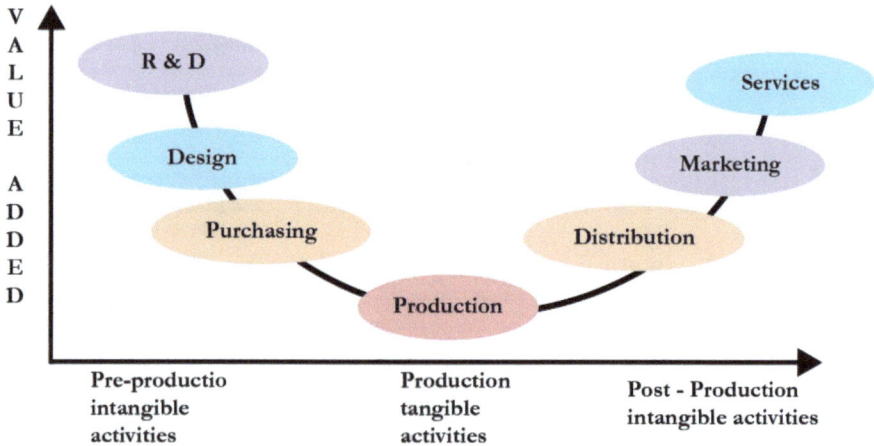

Shifting from the manufacturing (assembling) position requires the development of new competencies. This shift can only be implemented gradually:

- As a first step, the company can take over parts of purchasing and distribution.

- Later it can participate in design. The shift is possible through the cooperation with the buyer (example for this is presented in the exhibit).

EXHIBIT 3.7. FOXCONN, AN ODM COMPANY

We selected as an example Hon Hai Precision Industry Co. Ltd., trading as Foxconn Technology Group, a Taiwanese multinational electronics contract manufacturing company. With a turnover of 128 billion dollars, it is the largest contract manufacturing company in the world (and is said to be the largest private employer with about 1.3 million employees). Although the company is headquartered in Taiwan, most of its manufacturing activities are performed in China and other countries. Foxconn is one of the ODM (Original Design Manufacturer) companies. The brands manufactured by them include among others: BlackBerry, iPhone, iPad, Kindle, PlayStation, XboxOne. An ODM company differs from a simple CM (contract manufacturer) company in that it manufactures according to the

requirements of the buyer, it designs and manufactures the product or certain parts of it, which the buyer labels with its brand.

Source: Rekettye, et al. (2015: 259) Logo: By Foxconn - http://www.foxconn.com/, Public Domain, https://commons.wikimedia.org/w/index.php?curid=10543276

- The real breakthrough, however, could happen as a result of cooperation in the post- fabrication stages or of their taking over entirely. There are two options: The two companies continue their collaboration and develop new brands together, or the company develops new brands on its own and then markets them typically on domestic markets using different channels. The second option carries the risk of conflict with the original buyer (see exhibit below).

EXHIBIT 3.8. CONTRACT MANUFACTURING, A TWO-EDGED SWORD – OR IBM VERSUS LENOVO

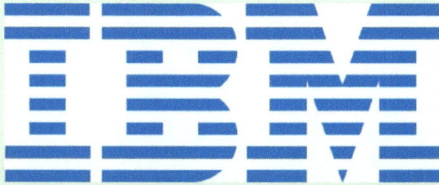

As Arrunada and Vazquéz concluded, contract manufacturing is a two-edged sword, because it can happen that the contract manufacturer 'bites the hand that feeds it', and by learning the technology it becomes the competitor of the original equipment manufacturer. Lenovo used to be the supplier of IBM, but it has become one its major competitors. For more information on how to protect against this read the article by these authors (Arrunada–Vazquéz 2006).

Lenovo Group Limited is one of the leading manufacturers of personal computers in the world. In 2012 Lenovo became a world leader with the number of units sold dethroning the former world leader Hewlett-Packard.

CASE I.1. BLOCKCHAIN TECHNOLOGY AS A RESOURCE FOR VALUE CREATION: THE CASE OF EVRY[1]

Ismaila Ola Ogundega

Disruptive digital technologJaiies, like blockchain, artificial intelligence (AI), digital reality (DR), and cloud, are initiating a new period of productivity for consumer products organisations. These technologies are not only assisting to propel effective internal processes, novelty, brand growth, and profitability, but also improving the consumer experience.

Disruptive technologies redefine the way consumer products companies do business. Blockchain can assist them in creating more value, attain operational efficiencies, and improve customer experience.

Company background

Evry, the largest Information Technology firm in Norway has extensive deliveries to Norwegian and Nordic business, financial, government and healthcare sectors. (Evry, 2017).

Evry intended to gain competency on blockchain technology, so they commenced a project to design a solution within their range. Peter Frøystad (a consultant at Evry Norge) says the first project commenced in fall of 2015 with a research project in which "the main objective was to study the technology and its nature. This study led to the appointment of Peter to commence a business project. Three persons were put in place to discover a project appropriate for Evry's operational space. They identified a project and how much resources they would require to implement it. In the fall of 2016, the team had recognised syndicate loans as a fit. They are now building a platform such that banks can interface and work jointly, to make the syndicate loans process digital and more effective.

Partners, customers and competitors

Peter recognises the merits of being a large organisation. They hold that reality by gaining meetings with the administration of larger banks that is presently their customers of other products. As of today, Evry hasn't signed any contract with customers or partners relating to their blockchain solutions, but they have some that have shown interest.

Evry are seeking for a customer or partner that wishes to develop the system together with them. As stated by Peter "the effect of the network is very essential

---

[1] Source: The logo image by EVRY - official company website, https://commons.wikimedia.org/w/index.php?curid=68406568.

in blockchain products that you can't sell it the traditional way, where you initially create a product and then sell it. You need to have committed people, staying on the project from the onset, or else it is not possible". R3 (a distributed database technology organisation leading a consortium of over 70 of the world's biggest financial institutions in research and development of blockchain database usage in the financial system) based their organisation on this reality - if they could not get the banks onboard from the start when developing new financial infrastructure, you will never get them interested later either. Evry is employing part of that idea to include the banks. Peter considers that this does make it more difficult, as it implies you have to get a person ready to engage the resources for development to make it, and there are not many firms prepared to do that in Norway today.

As stated by Peter "no one globally has blockchain deliverables today, at least none that has any operational revenue". There are only some supply chain solutions that are being developed globally, for instance, Wal-Mart, Mesk and Alibaba are testing creating solutions on the blockchain. As stated by Peter, the consulting firms in Norway are actually the organisations looking at blockchain and they do it to get knowledge of the blockchain technology so that they are ready when there is an interest from the market. "Consulting firms require competence on it, but few of them have no practical experience since there are no customers in the field so far", according to Peter. The ones that do work for customers are smaller consultancy companies involved in concept development and workshops for other smaller firms.

Within the syndicated loan space the US firm Symbiont (Symbiont, 2017) working with it, but Evry haven't researched into them or attempted to search for other competitors since their project was never meant to be a product in the initial instance. Nets is considered a competitor on various payment solutions, possessing their own ongoing blockchain project, but they are not a competitor in view of blockchain solutions.

Blockchain at Evry

As at the development of his white paper (Frøystad and Holm, 2015), Peter Frøystad envisaged the likelihood of blockchain, and what other people had done. Evry then intended to do own project, and the task of searching for that project commenced. Various use cases were suggested, and some of them were well researched on, for example, trade finance and international payments. Evry intended to use the technology on a real business problem, "it was not ideal, to begin with a technology and then discovering a problem, but that was what we did", said Peter. After brainstorming between Peter and his superior, Jarle Holm, where they viewed business processes and complementing it with products and competencies they had in Evry - they began considering syndicated loans. With Evry now possessing a product for syndicated loans, Peter thought it was suitable. Peter could see some business prospects, but they had no use case. After talks with some of Evry's staff working with syndicated loans, and delivering an annual customer forum on Evry's syndicated loan product about the prospects of Blockchain, they had some talks with customers about the issues of syndicated loans today. They decided on what they could do and began a development project in summer 2016.

First, they began with automatic payments making use of Ripple (a FinTech company), as payments appeared as the clear starting point, but the team soon discovered that payments work well enough today and is not a big issue. Norway has a developed payment system for very fast payments that is both effective and cheap, in comparison to other nations such as the USA and South-East Asia, where they "employ very slow carrying systems that are expensive and don't work" said Peter. Having gone in-depth on syndicated loans they discovered that such loans were a tradition to manual labour and a system based on trust. As stated by Peter, they resolved that syndicated loan was the ideal use case for Evry depending on these features.

As a part of the blockchain implementation process, Evry considered what Bitcoin does. It digitizes an asset and tracks it. The team discovered prospects for doing this on the syndicated loan, issuing out stocks to various banks for their shares of the loan. This could be digitized so that, one can see how much each of the partners possesses, and the sale and purchase of stocks would be made easy. Today, selling out loans to other banks is difficult.

It is done manually, there is little digitalization and it is time-consuming to find partnering banks since banks are specialist in loans for various use cases. To facilitate all of these, a platform needed to be created for syndicated loans with the invitation process and contract negotiations. This is when the team realised the basics of what blockchain technology authorises in the space of syndicated loans.

The basic issue banks have to agree on is contract status. Based on this, Peter said that the fall of 2016 is when they began to make a system for intention and agreement on contract status which made the whole process of negotiation digital and gave the same rights to the involved financial institutions. This made it feasible to define various roles by considering what type of access they would need to the contract.

Evry hasn't done an analysis of the project after it was completed. They didn't consider trade-offs of using blockchain versus more traditional databases. They knew that the platform they employed (Hyperledger) for the development was not ready yet, that it was an immature technology, so a centralized solution would have been better.

In Peter's viewpoint, it makes sense to employ blockchain as the infrastructure rather than a centralized database. In a centralized database, you would require a neutral third party as the operator for all the syndicated loans in this case, and the banks would have to contact this operator every time they need to create a new loan or change anything with the existing ones.

Value propositions and competitive advantage

Peter sees their blockchain solution's main value propositions to be decentralisation and sharing and restriction of information. Information sharing means that everyone can see the status on the syndicated loan. It gives information about how many are invited, if they said yes or no to contribute, how much money they are prepared to invest, and if they are complying on the contract today, Peter stated.

In addition to information sharing, Peter is keen on restrictions also. Information restriction is an essential aspect of an alliance between banks. Within the alliance no one would have greater control than the other, so no members would depend on a central administrator to keep everything in sync, as an argument for having a decentralized solution that no one owns more than anyone.

Very few startups in Norway work on blockchain technology. As stated by Peter, there are few in Norway with the know-how on advanced cryptography required to comprehend blockchain technology adequately. It is getting more impulsive to design applications on top of blockchain solutions, but as stated by Peter there are not many individuals globally that could build the blockchain protocol.

Analysis of Evry Syndicated Loans

Evry has a lot of prior experience working with syndicated loans, giving them the advantage to create the blockchain solution for it. Evry has no intention of building a product to be sold when they built it, they didn't search for competitors and how to differentiate their offering from them. In essence, their product only becomes one out of many solutions to manage syndicated loans, without a clear competitive advantage (Han et al., 1998). In Evry's case, there was a lack of people with long experience with blockchain in the team, and there was no passionate visionary founder. This decreased the ability of the team to see an issue to address, where blockchain technology would be useful beneficial.

Evry's competitors have a competitive advantage by strengthening their knowledge, but as blockchain knowledge expands, the importance of this advantage will be reduced and Evry will be more competitive. This implies that the firms which enjoy the competitive advantage because of superior know-how today might experience this resource seemly less valuable, relative to competitors, as the general knowledge strengthens.

Questions and tasks

1. Do you agree with the strategy of Evry to acquire experience in a new technology?

2. Please analyse the fields where blockchain technology will be important in the near future!

3. What should Evry do to establish a competitive advantage in the technology?

References

Blockchain Technologies, 2016. What are Blockchain Applications? Use Cases and Industries Utilizing Blockchain Technology., Available from: http://www.blockchaintechnologies.com/blockchain-applications [Accessed 8 Apr. 2016].

Evry, 2017. Om Evry. [Online] Evry.com. Available at: https://www.evry.com/no/selskapet/om-oss2/om-evry/ [Accessed 29 May 2017]

Frøystad, P., 2017. Peter Frøystad. [Online] Linkedin.com. Available at: https://www.linkedin.com/ in/peterfroystad/ [Accessed 14 Apr. 2017].

Han, J.K., Kim, N. and Srivastava, R.K., 1998. Market orientation and organizational performance: is innovation a missing link?. The Journal of marketing, pp.30-45.

R3members.com, 2017. R3 Alliance. [Online] http://r3members.com [Accessed 18 May 17].

Symbiont, 2017. [Online] symbiont.io. Available at: https://symbiont.io [Accessed 5 May 2017]

CASE I.2. EMPOWERING WOMEN'S SAFETY THROUGH TECHNOLOGICAL EMBELLISHMENT: TITAN'S SMART WATCHES IN INDIA

Rajashekharaiah Jagadeesh

Titan Company Limited is a leading manufacturer of lifestyle products in India, which is a joint venture between the Tata Group and the Tamil Nadu Industrial Development Corporation (TIDCO), (www.titancompany.in). The company commenced its operations in 1984 under the name Titan Watches Limited and is the fifth largest integrated own brand watch manufacturer in the world. Over the last three decades, Titan has expanded into underpenetrated markets and created lifestyle brands across different product categories. Titan is widely known for transforming the watch and jewellery industry in India. Belonging to the highly respected and reputed Tata Group, the company started its production unit in the southern part of India producing wristwatches in a big number. Within a short period, the company gained a significant market share in the growing watches market and started marketing luxury and jewellery watches that were expensive and exotic in design. Soon the company became a pioneer in introducing new types of watches at regular intervals and offered a huge product range catering to a wide segment of customers. It also ventured into other markets by producing fashion and lifestyle products mainly focused on the youth segment of the market. The other products include Titan Eye Wear, which is quite popular because of the trendy design.

Titan has introduced many novel designs in the watches that were unheard of in the market. As per the latest quarterly report ending in December 2018, the company has posted a profit of 41.6% after tax. Every year it has been a tradition with the company to introduce new designs and capture new markets. They also have a sophisticated forecasting system which can give hints about the changing styles and trends. The data for forecasting is usually obtained from the sales persons and the exclusively created "Titan World" showrooms across the country and outside, and using advanced models through customized software, it is possible to obtain a reliable forecast.

But has at any time the company thought of creating a design that would be triggered by a barbaric incident?

What happened on that dark, fateful night of December 16, 2012?

It was a horrific night and turned out to be fatal to Nirbhaya (a pseudonym given to the victim to protect her identity) and barbaric to her friend. They were waiting for a bus to get back to their place and boarded an off-duty bus with six men inside including the driver. Within no time they realized that the men were drunk and the bus was headed in the wrong direction. When they protested, they were assaulted and the girl was raped in turn by the men and finally fatally wounded beyond imagination. The two were thrown out of the bus and dumped on the pavement. Later some passers-by helped them to get medical help and police were informed. In a hopeless condition, Nirbhaya was later shifted to a hospital in Singapore but she did not respond to the treatment and succumbed to the fatal injuries.

Once the news broke out, the entire nation went on a protest mood and everywhere the safety of women was discussed. In the aftermath of such a heinous crime that involved a gang rape of a woman in the national capital of India, the debate on providing safety to women became the focus of public interest. The steps to be taken to protect women focused primarily on the possible safety measures or help enablers, so that, in case of a crisis the women can avail help and protect themselves.

The corporate world in India took note of the criminal incidents and in this context support systems in the form of technology-enabled products became the hot favourites for product development or enhancement. These gadgets were expected to provide the necessary help during a crisis by way of alerting the police. Thinking of the same lines, the Titan Watch Company launched a specially designed watch under the brand name the Sonata ACT - App Enabled Coordinates Tracker, to help women in an emergency situation. The safety feature of the watch which is connected to the user's smartphone, triggers emergency alerts to a network of pre-set recipients, and prompts them for help to a network of pre-set recipients. This product became a path-breaking innovation for Titan and great value addition to Indian women. Some models of the safety watch are shown below.

Alert Button

The idea behind ACT

In an official statement, S Ravi Kant, CEO, Watches and Accessories Division, Titan Company, said, "The Indian woman continues to evolve with the changing times. As she faces new challenges and responsibilities, Sonata is proud to present a unique offering for the new-age Indian women. With Sonata ACT, we are extending our offering to women and girls who are seeking new opportunities and are empowered to chase their dreams". A noble thought indeed. (https://cashkaro.com/blog/sonata-act-the-watch-that-ensures-women-safety/14617)

How is this product helps women?

Given the vulnerability of women particularly those staying or moving alone or moving through poorly lit areas, such gadgets would prove handy as the person can establish the contact quickly and seek help. As the location is automatically identified and registered, women need not give any oral description of the location and just press the button. This enables the help channels to get activated and ensure timely intervention at the place required. Considering the fact that working women largely belong to lower and middle-income groups in India, the pricing was made affordable by the company. Thus the breakthrough product was made available in the market between approximately 40 to 43 USD, (INR 2,749 and 2,999).

The pricing has also taken into account the budgets of women in tier 2 and tier 3 cities along with metros. Through this affordable offering, the Titan Company has taken a huge step towards the empowerment and safety of women. In addition, this watch offers the usual Titan advantages like technology, style and luxury. Thus, none of the users would have to compromise on style when buying this product.

Can this product be a differentiator in terms of corporate social responsibility (CSR)?

CSR is now a major topic of concern in the corporate world and can include the best practices (Kotler and Lee, 2005). A few years ago, the Indian parliament passed a new bill insisting on a compulsory contribution by the companies towards CSR initiatives. The idea was to encourage the companies to invest in activities that help society in general and bring better benefits to the public. Although what constitutes CSR is often debated without any consensus, there is at least an agreement that CSR activities should be towards the betterment of people and the environment. To a large extent, CSR activities were confined to philanthropy as described by Smith (1994) and also by Fels (2004).

As illustrated by Weber (2008), the lack of a universally accepted definition of CSR has not hindered the growth or applications of CSR. Companies are supposed to remain resource-friendly and ensure no harm to the environment, (Foster, 2009). However, the corporate world needs to move beyond the usual hype of spending money on typical activities like promoting sports, education, village adoption, and uplifting of downtrodden groups. While such activities are well appreciated, the creative part or the deeper focused application seems to be missing.

In this context, the development of a safety watch for women deserves special appreciation and signifies out of the box thinking.

Has the company enjoyed a commercial success? This is more difficult to answer as the data related to the sales of this particular product is hard to get from the secondary sources. Although the CSR activities are not aligned towards business development or commercial success, as indicated by several authors like Margolis and Walsh (2003), Knox and Maklan (2004), and Salzmann, et al. (2005), it should not be forgotten that profit is not the intention behind a company adopting the CSR initiatives.

Questions and tasks:

1. Analyse and discuss the target market of the Sonata ACT watches!

2. Could this idea be used for other purposes?

3. Can companies' CSR activity increase the customer value of its products? If yes, how?

References

Fels, A. (2004). Corporate Philanthropy: New Models for the 21st Century, AQ: Australian Quarterly, 76(1), 30.

Foster, D. (2009). Green manufacturing an introduction from TDK Lambda, retrieved www.uk.tdk-lambda.com

https://en.wikipedia.org/wiki/2012_Delhi_gang_rape

Knox, S. & Maklan, S. (2004). Corporate social responsibility: Moving beyond investment towards measuring outcomes,European Management Journal, 22(5), 508–516.

Kotler, P. & Lee, N. (2005).Corporate social responsibility, Hoboken, N.J.: Wiley.

Margolis, J. D. & Walsh, J. P. (2003). Misery loves companies: Rethinking social initiatives by business,Administrative Science Quarterly, 48(2), 268–305.

Salzmann, O., Ionescu-Somers, A. and Steger, U. (2005) The business case for corporate sustainability: Literature review and research options. European Management Journal, 23(1), 27–36.

Smith, C. (1994). The New Corporate Philanthropy, Harvard Business Review, 72, 105–16.

Weber, M. (2008). The business case for corporate social responsibility: A company-level measurement approach for CSR, European Management Journal,26, 247– 261.

PART II

THE COMPONENTS OF VALUE

CHAPTER 4

MARKETING DIMENSIONS OF CUSTOMER VALUE

We are surrounded by a myriad of products and services in today's modern world. The basic element of a company's offerings is called "product" in marketing. Although this term implies some kind of physical appearance, the notion of a product extends to services as well, not only to tangible goods. All elements of a company's offerings include both tangible (physical) and intangible (non-physical) components. The share of tangible and intangible components obviously differs from product to product. Products in which the share of non-physical components exceeds the physical ones are called services. The divide between tangible products and intangible services is not too big: we can rather talk about a kind of continuum (Figure 4.1.).

> A product is anything that is offered on the market, satisfies a need and can be a subject of exchange.

Although we cannot draw a sharp distinction between tangible products and intangible services, they must be distinguished from a marketing point of view. Services have particular features which require a different marketing approach than tangible products. What are these characteristics? First of all, their physical appearance. While tangible goods are "physical objects", "materials" or "things", services mean "action", "effort" or "performance". Due to their non-physical nature, the production of services is characterized by the presence of humans, and in many cases by the presence of customers or consumers. Services, in general, are produced and consumed simultaneously. As a result, services are more difficult to standardize than tangible goods, their quality is harder to assess, and they cannot be stocked or transported in most cases.

Figure 4.1. Continuum of tangible and intangible products

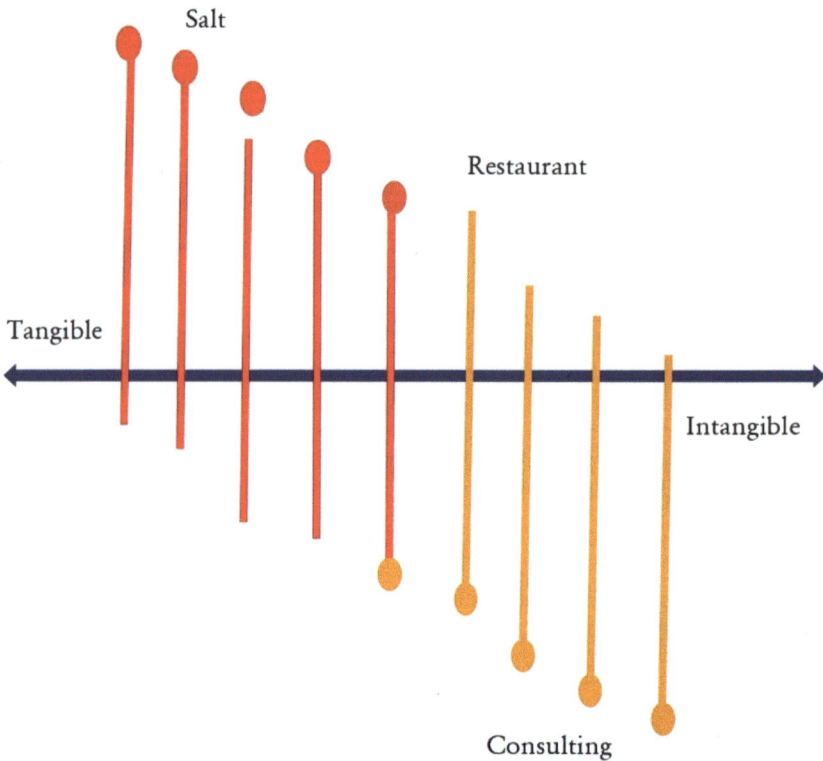

EXHIBIT 4.1. A HEALTH SERVICE PROVIDER - CLINIC ABOVE THE CITY

The Da Vinci Private Clinic is one of the most exclusive private hospitals in Hungary. The joint medical practice of renowned specialists of the Medical University of Pécs and the state-of-the-art glass and concrete hospital built on the Mecsek Mountain just above the city offers a unique opportunity. The facility spreads 1,200 m2 and includes eight surgeries, three dental surgeries, two large operating theatres and seven patient rooms, all serving the work of 50 doctors. The parking lot for patients has 18 spaces and is located directly at the entrance. The 5-storey modern building inaugurated in 2011 with its extensive green glass surfaces is an excellent example of the modern technology of the 21st century; its rooms and

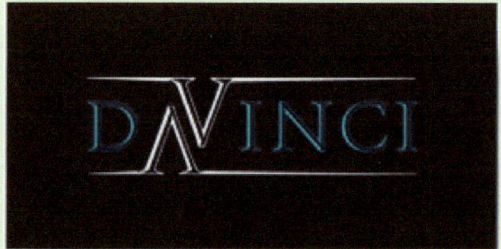

surgeries offer a spectacular view of the pine forests surrounding the clinic and the city of Pécs at the foot of the Mecsek Mountain.

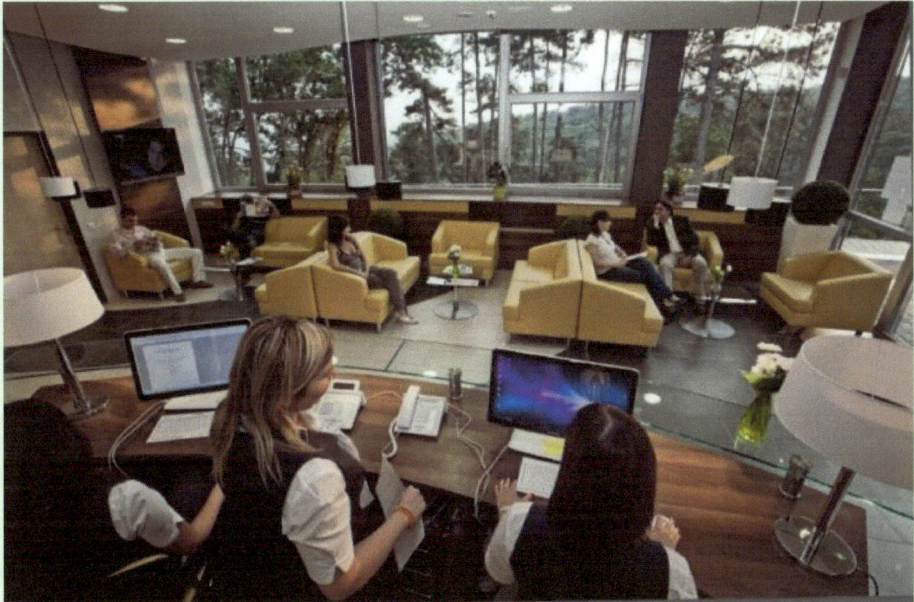

The doctors working at the clinic are leading medical professionals in their respective fields, who, in addition to their therapeutic work, are also involved in training the future doctors at the Medical School of the University of Pécs and in doing scientific research into new technologies.

Source: http://davincimaganklinika.hu/en

The market-oriented approach emphasizes that the product must be examined from the point of view of the customers, the consumers or the users. No matter how obvious this requirement sounds, reading about it in a book, practice shows that most manufacturers have not yet come to this realization. The product for a manufacturer means nothing but the totality of materials, parts, work processes, technologies, technical parameters, packaging materials, etc., which is totally understandable from their point of view. The customers, especially the buyers of consumer goods, however, are not interested

> **The product must be examined from the customers' point of view.**

in these. They care about buying need-satisfaction. Customers make buying decisions based on what they know or think about the product, or about the extent the given product will satisfy their need.

4.1. THE CORE PRODUCT

The marketing literature examines several dimensions of products. The focal points of this approach are the so-called *core product, the core benefit of the product, and* more recently *the core customer value.* The product is purchased because of the core benefit it offers. In the case of services, we can distinguish the core benefit, which can also be called core-service. The core benefit of hotels, for example, is that the guests can spend a night in a guestroom. Some accommodation providers do not intend to offer more than that. For example, low-cost hotels built on the model of low-cost airlines. The marketing literature refers to the products satisfying basic needs, i.e., offering only "core benefits" as "generic products". The best example for the business model, which offers only no frill low-cost products and services, is the Easy Group (see Exhibit 4.2.!).

EXHIBIT 4.2. THE LOW-COST FAMILY OF EASY BRANDS

In 1995 a 28 years old entrepreneur Stelios Haji-Ioannou (from 2006 already Sir Stelios), with easyJet, started a new business offering only no frill, low-cost services. This business model with its anti-augmentation policy has become a success proving that an idea going against the recommendation of the theory may also be effective.

After the inaugurating flight between Luton and Scotland in November 1995, he started to widen his business to the hotels, cars, buses, energy, coffee, gym, and other areas. The easyGroup was established in 1999. With investments and licensing out, it has become a huge entity working under the following principles (according to The easyGroup strategy):

(1) Great value,

(2) Taking on the big boys,

(3) For the many, not the few,

(4) Relentless innovation,

(5) Keep it simple,

(6) Entrepreneurial,

(7) Making a difference in people's lives and

(8) Honest, open, caring and fun.

One of its flagship is the easyHotel, which opened hotels in 35 locations. The room prices in London for example start from 12.99 pounds. A typical room looks like it, the socalled 'easy-orange colour' is dominant here as in the other easy brands.

The first Hungarian unit of easyHotel chain was opened in 2007, with room prices starting 29 euros.

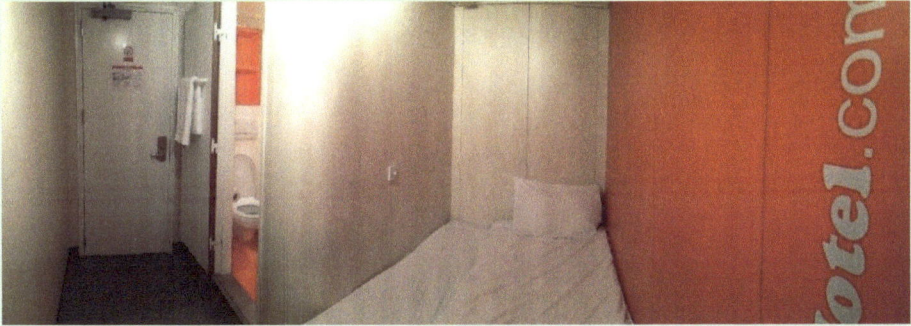

As one Hungarian paper described: It's hard to imagine anything simpler than the budget rooms built from metal and plastic and decorated in orange and white. The rooms of the hotel are equipped only with a bed, a bed-side table and a shower made of pre-fabricated panels, and you must pay an additional charge for the use of television, luggage storage and internet access. There are no other extra services available, not even breakfast.

The concept of easyHotel.com belonging to the easyGroup company is exactly the same as the operational concept of low-cost airlines: the earlier you book, the less you must pay, and you only need to shell out more money depending on the hotel's occupancy rate. Similarly to airplane tickets, these hotel rooms can only be booked online.

Source: http://utazgato.blog.hu/2007/10/06/fapados_hotel_nyilt_magyarorszagon

4.2. THE EXPECTED OR ACTUAL PRODUCT

The physical appearance (specific presentation) of core benefit includes the *actual* or *expected* product. The expected, visible manifestation of a product can vary across markets (market segments), countries, and according to the level of economic development, or even over time. The minimum expected level of hotel services in Europe include reception services, room reservation, towels and television in the room, and breakfast in addition to the guest room. In Japan, breakfast is not part of the expected services; however, slippers, the daily changing of toothbrushes and razors, as well as soap and toothpaste are. A product or service offering less than the minimum expected benefit cannot be competitive and successful on the market.

4.3. THE AUGMENTED PRODUCT

In addition to offering the services expected from a product, market participants are trying to make their offerings more attractive by providing new ones. These additional services constitute the notion of augmented product. Theodor Levitt already concluded 45 years ago that:

> Theodor Levitt (1925-2006), the legendary professor of the Harvard Business School. His most well known articles having a fundamental impact on marketing thinking include:
>
> - *Marketing Myopia, Harvard Business Review,* 1960
> - *Creativity Is Not Enough, Harvard Business Review,* 1963
> - *Marketing Intangible Products and Product Intangibles, Harvard Business Review,* 1981.
> - *After the Sale Is Over, Harvard Business Review,* 1983,
> - *The Globalization of Markets, Harvard Business Review,* 1983.

"We live in an age in which our thinking about what a product or a service is must be quite different from what it ever was before. It is not so much the basic, generic central thing we are selling that counts, but the whole cluster of satisfaction with which we surround it." [Levitt, 1973].

Theodor Levitt (1925-2006) is credited with popularizing the term globalization in the world.

The marketing literature most often presents these product levels in a three-way structure as in Figure 4.2.

Figure 4.2. The product onion

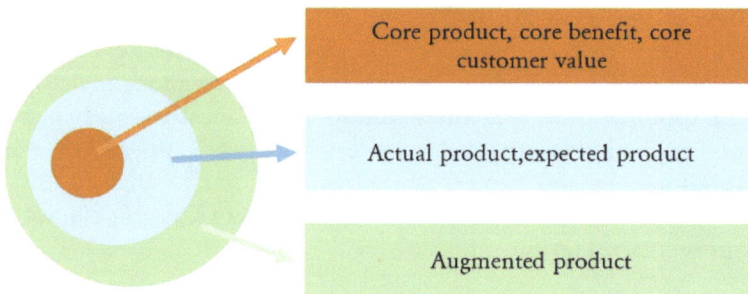

Such a structure is presented, for example, by Kotler and Opresnik in *Marketing - an Introduction* (Pearson, 13e, p. 232) published in 2017. Works analysing the topic in more details, like Kotler and Keller's *Marketing Management* suggest five-way structure (core benefit, core product, generic product, expected product, augmented product and potential product), Pearson 12e, 2006, p. 372.

4.4. A NEW CONSTRUCTION OF THE MARKETING LEVELS OF THE PRODUCT

Looking back at the value-creating functions discussed in the first chapter in Figure 1.5, and projecting them onto the customer-oriented product levels, we have arrived at a different product onion structure than the one presented in Figure 4.2. The levels of this new construction of the product onion (Figure 4.3.) express the tools required to achieve the marketing objectives of the producers:

- The attractiveness of the product helps the customers to buy the product for the first time, and with that, it serves even faster penetration of the product to the market.

- The high quality needs satisfaction aims to strengthen the rebuy process and helps to establish customer preferences for the product and with that to maintain and to grow the market share even in the maturity phase of the product life cycle.

- The good level of customer experience assists in developing a sort of loyalty, which is very important from the point of view of the rebuy and more importantly for the recommendations to others.

It is, however, important to mention that these three constructs work together, and have to be in harmony; their separation serves only didactical objectives. For example, good design or a useful and nice packaging plays a crucial role also in the needs satisfaction, and a good recommendation from others can also help the first time buyers to make their purchasing decision.

Figure 4.3. The new construct of the product onion

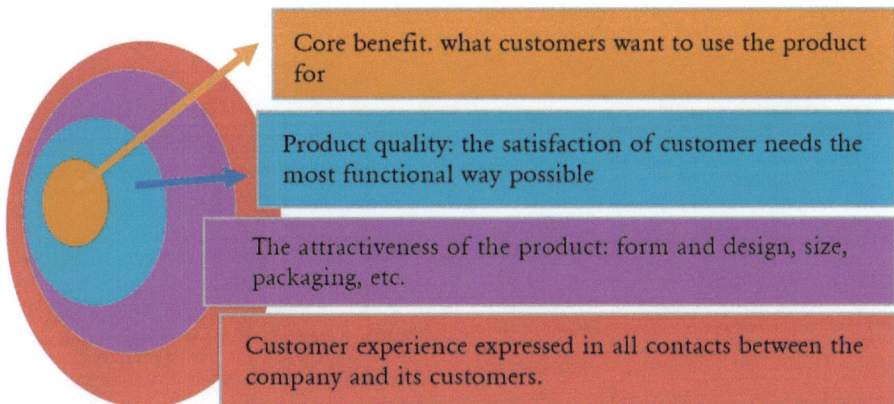

Core benefit. what customers want to use the product for

Product quality: the satisfaction of customer needs the most functional way possible

The attractiveness of the product: form and design, size, packaging, etc.

Customer experience expressed in all contacts between the company and its customers.

In the following chapters, the three levels surrounding the core product will be discussed in details.

CHAPTER 5

QUALITY, THE ESSENCE OF CUSTOMER VALUE

HIGH LEVEL NEED SATISFACTION

Providing high-level need satisfaction is only possible by offering a level of quality, which meets customer needs.

Quality is one of the most often discussed terms in management literature, yet to define it is not easy at all.

When discussing quality, it is compulsory to mention the names of three scientists whose work has after World War II totally changed the quality and reliability concepts worldwide. These are *Crosby, Juran,* and *Deming.* It is worthwhile to mention that Juran and especially Deming was active also in Japan and they contributed a lot to the shocking quality improvement of the Japanese manufacturing industries primarily in the seventies of the last century. The *zero-defect* theory described in Crosby's famous book "Quality is Free" has led to the creation of Six Sigma employed first by Motorola and since that has disseminated worldwide.

The quality definition of these three scientists is listed in Figure 5.1. together with the philosophical description and the definition of the American Society of Quality.

Looking at Figure 5.1., it is easy to conclude that defining the quality of products and services requires that the expectations of the customers should be taken as the starting point. While engineers talk about quality, marketers use the expression *perceived quality.* Customers' perception of the quality of products and services can be influenced by several factors. Some of these are presented below using also the opinions of operations management gurus like Krajewski, Malhotra or Ritzman (Krajewski and Ritzman, 2004, or Krajwsky et al., 2018).

Figure 5.1. Quality definitions

Philosophical definition:
The entirety of features that characterize the substance of things

The definition of Philip Bayard Crosby (1926 – 2001):
Quality is conformance to requirements

The definition of Joseph M. Juran (1904 - 2008):
Quality is fitness for use

The definition of W. Edwards Deming (1900 - 1993):
Good quality means a predictable degree of uniformity and dependability with a quality standard suited to the customer

The definition of the American Society of Quality:
Quality denotes an excellence in goods and services, especially to the degree they conform to requirements and satisfy customers

Source: the works of Szintay et al., 2011 and Chandrupatla 2009 were used to create this Figure.

5.1. MEETING THE SPECIFIED PERFORMANCE

It is a natural expectation of customers that the product or service should meet or even exceed the specifications the manufacturer or distributor companies claim about their products/services in their promotional materials. Some of these can be measured: in the case of cars, for example, these include consumption, acceleration, top speed, and so on. Services should also meet the specifications, although these cannot always be measured clearly. If, for example, the food delivered by Domino's Pizza is cold,

it does not meet the promised specification.

EXHIBIT 5.1. THE REAL PETROL CONSUMPTION OF CARS COMPARED TO WHAT WAS DECLARED

In 2014, ICCT (International Council on Clean Transportation), a little-known company at the time, proved that VW substantially manipulated the emission tests of their cars, and they were not the only manufacturer to do so.

Data compiled by ICCT have since proved that there is a growing gap between the real fuel consumption of cars and what was declared by the manufacturers. The following diagram shows this shocking result based on European data.

Figure 5.1.1. Gap between real fuel consumption and manufacturers' declared fuel consumption

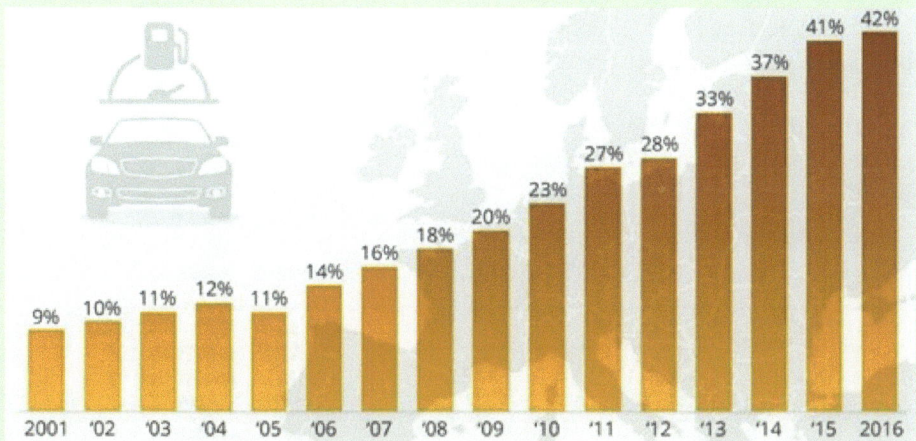

Source: https://www.statista.com/chart/11691/real-fuel-consumption-of-passenger-cars-in-europe-and-manufacturers-specifications/

5.2. MEETING THE VALUE EXPECTATIONS OF CUSTOMERS

Customers often assess the quality of a product based on how the product meets their preliminary expectations at the given price as regards to its use. If, for example, we can have a tennis racket restrung for £ 25 allowing us to play through a season without breaking the strings, the string has met our preliminary expectations, and „was money well spent". If, however, the string breaks during the second game, we are right to be disappointed and can think that the *value* (quality) of the string was not satisfactory.

5.3. MEETING THE INTENDED PURPOSE

Customers judge a product according to what extent it fits the intended purpose it was designed for or was purchased for by the customer from technical and convenience points of view. Customers may have other considerations when evaluating the fitness of the product, such as the appearance of the product, its form, its durability, its dependability (see next exhibit), its reparability, ease of operation, and so on. Services are often judged based on the external features attached to them, for example, the technical infrastructure of automobile repair shops.

EXHIBIT 5.2. J. D. POWER DEPENDABILITY STUDY AMONG CAR OWNERS

In a study conducted the first time 28 years ago, the owners of three-year-old cars were asked in 2017 what sort of problems they had been experiencing with their vehicles in the previous 12 months. The study involved 35,186 owners and altogether 224 different car brands.

Lexus and Porsche tied for first place with 110 defects per 100 vehicles. Toyota came third with 123 problems, but Camry, the 2014 model by Toyota, produced the fewest problems all segments considered.

The industrial average was 156 defects per 100 vehicles, while more than 40% of respondents said they had no problem at all with their cars during the year before. Fiat ranked last with a very disappointing result of 298 scores.

Source: J.D. Power — quoted by Origo

(http://www.origo.hu/auto/20170224-a-legmegbizhatobb-autok-friss-listaja.html)

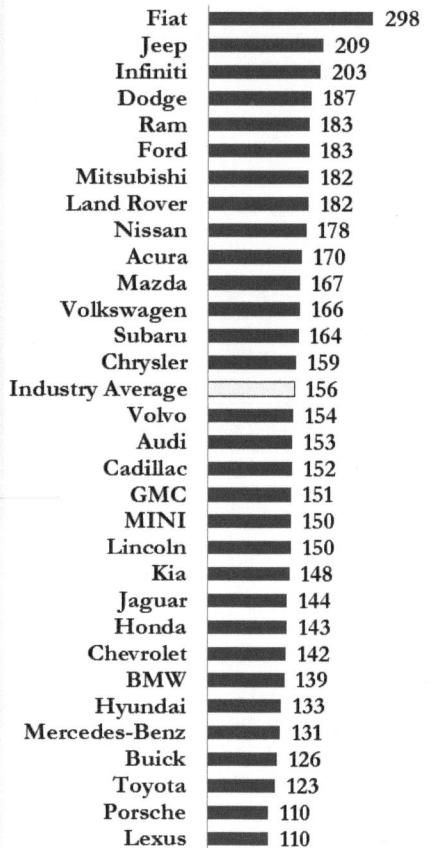

Brand	Score
Fiat	298
Jeep	209
Infiniti	203
Dodge	187
Ram	183
Ford	183
Mitsubishi	182
Land Rover	182
Nissan	178
Acura	170
Mazda	167
Volkswagen	166
Subaru	164
Chrysler	159
Industry Average	156
Volvo	154
Audi	153
Cadillac	152
GMC	151
MINI	150
Lincoln	150
Kia	148
Jaguar	144
Honda	143
Chevrolet	142
BMW	139
Hyundai	133
Mercedes-Benz	131
Buick	126
Toyota	123
Porsche	110
Lexus	110

5.4. THE EXTENT OF PRODUCT SUPPORT

Consumers also draw conclusions about the quality from the amount of support they get from the manufacturer or distributor of the product. An incorrectly issued invoice or warranty, incomprehensible manual instructions, a misleading advertisement are not signs of good quality.

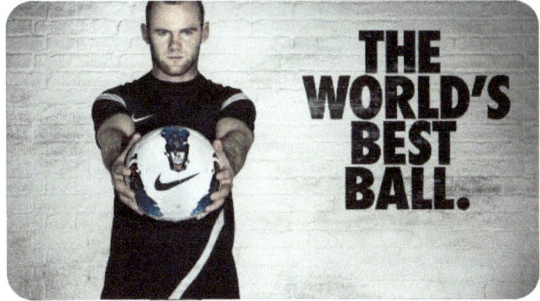

Many brands use world-famous people (sportspeople, actors and actresses, etc.) to promote their products. In the pictures Wayne Rooney, the English footballer advertising Nike and Usain Bolt, the Jamaican athlete and multiple Olympic champion promoting Nissan create the impression that these products are just as excellent as they are.

Well thought-out product support can offset the actual defects of the product; if the seller repairs the defect of the product straight away and without any trouble, the customer can take it as an accidental problem and will not formulate a general bad judgment about the quality of the product.

5.5. PSYCHOLOGICAL IMPRESSIONS

People often assess the quality of a product based on psychological impressions; image, the ambiance of the place of distribution, the aesthetical appearance of the product, etc. are all important influencing factors. It is especially true for services. A dowdily dressed, a sweaty waiter can greatly deteriorate the quality of a restaurant even if the meals served are excellent. Let us see the example of two famous restaurants (Exhibit 5.3.).

EXHIBIT 5.3. THE BEST RESTAURANT IN LONDON AND BUDAPEST

LONDON

THE RITZ RESTAURANT

By Herry Lawford from Stockbridge, UK, CC BY 2.0, https://commons.wikimedia.org/w/ index. php?curid=38428551

With sparkling chandeliers, towering marble columns and soaring floor to ceiling windows overlooking the calm oasis of Green Park, the elegant Ritz Restaurant is widely considered to be one of the most beautiful dining rooms in the world.

In charge of creating magnificent Michelin-starred meals is the Executive Chef, John Williams MBE, who is passionate about using the best seasonal British ingredients.

The Ritz prides itself in delivering the highest of service standards and in maintaining the traditional values.

Source: https://www.theritzlondon.com/dine-with-us/the-ritz-restaurant/

BUDAPEST

GUNDEL RESTAURANT

Thaler Tamas CC BY-SA 4.0, https://commons. wikimedia.org/w/index.php?curid=72008465

Gundel is much more than just one of the most well-known and oldest Hungarian restaurants.

The Gundel has built its reputation for creating an amazing gastronomic adventure. A combination of creative culinary highlights with the perfect service underlined with the sounds of a live gypsy band. Altogether a unique experience not to forget.

The name has become synonymous with an haute cuisine dynasty, a committed school, a prestigious institution, a real Hungarian specialty, and of course an internationally renowned pancake.

That's what makes Gundel.

Source: https://gundel.hu/en/about/

As you can see, judgment about the quality (value) of the product is formulated based on the overall impact of the physical and non-physical characteristics of the product. It is the task of product policy to continuously test and analyse the value properties of products and services and make continuous efforts to improve them. We will come back to the methods of analysis in the following chapters of the book.

CHAPTER 6

THE ATTRACTIVENESS OF THE PRODUCT

6.1. THE APPEARANCE OF THE PRODUCT - DESIGN AS VALUE CREATING FUNCTION

ATTRACTIVENESS

Looking at the wide range of goods surrounding us and affecting most of our everyday lives, we can immediately notice how varied the formal appearance of these goods and their packaging are. Products serving to satisfy the different needs are given a form or packaging which is essentially determined by their practical function. This determination, however, is not a direct one. The same practical function can be performed and expressed by several different forms or packaging too. Throughout the history of product manufacturing goods having the same functions have appeared one after the other and have been characterized by technical and functional improvements as well as changes and enhancement in their forms intended to express the nature and substance of the goods and reflected the different tastes of different times. This direct determination of substance and form is not only confirmed by retrospective analysis; we can draw the same conclusion by examining the design of today's products which have the same function. Even products on the market of a given country having the same functions are characterized by a multitude of forms, and the picture becomes even more diverse if we compare the products offered on the markets of different countries.

> Design (including the design of packaging) refers to the formal properties of the product which offer utility, enjoyment and symbolic benefits to the consumers.

The importance of design

Design (including the design of packaging) refers to the formal properties of the product which offer utility, enjoyment and symbolic benefits to the consumers of the product (Bloch, 2011: 378).

It is an objective fact that there is a growing demand for "beautiful" products with form and function in harmony; however, the assessment of form itself is fairly subjective, which means that it cannot be measured with precise parameters. So we can say that form becomes an important consideration for groups of products where the assessment of the product characteristics and the product itself, as well as the purchase decision are all based on subjective, emotional factors.

The classification introduced by Hillmann [1971, 61-62 pp.], according to which judgments about the characteristics and distinguishing features of a product are impacted by rational and emotional motives, still holds true. In order to illustrate the role and the changing role of these two decision making motives, he classified the goods into ten categories according to their main areas of use (Figure 6.1.). Moving along this classification the importance of the emotional elements increases more and more, while the purchase decision, is based more and more on less "smart" or rational methods.

Figure 6.1. Increase in the rate of emotional judgment according to product categories (adapted from Hillmann, 1971)

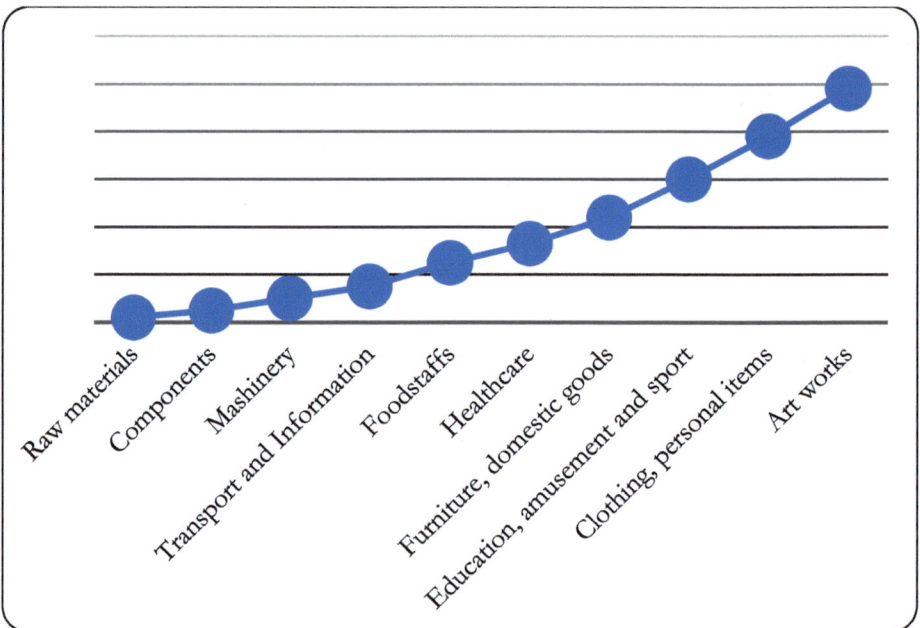

It has become clear from that above that product design can be a relevant factor in the competition between products and between companies. Companies which do not include design in their marketing policy arsenal will automatically be in a disadvantageous position compared to their competitors.

Fifteen years after the first publication of his article cited by us, Bloch concluded that marketing professionals were not really aware of the importance of design at the time and no research was done on this topic. Things have improved a lot by now, although the issue is still not given the importance it deserves. The reason according to Bloch is that „marketing professionals are outsiders in the aesthetic and engineering work closely related to design" (Bloch, 2011: 378).

EXHIBIT 6.1. THE BUSINESS VALUE OF THE DESIGN - THE MDI (McKinsey Design Index)

Not much after the critical words of Bloch the McKinsey & Company carried out comprehensive research lasting for five years about the companies' behaviour toward design. The findings of this research were published in October 2018 (Sheppard et al., 2018).

To illustrate the magnitude of the research: they followed the design activity of 300 public companies in three industries (medical technology, consumer goods and retail banking) over five years , collected two million financial data and recorded over hundred thousand design actions.

They created an index measuring the efficiency of the design activity, called MDI, and gave an MDI score to all companies participating in the research. After that, they analysed how MDI scores and the financial indicators of the companies correlated within these five years.

The findings of the research can be summarized in three points:

1. The study provided strong evidence for the business value of the design. Those companies that had a high MDI score (belonging to the first quartile) could achieve during these five years a 32 percentage point higher revenue growth and a 56 percentage point higher return to their shareholders than the others in the same industry.

2. The above results were somewhat similar in all the three industry proving that it does not make any difference if the design is directed to tangible goods, services, digitals, or any combination of them.

3. An exciting result of the research is that the markets rewarded only the bests. The revenue and the shareholders' return differences between the fourth, third, and second quartiles were marginal. The difference described in the first

point was the result of the companies belonging to the first quartile of the MDI scores.

The recommendations of the research (which actually made the components of the design index) are summarized in the next Figure.

Analytical leadership
• Measure and drive design performance with the same rigor as revenues and costs!
Cross-functional talent
• Make user-centric design everyone's responsibility, not a siloed function.
Continuous iteration
• De-risk development by continually listening, testing, and iterating with end-users.
User experience
• Break down internal walls between physical, digital, and service design.

Source: Based on Figure 4a on page 5 of the McKinsey report "The Business Value of the Design"

After the research, the firm established the McKinsey Design, its dedicated design wing, which encompasses teams focusing on product design, experience design, and service design. With some 350 designers already spread across ten global studios, "we're the biggest design firm you've never heard of," says Hugo Sarrazin, senior partner at McKinsey Design in Silicon Valley.

Source: https://www.architecturaldigest.com/story/mckinsey-design-consulting-group-confirms -the-importance-of-design-to-business

There are many ways the form and/or the packaging of the product can contribute to the success of the product on the market:

- Today's markets are characterized by the abundance of brands which satisfy similar needs. The form of the product (its exterior appearance) can largely contribute to drawing the attention of prospective customers to the product. Several examples demonstrate that a specific product was made famous by its form (such as Swatch watches, or the success of Apple products owe a lot to their appearance and even to their packaging).

- The form of the product can convey essential information to the customers. Customers can infer quality from the exterior form of the product (the same way as from its price).

The fundamental requirements of design

For design to be able to meet these important company objectives, designers should always keep in mind certain fundamental requirements during their activities. Such fundamental requirements of industrial design include:

1. the utmost purpose of a product;

2. the conditions of profitability;

3. the aesthetic aims.

Design is not an end in itself, but rather an activity which highlights the essence of the product and increases its use value. It means that "beauty" as a requirement can only be a partial objective, and "beauty" should never be separated from "goodness". Utmost purpose requires that the form of the product should help and express the functions of the product in the best way possible. A few partial requirements need to be set out to serve this purpose. Some of these are presented in Figure 6.2.

Figure 6.2. The requirements of design

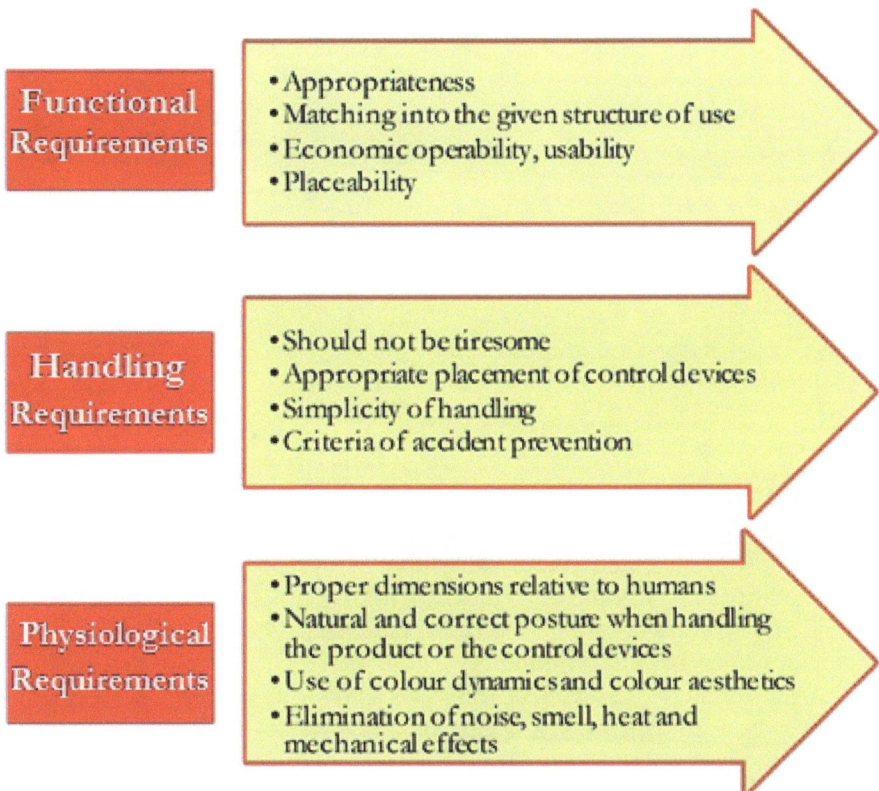

Functional Requirements
- Appropriateness
- Matching into the given structure of use
- Economic operability, usability
- Placeability

Handling Requirements
- Should not be tiresome
- Appropriate placement of control devices
- Simplicity of handling
- Criteria of accident prevention

Physiological Requirements
- Proper dimensions relative to humans
- Natural and correct posture when handling the product or the control devices
- Use of colour dynamics and colour aesthetics
- Elimination of noise, smell, heat and mechanical effects

Ergonomic aspects are given more and more emphasis in product design, as revealed by the partial requirements. Design engineers and designers must therefore always keep pace with the results of ergonomic research in order to make the machines and devices suitable for the physical and intellectual aptitudes and abilities of their users.

Design plays a key role in the manufacturing of Hyundai cars, as Woong Chul Yang, Vice Chairman of Hyundai said: "The cutting edge technology and design inspired by nature and water reflect the continuously growing attractiveness of the Hyundai brand."

Source: http://www.hyundai.hu/a-hyundairol/rolunk, Photo: By M 93, CC BY-SA 3.0 de, https://commons.wikimedia.org/w/index.php?curid=47224841

The requirement of utmost purpose clearly refutes the previously prevailing view that a product can be made "beautiful" subsequently using exterior decorations. It is becoming increasingly apparent that a nice form must be a "structural characteristic" of the product. (It also anticipates that the technical engineer and the industrial designer must work in cooperation from the early stages of product development.)

(2) The cost-effectiveness of product design is closely related to what was described in the first point, that is, if the form can assist in improving the quality of the product (offering higher quality utility value), it will be reflected in the marketability of the product and ultimately in the price of the product, therefore design will become a source of additional revenue in some way. Developing the form of a product and its continuous manufacturing however entail costs. The task of the industrial designer in this regard is to choose or design from the possible product forms reflecting the functions of the product the one which can be manufactured in a cost-efficient way even in modern mass production, which can, therefore, contribute to the "overall viability" of the product. To achieve this, the industrial designer should always take into consideration the

following principles when designing the form of production assets and most of the consumer goods:

- an effort to minimize costs,

- an effort minimize weight,

- an effort to reach optimum volume,

- an effort to apply "modular" design and

- an effort to cause the least possible damage to the environment. This latter one is also called "ecodesign" or "green design" (Eppinger, 2011).

An attempt to respect these principles requires that each case should be assessed individually and the quality of the product should never be compromised.

ARE PRODUCTS SHRINKING?

According to the report of the UK's Office for National Statistics published on July 24th, 2017 the analysis of product costs revealed that 2529 of the articles examined had become smaller in the five previous years and only 614 of them showed some increase.

(3) Adherence to the aesthetic objectives basically results in a "beautiful", attractive form attached to a good design. Artists should be entirely free, in this regard, to create within the framework of the above principles. Artistic freedom is, however, limited by certain specific laws. Such laws prevail, for example, concerning:

- proportion, dimension, and size of the products,

- symmetric and asymmetric balance,

- the importance and impact of colours, etc.

We do not intend to discuss these aesthetic requirements or the apparent principles in more detail; this is the *area where the management of a company should give the designers,* knowing these principles *a free hand.* The only reason we need to emphasize artistic freedom again is that design is the area where everybody feels to be an expert and feels competent to make decisions even without having the necessary qualifications or practice. This type of "interference problems" can be avoided by organizing the design process well and by positioning the designer at a suitable level in the organization.

A very interesting dimension, which was observed in nature and which creates the most favourable impression in objects is the so-called *golden ratio*. The ancient Greeks already knew its; the famous Parthenon on the Acropolis (see photo) or the Great Pyramid of Giza was built on a rectangular area the size of which correspond to

$$\frac{a}{b} = \frac{a+b}{a}$$ that is

the 1.618 ratio.

Photo: By Harrieta171 – own work by the person uploading the photo, CC BY-SA 3.0, https://commons.wikimedia.org/w/index.php?curid=594036

Consumer response to design

The form of the product can evoke a set of psychological and behaviour responses from people. These are presented in the figure below.

Figure 6.3. Response to the form of the product

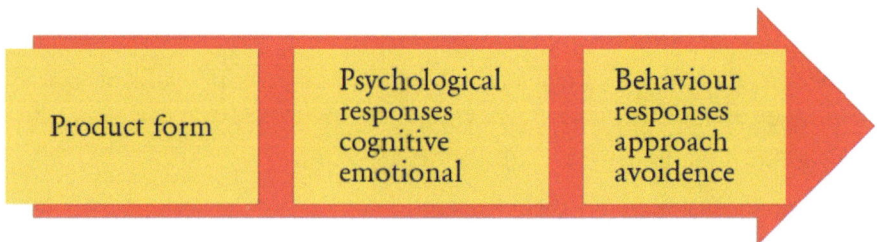

| Product form | Psychological responses cognitive emotional | Behaviour responses approach avoidance |

Response to the form and/or packaging can be either *cognitive or emotional*. Cognitive response refers to the type of conclusions a potential customer draws about the whole of the product based on its form. Customers can formulate judgments from the form about the product's durability, value, technical complexity, the prestige of use, or whether it was designed for men, women,

98

children, and so on.. Customers may arrive at a completely different *"sense of the product"* than what was intended by the designers.

Another form of cognitive response is *categorization:* consumers immediately try to classify the product into an already existing product category purely from its form. (For example, a product whose form suggests high quality will be categorized as a luxury good.) It is the interest of the company that customers position the product according to the expectations of the company; it is, therefore, important that cognitive responses related to categorization be taken into consideration during the design phase. If the form of the product is very innovative customers may find it difficult to classify the product into a category. According to the relevant theory, the innovative nature of product form can be favourable only to a certain extent: entirely new product forms can often evoke negative responses from customers precisely for the lack of categorization possibilities.

> There is no consensus among psychologists whether the cognitive responses to a product stem from the holistic image of the product or are composed of the individual features. According to Gestalt psychology, people do not perceive objects atomistically, but rather as a „whole". Judgments about a car will result from the whole of its form, rather than from the combination of judgments about the wheels, the dashboard, the bodywork, and so on. Other directions of psychology, on the other hand, emphasize the importance of details. The truth probably lies somewhere in between these two theories.

The other form of response is *emotional,* which can be aesthetic or any other type of positive or negative impact. The emotional response can range from dislike to neutral treatment, from simple like to fascination as is typical with works of arts.

The psychological responses given to the form of a product are affected by a number of factors. Among them, the *individual, social and cultural determinations, and all those situational factors* must be emphasized, in which the potential buyer meets the new form.

The psychological responses of customers manifest themselves in their *behaviour with regard to the product*s. According to Bloch (1995), these forms of behaviour can be interpreted as an 'approach-distance continuum'. If a given product form elicits positive psychological responses, the customers begin an "approaching activity". They look at the product for a longer time, observe it, touch it, gather information about it. (If they like the product displayed in the shop window, they will enter the shop and look at it more closely, they feel it, etc.)

EXHIBIT 6.2. ADDITIONAL ROLES OF INDUSTRIAL DESIGN IN CORPORATE MARKETING

Industrial design defined correctly – in the broad sense, that is at the level of industrial aesthetics plays a key role in marketing. The most important area is that of the products. Design can be used even by companies where product form design is not possible due to the nature of the products (e.g., companies operating in the extractive industry, and so on).

Design is at the heart of a creating corporate identity (CI) in companies with a resourceful marketing policy. Certain typical (sometimes traditional) forms and motifs, which usually refer to the main products of the company, are continually present and dominate all the relations of the company (material and communication) conducted with the outside world. In addition to the products, the areas of corporate PR, market manipulation and promotion should be highlighted. The role of design in these areas is to assist in creating a coherent corporate image.

Products	PR	Communication and promotion	Packaging
• Developing common characteristic design for the product lines • Redesigning product forms • Designing the trademarks, signs, fantasy names and other designations appearing on the products • Etc.	• Creating company name, logos, symbols • Showrooms, meeting rooms, • Designing the interior of retail outlets • Designing of company uniforms • Designing letterheads and logos for company correspondence • Etc.	• Designing the stands in fairs and exhibitions and shows as necessary • Advertisements • Designing films and other visual instruments • Creating POS materials • Etc.	• Designing the • material • form • colour • size • usability • handling • etc. • of the packaging

The endpoint of the "approach process" for the company is the purchase. For the customers, however, this process has not yet completed: if they like the form of the product, they will continue to take delight in it long after they have purchased it; they will put it in a place where the other members of the family and even their guests can see it. All this constitutes part of the aesthetic experience and will ultimately contribute to the success of the product on the market by word of mouth advertising.

> György Lissák calls the touching of the product intimization. The intimization of the product is closely related to touch. It seems that the product will not be to our liking upon mere visualization; we need to touch it and feel it before we believe our eyes. Deeply rooted traits are brought out of people: we own something by holding it in our hands. What we don't hold, we cannot intimizate; one would not think how important touching is" (Gyöngyössy, Lissák, 2005, p. 90.).

6.2. PACKAGING AND LABELLING

Although the discussion of design meant to include packaging as well, due to its importance, it should briefly be addressed separately together with labelling which appears on the packaging. More and more tangible goods placed on the market need to be packaged and labelled. The products need to be covered in materials which allow customers to obtain them in a comfortable way. From a marketing point of view, it is also very imperative that the packaging should carry messages. There is a strong relation between packaging and branding because packaging can help convey a lot of information which refer to the brand as well. Packaging allows the company to provide information on the wrapping material about the product which is necessary for the customers to make their buying decisions; that is the role of labelling. In the next part, we will discuss the marketing approach to packaging and labelling.

The functions of product packaging

The packaging of a product is an activity during which the wrapping material of the product is designed. Packaging has recently become a very effective marketing tool. A well-designed packaging can represent comfort value for the customers and promotional value for the manufacturers. Many market players consider packaging as the fifth element of the marketing mix in addition to product, price, place and promotion. Packaging involves all those activities which are aimed at making design or wrapping material for the product. It doesn't always play an important role (in the case of cheap products, for example), but other times it does (in the case of beauty products, for example).

Packaging must perform several functions, which are summarized in Figure 6.4.

Figure 6.4. The functions of packaging

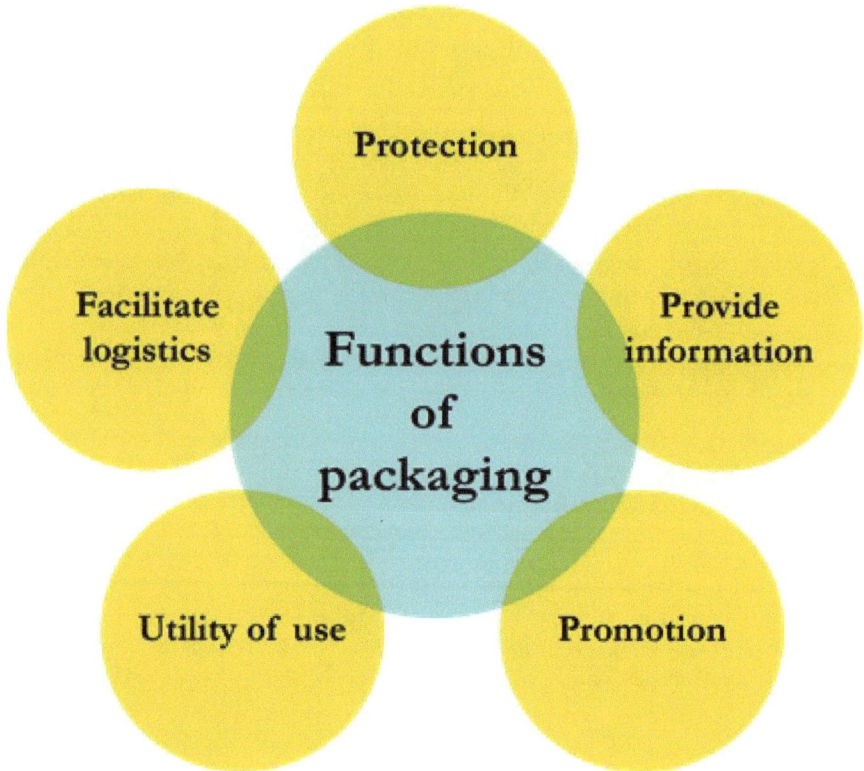

Packaging as a marketing tool

- Increases the utility of the product
- Informs the customers
- Stimulates purchase
- Identifies and differentiates

EXHIBIT 6.3. THE 2018 YEARS RECOGNITION OF MUTTI ON PENTAWARDS

WORLDWIDE PACKAGING DESIGN COMPETITION

Created in January 2007, the Pentawards are recognized as the most prestigious worldwide competition exclusively devoted to packaging design. They are open to all those who are associated with the creation or marketing of packaging from every country in the world. The primary mission is to increase the stature of packaging design and those who create it.

In 2018 the 12th edition of the Pentawards was held at the Solomon R. Guggenheim Museum in New York. The international jury of Pentawards selected this time Mutti designed by the Italian studio Auge Design the Best of The Show - Diamond Pentaward winner 2018.

DIAMOND PENTAWARD 2018 MUTTI - AUGE DESIGN

The limited-edition range of traditional Italian tomato-based ingredients have been given a new lease of life, with a blend of past and future through an intricate system of symbols, that not only represent the different types of tomatoes and sauces in the range but that also become a powerful pattern, resonating throughout the entire range. Starting from the original format, the range has been adorned with a new glamorous and luxurious feel, with a high-end gold foil finish contrasting with the ivory silkscreen surfaces. This is a design that will now join an exclusive Pentawards club, being only the 13th recipient of the Best of The Show - Diamond Pentaward crown since the Pentawards began.

Source: http://www.pentawards.org/winners/?cat=16

EXHIBIT 6.3. INFORMATION ON THE PACKAGING AND LABELLING OF PRODUCTS - TOO MUCH OR TOO LITTLE?

"Consumer protection legislation stipulates that manufacturers and distributors are responsible for providing appropriate information to consumers. Consumers must be informed about the function, quality and the main characteristics of the product. Depending on the nature of the product, the main characteristics include the size, the net weight, the composition, the origin, the sell-by date, the storage conditions, the technical specifications, the methods of use and handling" (Stágel Imréné, 2008: 2-3).

The material by Stágelné presents in detail the type of information that must be communicated about the different types of products, and in what way and in what language this information must be displayed on the products or their packaging.

The principle of economy, which was emphasized in design, also applies here. Well, a rather significant part of Europe is made of small countries whose markets are not big enough to have separate packaging. Manufacturers, therefore, wish to put the required information in many different languages on the same packaging, which in most cases makes the whole thing unreadable.

The bag shown in the picture is big enough to allow the information to be read in twelve different languages (EN, DE, FI, HU, PL, LT, RO, BG, RU, HR, IT, GR) on the back.

In the case of smaller products, however, even a magnifying glass won't be much of a help, especially if the trader sticks the price tag on top of the required text.

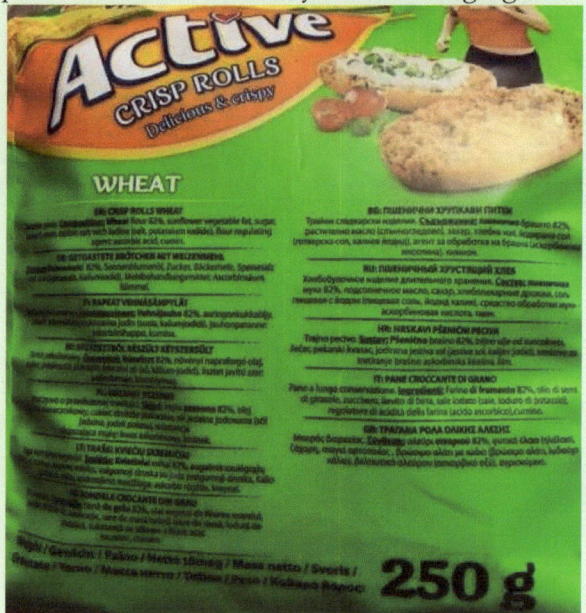

CHAPTER 7

THE ROLE OF CUSTOMER EXPERIENCE

7.1. CUSTOMER EXPERIENCE

CUSTOMER EXPERIENCE

Numerous studies have been published about customer experience (CX) in marketing literature over the past decade. The common view is that successful companies apply an additional layer to the quality representing the essence of their products and to the attractiveness of the appearance thereof, as it is well illustrated by the newly modified product onion; and this additional layer is none other than customer experience, *positive customer experience*.

But what does customer experience mean? It is not easy to define. As Adam Richardson, the author of the first part of the series of articles on customer experience published in the Harvard Business Review writes: „people have been grappling with a definition of customer experience for several years. Sometimes it's defined as digital experiences and interactions, such as on a website or a smartphone. In other cases, customer experience is focused on retail or customer service, or the speed at which problems are solved in a call center."

According to Richardson all these things should be part of it, but customer experience is more than that. Customer experience is not only a snapshot of the relationship between the customer and the company, but the totality of the emotions built up in the customer with regard to the brand and the company throughout the entire arc of being a customer (Richardson, 2010).

Looking at this definition, we can realize that most of the customer experience can be traced back to the touchpoints with whom the customer gets in contact with, notably the people involved in handling, manufacturing and distributing the products. It gives a kind of "service character" to it all. Indeed, most of the examples cited by the literature are services. Nevertheless, customer experience is the key to success in the case of tangible goods as well.

Well, we are facing a kind of paradigm shift here as well. We must agree with Kenesey and Kolos (2017) who said that the new paradigm, the *"service-dominant logic"* (SDL) described by Vargo and Lusch (2004) should be understood in such a way that the tools of service marketing are to be introduced into the world of physical products. So perhaps one of the most critical tools in services marketing are the appropriate people (P – People).

Research conducted by Bhattacharjee et al. (2016) shows that those having positive customer experience are three times more likely to repurchase and recommend the product than others. Customer experience, therefore, should become a strategic priority. The global survey of Acquia Consulting Company shows however that the endeavour of companies even in the most advanced countries is lagging behind the expectations of customers (see in Exhibit 7.1.).

EXHIBIT 7.1. CLOSING THE CX GAP – FINDINGS OF THE ACQUIA RESEARCH

To get a global view about the present state of CX the Acquia the London based consulting company did a survey among 5000 customers and 500 marketers in some selected advanced countries (USA, UK, France, Germany and Australia). The results prove that there is a huge gap between the customers and marketers' opinion about the efficiency of customer experience.

While marketers are overwhelmingly confident that they deliver excellent customer experience, yet nearly half of consumers say that brands they use do not meet their expectation for a good experience. Sixty-six percent of the customers cannot even remember the last time when a brand exceeded their expectations.

The final goal of CX is to make customers loyal to the brand. According to the survey, marketers know that every touchpoint of the customer decision journey must be well thought out and carefully curated to convert a sale seeker or impulse buyer into a life-long loyalist. Customers are however rather divided in the loyalty issue. Fifty-four percent of them does not consider themselves loyal. However, even the loyal customers' commitment is somewhat fragile Seventy-six percent say that they will move on from a brand after a bad experience.

One would think that the new technology should make the online experience with brands better. Nevertheless, according to the survey, the truth is not so cut and dry. Even though marketers have invested a lot in marketing technology and want to continue it also in 2019, 74 percent of them feel, that technology has made it harder to offer customers a personalized experience.

Another catch 22 for marketers is the trust of customers concerning their privacy. To get a good experience they expect personalized offer, however, they strongly defend privacy. This 'trust gap' is illustrated in the following figure.

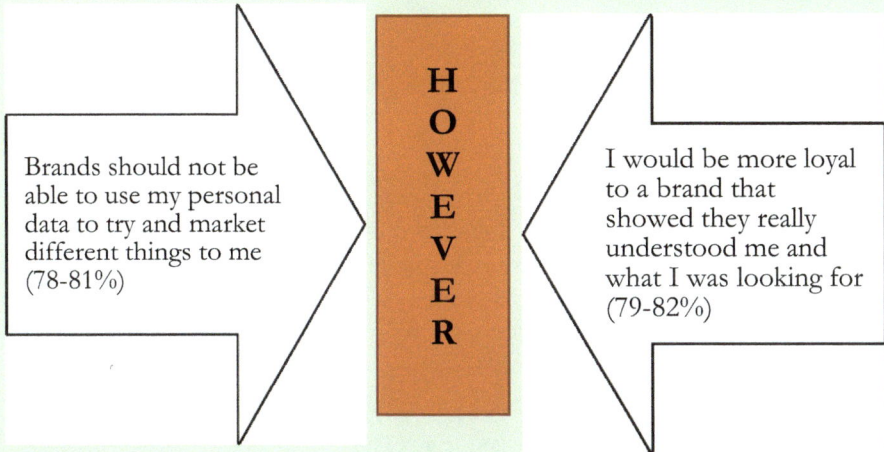

Brands should not be able to use my personal data to try and market different things to me (78-81%)	HOWEVER	I would be more loyal to a brand that showed they really understood me and what I was looking for (79-82%)

The Acquia report concludes that customers are now more informed than ever before, they prefer brands that understand and respect them. Marketers have also more tools, but with them come greater responsibility. This fragile balance will decide the success of customer experience.

Source: Excerpts from the Acquia Report (2018)

Customer experience, as it will be discussed in more detail later, is created as a result of the satisfaction of the buyer with the so-called touchpoints of the supplier. Some of these touchpoints are of a personal nature. It is an obvious objective of managers to make customers satisfied with the behaviour of the company's employers, particularly front-line people. But it is not that easy to achieve. It is not easy to realize the vision of the management by the people working in the front lines.

The WORKCENTER Employment Agency was created with the aim to provide services handling the needs arising in the field of human resources in a flexible way, taking off the burden of the "HR challenge" from the shoulder of companies and thus ensuring that the companies can operate more efficiently in their own special fields and industries.

Our progress and success is primarily owed to our attempts to meet our partners' requirements in both quality and quantity with short deadlines and maximum efficiency.

Source: http://workcenter.hu/hu/rolunk-t43/

This is where human resource management (HRM) comes into play. People with *emotional intelligence* should be hired for these positions and should be trained for these tasks, who possess the appropriate attitude towards the customers (Boxer and Rekettye, 2010). There are specialist companies for such HR tasks (see the photo above). Those interested in emotional intelligence (EQ) should read the book of Daniel Goleman published by Bantem Books.

Not all products require intensive human involvement for delivering excellent customer experience though. The closer we move from the convenience goods towards the specialty (premium, luxury) goods, the higher the need for personal involvement (Figure7.1.).

Figure 7.1. Increase in the importance of personal involvement

7.2. CONSUMER DECISION JOURNEY — TOUCHPOINTS

Traditional marketing has taught us that consumers take a particular journey before making their purchase decisions. This journey was illustrated with a funnel metaphor, where the number of potential brands gradually decreases. As Kotler and Keller describe in their 'five-stage model' (Kotler and Keller, 2006: 191), it starts with the problem recognition, followed by the information search, evaluation of alternatives, and decision. The decision means the purchasing of the product, followed by the post-purchase behaviour of the customer, which can ideally manifest itself in *loyalty, or even in evangelism.*

Source: Ceresa, A.: Marketing Profs.com December 15th, 2014

@lphascript publishing

Apple Evangelist

High Quality Content by WIKIPEDIA articles! An Apple evangelist, also known as Mac(intosh) evangelist, Mac advocate or Apple fanboy is a promoter of the Apple Macintosh platform. The most well-known Apple evangelist is ex-Apple-employee Guy Kawasaki. Kawasaki is credited as being one of the first to use evangelistic methods to promote a computer brand through a blog. Apple formerly had a "Why Mac?" evangelist site [1]. The page no longer exists, but the company ran Get a Mac, which gave numerous reasons why "PC users" should switch to Macs. Several third-parties still host and maintain Apple evangelism websites.

Frederic P. Miller, Agnes F. Vandome, John McBrewster (Ed.)

Apple Evangelist

Macintosh, Third-party Developer, Get a Mac, Evangelism Marketing.

9 786132 802392   978-613-2-80239-2

High Quality Content by WIKIPEDIA articles!

The picture above shows the cover of the book published by Wikipedia, which describes the activities of Guy Kawasaki, the Evangelist of Apple.

Representing the decision journey of consumers as a funnel implies that the initial list of brands considered worthy of attention by the consumers (initial consideration list) is gradually narrowed down in each step until *only one* remains at the point of purchase. Companies, through their marketing activities at the touchpoints, try to "push" their own brands down the funnel.

The research conducted by Court et al. (2009) found that something different was happening on the decision journey in today's digital world. For example, due to (or despite) the proliferation trend of products and media discussed in Chapter 1, the *initial consideration list* has become narrower than before; and the whole decision-making process can be described more like a circular movement (Figure 7.2.), in which the *initial consideration list* is followed by *the active evaluation phase*. In this phase, brands can be subtracted from or new brands can be added to the list. It is followed by the closing, the purchase itself, and then the post-purchase phase. During this last phase the consumer gains experiences by using the product, he/she evaluates it and ideally enters the so-called loyalty loop.

Figure 7.2. The consumer decision making journey

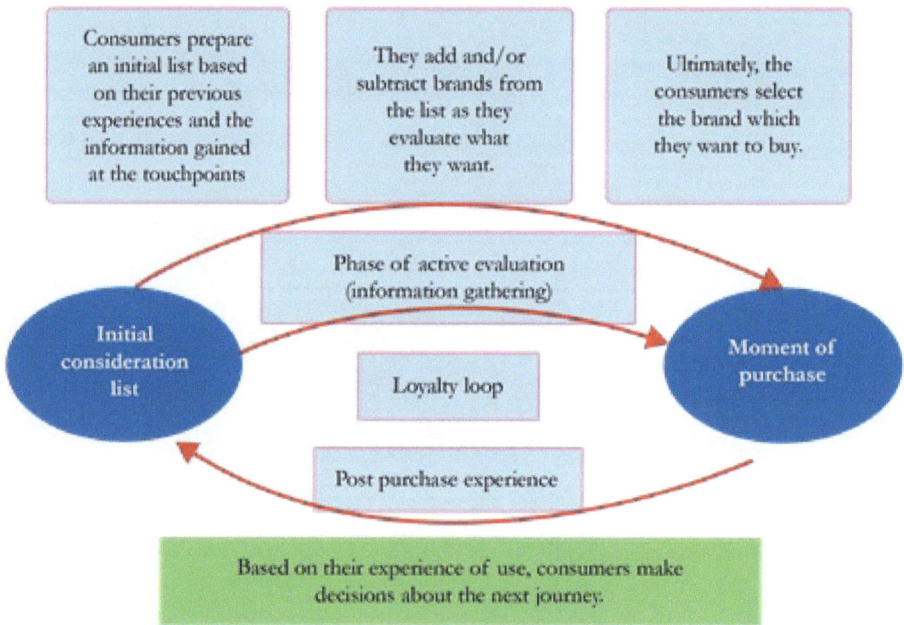

Source: Court et al. 2009: 5/13

The research has provided several important findings:

Contrary to the funnel model, the initial consideration list most of the times does not get narrowed down in the active evaluation phase, moreover it gets expanded as a result of an intensive search for information. For example, the initial consideration list in the case of cars was typically 3.8 to which was added a further 2.2 during the intensive information search.

The second important finding is that the touchpoints of the active evaluation phase were not dominated by the marketing activities of the suppliers, but rather by the customer-driven ("pull") activity, particularly by online reviews, recommendations by friends and family members, as well as the interactions experienced in the shops. Traditional, supplier-driven marketing has a more important role in the creation of the initial consideration list, but its importance diminishes during the phases of active evaluation and final decision.

The final decision is principally influenced by two factors: the personal interaction of the shop, the dealers and the agents, and the customer-driven marketing (word of mouth advertising, online search, offline search).

> "Positive customer experience can be created through permanent good experience with the brand and by providing consistent services in the different channels either online, in the shop, or from the distance." Andrea Fishman, partner, PwC Digital Services.

The research has also revealed that there are two kinds of loyalty. Some of the customers are what we call active loyalists, who do not only keep buying the same brand, but they also recommend it to others. The passive loyalists keep stuck to the same brand either for convenience's sake or for fear of the misleading variety of choice, but they are not necessarily fond of it.

A fundamental conclusion can be drawn from the results of the research about the creation of positive customer experience:

1. Company marketing must be present at the touchpoints generated by the customers. To achieve this, all the touchpoints for each product must be known, and the active loyalists must be continuously provided with appropriate content.

2. It is important to ensure that customers, consumers are not to be disappointed at the personal touchpoints. Its increases the importance of human resource management.

3. One of the priorities is to make sure that the product is included in the initial consideration list, and after that to provide the potential customers with appropriate and personalized information during the active evaluation phase. Finally, by identifying the appropriate touchpoints, the company should ensure that the customers' post-purchase experience is positive as well and they immediately enter into the loyalty loop during the repurchase.

EXHIBIT 7.2. A POST PURCHASE EXPERIENCE - WITH SAMSUNG'S CALL CENTRE

The author had a Samsung smart television, and he noticed there was something wrong with the intelligent part of the TV. He looked up the number of Samsung's customer centre on the Internet and called them. He could talk to a very kind female voice relatively fast. She suggested that he should first contact his internet service provider because the problem might be on their end. (SO FAR SO GOOD!)

He did so. Those who have ever tried to talk to the customer service of Telekom know how difficult it is to reach a human. However, this time it happened rather fast. Soon he was connected to the department offering paid services, where he was told very politely that if they manage to troubleshoot the fault with his cooperation over the phone, he would only be charged HUF 1,200 as he was a platinum customer. Well, they did not manage it. They offered to send a specialist whose success fee was HUF 6,500. He accepted. They agreed to 10 am on July 3rd. A very polite young man appeared at the time agreed. (EVERYTHING WAS STILL ALL RIGHT)

The expert very quickly concluded that the problem was not with the internet service, but with the television, and suggested to call the customer service of Samsung again. He dialled the same number with the area code 80 that the author had found on the Internet and called three days earlier. "The number you have dialled is not in service" was the automatic response for both of them. (SOMETHING DOES NOT FEEL RIGHT.)

The young man gave the author the TV's module number, so he should know it if he managed to get through to Samsung. He left and didn't ask for any money.

The following day (at 10 am on July 4th, 2017) the author called the number again, and it just so happened that somebody answered. He again explained his problem. "Are you from Pécs", asked the lady (not necessarily the same one as before). Yes, the author said. "Great. We have a repair service in Pécs. Oh… I can see from your module number that you have a large TV set and the repair service in Pécs can only handle small sets. It would be best if you turned to Kaposvár. Hold on; I'm sorry I was wrong, you should turn to our repair service in Szekszárd." (IT REALLY DOES NOT SEEM VERY PROFESSIONAL.)

"I will give your telephone number to the service in Szekszárd and they will get in touch with you. In the meantime I will check how much the repair will cost" – she said. "You know what?" – the author said. "Why don't you give me their number and I can call them." "I am afraid I can't do that - she said - because the *service has no telephone availability*". (IS IT POSSIBLE IN THE 21ST CENTURY? SOMETHING SMELLS REALLY FISHY HERE.)

So, he asked her to give the number of this call, because – he explained - he was writing a book, and it would come handy for an exhibit. She said that Samsung would not consent to record the conversation (THIS IS ALREADY TOO AWKWARD). The customer had given his consent, but they wouldn't give theirs. (WHOA).

"Oh, and by the way, the service fee would be HUF 50K." A few days later he got a call from somebody from the repair service, who came and concluded that the Wi-fi reception of the TV was not good. "If this was the only problem it would cost only HUF 12-15K, but if the motherboard was faulty, it would really cost around 50 K. You should decide" he said and left.

One-day later the author's 13-year-old grandson came to visit and said: "Grandpa, why don't we buy a cable and connect the TV directly to the router." The cable cost only HUF 800, and everything has been working fine ever since.

The above happened to the author in the first week of July 2017.

7. 3. THE WOW EFFECT

Let's return to customer experience, the decision journey and the touchpoints. It is evident that customers take a very different journey to purchase the various product categories; the touchpoints may be different, and customer experience needs to be created in a different way too.

The purchasing of convenience goods (especially the daily households items) is done mostly routinely, so the decision journey is much shorter, the number of touchpoints is fewer and is limited in most cases to one-sided communication using traditional tools. The question is whether these products can create a strongly positive customer experience, or whether they can have the same WOW effect that Apply products have on many customers.

István Sas, the well-known advertising psychologist, identified the AHA and the HAHA effects in addition to the WOW effect. According to him, the WOW effect refers the unique experience arising from the recognition of a surprising, bold, or even norm-breaking solutions; the AHA effect is the experience of recognizing a new relationship between two known things, while the HAHA effect is the pleasant experience arising from the recognition of the strange and funny relationship.

Source: presentation material by István Sas (http://www.sasistvan.hu/files/reklampszichologia/6_feldolgozas.pdf)

Source: Pickit Free Images

The answer is yes. The packaging alone can distinguish a brand from the huge set of products and can create a WOW effect in itself. If it is accompanied by the satisfaction with product quality, the WOW effect can be doubled. And there is one more thing that can add to this: the image of the retail outlet, the attitude of the people working there.

EXHIBIT 7.3. THE NET VALUE SCORE (NVS) OF B2B INTERNATIONAL

The research institute created a metric system for measuring the perceived value of the products offered by companies on the market (mainly, but not exclusively, on the B2B market) compared to their competitors. According to the company, the NVS indicator is used by more than 100 big companies, and the surveys conducted led to the development of an NVS ranking not only among companies but among specific industries as well.

The score asks three relatively simple questions from the buyers of the product (see table below) and calculates a benchmark score for companies and their brands.

	Significantly better	Somewhat better	Neither better nor worse	Somewhat worse	Significantly worse
How would you rate **COMPANY X** *on the product or service benefits the company offers, compared to the product/service benefits offered by other suppliers of similar products/services?*					
How would you rate **COMPANY X** *on its prices, compared to the prices of other suppliers of similar products/services?*					
How would you rate **COMPANY X** *on the total value the company offers, compared to the total value offered by other suppliers of similar products/services?*					

The score can be calculated *from the third question* as follows:

$$\text{Net value score} = \frac{(2 \times \text{Significantly better \% + Somewhat better \%}) - (2 \times \text{Significantly worse percentage + somewhat worse \%})}{2}$$

The results can be presented on a scale of 100 (the best possible score) and according to them:

- 60 and above: Outstanding rating

- 40 to 59: Excellent rating

- 30 to 39: Good rating

- 20 to 29: Moderate rating, acceptable but average

- Below 20: Poor rating, improvement required
  Source: https://www.b2binternational.com/research/methods/pricing-research/net-value-score-nvs/

EXHIBIT 7.4. THE WOW EFFECT OF HONDA CIVIC'S 10th GENERATION

The tenth generation Honda Civic was based on a brand-new platform from the first bolt to the last, which did it much good. It got very close to being perfect.

It is longer and a bit flatter than its predecessor, and has a boogie and cool, young and dash character. *It has a design inviting you to hop in, a design you smile at when you park it in the evening on your driveway and to which you throw a parting glance from your doorstep.*

Source: G. Nagy: The new Honda Civic busts the door on the lower-mid category of cars, 11 /05/17. ttp://player.hu/auto-motor-2/honda-civic-teszt-cvt-2017/

CASE II-1. TESTING TIMES FOR VALUE CREATION: THE CASE OF HELIOS

G. M. Pandya, S. Ganguli, R. Taparia, N. J. Shah and T. Tewari

Titan Company Limited started its operations in 1986 under the name Titan Watches Limited as a joint venture between the Tamil Nadu Industrial Development Corporation (TIDCO) and Tata Group. Titan Industries is now the world's fifth largest wristwatch manufacturer[1]. In 1994, Titan diversified into jewelry by introducing brand Tanishq, and very soon ventured into eyewear with Titan Eye Plus[2]. Titan also entered the fragrances segment with SKINN in 2013. It also introduced Fastrack, a brand for youth. The wristwatch segment included brands Xylys, Octane, Raga, Regalia, Nebula, Sonata and Fastrack[3]. The company acquired license for marketing and distribution of international brands viz. Tommy Hilfiger, Police, Coach, Kenneth Cole, and Ann Klien[4]. It started exporting watches to about 32 countries around the world with manufacturing facilities in Hosur, Coimbatore, Dehradun, and Goa in INDIA. By 2018, the watch segment accounted for Rs. 2126 Cr[12] in revenue, 10% of its total revenue[5].

Homepage of Helios (https://www.helioswatchstore.com/

Titan Industries entered the high-end watch market with the launch of Helios[6], a multi-brand watch store in Bangalore. Helios is a one-stop shop for

---

[1] Note: Rs or INR stands for Indian Rupee (In April 2019 one USD was 69.24 INR.)

[2] Note: According to the Indian numbering system **Lakh** means 100 000 (hundred thousand) and **Crore** (Cr) 10 000 000 (ten millions)

premium watches in India, offering more than 30 international brands. It has 70+ stores across 30+ cities in India. It has over 300 watch experts who help people to choose the best brands among TAG Heuer, Movado, Frederique Constant, Victorinox, Swarovski, Guess Collection, Versace, Alpina, Luminox, Seiko, and Citizen, etc.

Transparent pricing, special offers, and unmatched service differentiated Helios from other stores. Easy exchange, free shipping, loyalty program (Encircle[7]), expert sales staff and TATA brand helped Helios double its reach very fast. The customer experience was magnificent. The multi-brand format had double-digit growth resulting in a good market share[8]. The downside is low margins, the huge cost of maintaining experts, high rental and set up costs.

Market Trend

The Indian watch market for timepieces had grown at a rapid pace. The demand for timepieces includes wristwatches, table clocks, alarm clocks, and wall clocks, with wristwatches contributing highest[9]. The introduction of technology in products like smartwatches and wearables boosted the wristwatch industry. The luxury watch market is also growing very fast[9]. As the size of the population with high disposable income went up, the demand for luxury goods increased proportionally.

Based on the price, the market in India can be broadly classified into three categories that are the Mass, Mid and Premium segment[9]. Concerning volume, the mass segment dominated. On the other hand, in terms of value, both mass and mid-price segments contribute 38%. The rest includes the premium segment of the wristwatch industry in India. The super luxury segment was expected to increase at a CAGR of about 16.7%[10].

Competition in the Indian market

Helios is now at crossroads, where it is not about comparing itself with the competitors but about creating innovative ways to attract new customers. Helios had its presence mainly in Tier1 cities with limited brick and mortar stores. Its offline reach is less compared to that of combined unorganized competitors. Due to the limited number of stores, consumers preferred nearby local sellers in different cities over the far-off Helios stores. Introducing new stores was not in their cards because of the considerable setup and maintenance costs.

Introduction of e-commerce led to a competitive environment for the watch industry. The online platform showcased the same products by different sellers with a vast difference in prices. With various online offers, consumers became price sensitive and opportunistic. Along with this, several sellers sold fake products (AAA copies) at a discounted price which further hampered consumer confidence in high-value online products. Due to the positioning of Helios stores, with the availability of international brands, it became a myth that Helios focused only on the super-premium segment customers. However, Helios products start from Rs. 4,000. Due to customer-focused services, Helios created loyal customers but faced challenges to acquire new customers, compared to its competitors.

Customer Analysis

Luxury watch market garnered massive attention because of the rise in urban elite class coupled with the growth of Indians in the billionaire's club. India had a large middle-class population where almost 50 percent of its population belonged to the age below 25 years. Hence attracting and selling customers in this age group is the focal point for the luxury watch market.

Price-conscious Indian consumers always look for good bargains. Their expectations include specifications like colour, dimensions and technical aspects, along with outstanding aftersales service. Since customers also look for detailed information related to the product, maintaining a high degree of knowledgeable sales and service experts became inevitable for Helios.

The social value of owning a premium and genuine brand helped Helios establish loyal customers. Helios gained popularity among people who were conscious of their casual and professional looks. The younger generation also considered luxury watches as a mark of their social status. The premium segment wristwatch market in India can be further subdivided into three price categories: affordable luxury, luxury and super luxury. The most popular category was an affordable luxury which was economical for young professionals (see the table below).

Categories	Prices	Expected Growth	Other information
Fashion	Upto Rs 50,000	22-25%	
Affordable luxury	Rs 50,000 to 2,00,000	23.3%	Highest market share. Main customers are rising urban class with higher spending income.
Luxury	Rs 2,00,000 to Rs 6,00,000	15-20%	Rolex and Omega are major players
Super Luxury	Greater than Rs 6,00,000	16.7%	Is increasing because of the rise in the number of billionaires in the country.

Source: https://www.kenresearch.com/consumer-products-and-retail/luxury-goods/india-watch-market-research-report/419-95.html

Strategies Implemented for creating Brand Awareness & Value

Helios, brought around 40 international watch brands under one roof, bringing watches and watch-lovers together. It has an excellent collection of masterpieces exhibiting craftsmanship and timeless traditional designs[11]. Its parade featuring top international brands inspired people to add to their existing watch collection[11]. As India's leading retailer of international watch brands, Helios took a personal interest in those who wore and cherished quality timepieces thus creating value for them. Helios had set an international standard in multi-brand watch retailing in India targeting the affluent upper-middle and above class of population. It also opened stores in major airports which created footfall from all walks of life.

Helios actively encouraged customers to use only original spares to ensure quality and satisfaction. Helios also used the data from loyalty program to get consumers from purchaser other Titan brands viz. Tanishq, Eye Plus & World of Titan, resulting in successful migration of consumers. Helios relied more on superior customer service than on the advertisements. However, it still used various usual modes of promotions like SMS, WhatsApp, Radio, etc. Advertisements through print media incurred a considerable cost and low visibility because of the cluttered space. All these reaped benefits in creating loyal customers but did not result in new walk-ins.

The primary concern was that the usual promotional activities did not garner new customers. Inviting customers to product launches also helped little. To increase the footfall, Helios implemented innovative ideas like asking professionals such as dieticians, beauticians to give free consultation to the customer to enhance the overall value creation experience. Loyalty program (Encircle) launched by Titan rewarded members who choose to shop from any of the Helios stores and allowed them to earn reward points and exclusive privileges on every purchase, all with one membership. It also initiated the referral programs to increase the customer base. It did not yield expected results as far as gaining new customers, because of low involvement purchase. Helios even tried cross-promotion with other retailers to increase footfalls but execution level challenges at partner stores (other retailers) were high, and overall activity did not yield fruitful results.

Promotional Dilemma and Road Ahead

One of the issues faced by Helios was that it could not implement a marketing strategy for a brand, as it would increase sales of that specific brand rather than Helios as a store. Advertising a brand would only help directly that brand, not Helios, since customers would purchase the brand from any store and not just Helios. Other brand outlets like World of Titan had an advantage of promoting its products and increase the store footfall.

The high retention rate ensured that old customers were revisiting the stores, thus maintaining good sales. However, attracting new customers to the stores remained a daunting task. Joint ventures with top brands gave Helios an upper edge in India as an official partner. However, getting exclusive distributorship of brands was not possible since most of the well-known brands are already retailing in India.

If a consumer has purchased in any of the Titan formats, he will automatically become part of Titan family through Encircle. However, data sharing between TATA companies is not possible. It's a lengthy process with the risk of privacy dilution. Cross promotion with other retailers was tried but failed. Doing activities as Leaflet distribution is against Helios brand image.

Questions:

1. What do you think should Helios do to attract **new customers** (not part of Encircle) without compromising on the value propositions and premium brand image?

2. Do you think that focusing more on online sales is an option? What challenges do you foresee in this scenario?

3. In short, how to highlight the value of buying from Helios stores?

References

1 - https://www.business-standard.com/company/titan-company-1016/information/company-history
2 - http://research.adityatrading.com/Reports/Titan%20Company.pdf
3 - https://www.titan.co.in/shop/watches/brand=titan
4 - https://www.titan.co.in/shop/international-brands
5 - https://en.wikipedia.org/wiki/Titan_Company
6 - https://www.helioswatchstore.com/aboutus
7 - https://www.titan.co.in/encircle
8 - https://www.indiainfoline.com/company/titan-company-ltd/management-discussions/1016
9 - https://www.kenresearch.com/consumer-products-and-retail/luxury-goods/india-watch-market-research-report/419-95.html
10 - www.craftingluxurylifestyle.com/time-redefined-in-luxury
11 - http://www.highstreetphoenix.com/store/helios

CASE II-2. TECHNOLOGY-DRIVEN VALUE CREATION AT HUAWEI: SMARTPHONES

Bo YANG and Xiaoliang FAN

Huawei was established in 1987 with headquarter located in Long Gang District, Shenzhen, China. ICT (Information and Communications Technology) innovation is the foundation of Industry 4.0, and comprehensive internet connectivity is essential. Currently, Huawei provides connectivity services to one-third of the world's population, with customers in more than 170 countries. Huawei can be said to be a world-class "Connecting Expert". The company has not only become the benchmark in China's high-tech field but also has attracted the attention of other countries. Huawei ranked 72nd on the list of the 2018 World Top 500 Company released by Fortune.

Huawei released its financial report for 2018 on March 29, 2019. The company reported 721.2 billion Yuan (1 Chinese Yuan was around 0.15 US dollars at the time of the report) in global sales revenue, a YOY growth of +19.5%; net profits of 59.3 billion Yuan, an increase of +25.1%. The consumer business's annual revenue was 348.9 billion Yuan, a YOY +45.1%, accounting for 48.4% of the total revenue, making this business the largest source of revenue for Huawei for the first time. The growth of the consumer business was driven mostly by technological innovation and value creation for the consumers.[3]

Huawei's smartphone business

According to the 2018 global smartphone sales data recently released by IDC (International Data Corporation) , the world's top three smartphone manufacturers were ranked as the following: Samsung, Apple and Huawei. However, Huawei is the only one that achieved significant growth in 2018, with shipments up by 33.6% from the previous year. Samsung and Apple sales fell by 8% and 3.2% respectively. For the YOY see table below.[4]

Among suppliers, the gap between Huawei and Samsung narrowed from 11.2% in 2017 to 6.1% in 2018, and in July 2018, Huawei's sales of smartphones surpassed Apple for the first time making the company the second largest smartphone brand in the world. Moving up on the value/quality ladder: Mate 7, the first Chinese-made premium mobile.

---

[3] 2018 Annual Report, Huawei Investment Holdings Co., Ltd., https://www.huawei.com/en/press-events/annual-report/2018?ic_medium=hwdc&ic_source=corp_banner1_annualreport

[4] IDC Announces 2018 Global Smartphone Shipment: Huawei is slightly lower than Apple and Xiaomi is ranked fourth, Sohu, http://www.sohu.com/a/292611184_115565

Top 5 Smartphone Companies, Worldwide Shipments, Market Share, and Year-Over-Year Growth, Calendar Year 2018 (shipments in millions of units)

Company	2018 Shipment Volumes	2018 Market Share	2017 Shipment Volumes	2017 Market Share	Year-Over-Year Change
1. Samsung	292.3	20.8%	317.7	21.70%	-8.0%
2. Apple	208.8	14.9%	215.8	14.70%	-3.2%
3. Huawei	206	14.7%	154.2	10.50%	33.6%
4. Xiaomi	122.6	8.7%	92.7	6.30%	32.2%
5. OPPO	113.1	8.1%	111.7	7.60%	1.3%
Others	462	32.9%	573.4	39.10%	-19.4%
Total	**1,404.9**	**100.0%**	**1,465.5**	**100.0%**	**-4.1%**

Source: IDC Quarterly Mobile Phone Tracker, January 30, 2019

Source：http://www.sohu.com/a/292611184_115565

In the history of Huawei's mobile phone development, Model Mate7 is an important milestone. In 2014, Huawei released Mate7, which was the first Chinese-made premium mobile phone. Mate7 sold 1 million-units within a month, which was the first time that a Chinese domestic mobile phone brand won successfully against Apple and Samsung in the phone price range of RMB 3K to RMB 4K.[5] (RMB = Chinese Yuan).

Compared to its competitors, Mate7 offers some unique product features. For example, it has an 83.1% screen ratio, a 6-inch 1080P screen, a safer press-type fingerprint recognition, and a self-developed Kirin 925 eight-core processor, a more powerful signal receiving capability, an ultra-large capacity 4100mAh battery, and an EMUI3.0 software operating system. Supported by a comprehensive upgrade of hardware and software, Mate7's screen display is more amazing, its touch is more sensitive, so that users can enjoy a new experience.

In order to rapidly expand the marketing share of the high-end mobile phone in China, Huawei set a lower price for Mate7, even though the model had certain feature advantages. Compared to its competitors like Apple iPhone 6 plus (which was priced at RMB 6,088, RMB 6,888 and RMB 7,788), the phone price of Huawei Mate7 were RMB 2,999 and RMB 3,699, only about half of its competitor's price.

With the unprecedented success of Mate7, Huawei has determined the core functional criteria of the Mate series, called DNA: Large screen, Long battery life, High performance and Security. Every generation of Huawei product since then have been constantly optimized according to the DNA.

---

[5] Huawei Mate7/Apple 6 Plus comparison, mobile.zol.com.cn, http://mobile.zol.com.cn/483/4836455_all.html#p4857078

Comparison of cost and pricing

On November 10, 2017, TechInsights published a report comparing the component costs of the Apple iPhone 8, the Huawei Mate 10 and the Samsung Galaxy S8[6]. As can be seen in the next table, the manufacturing cost of the Apple iPhone 8 and Huawei Mate 10 have very similar costing models. The parts costs of the iPhone X and the Galaxy S8 are close, but their list prices are significantly different.

List prices and manufacturing costs of some competing smartphone models.

	Apple iPhone X	Apple iPhone 8	Huawei Mate 10	Samsung Galaxy S8
Teardown Date	November 2017	October 2017	October 2017	April 2017
Product Price	$999.00	$699.00	$710.00	$725.00
Manufacturing Costs	$357.50	$285.00	$290.00	$326.50
The share of Costs in Price	35.8%	40.8%	40.8%	45.0%

Source: https://techinsights.com/about-techinsights/overview/blog/cost-comparison-apple-iphone-x-apple-iphone-8-huawei-mate-10-samsung-galaxy-s8/

On the Way to the Premium Segment: Mate 20 Pro

In October 2018, Huawei released the Mate20 Pro[7]. The product has achieved a complete break-through in technology; especially the camera functionality has a significant advantage. Mate20 pro has 40 million wide-angle + 20 million super wide-angle + 8 million zoom cameras, which can achieve super wide-angle and super macro camera functions at the same time.

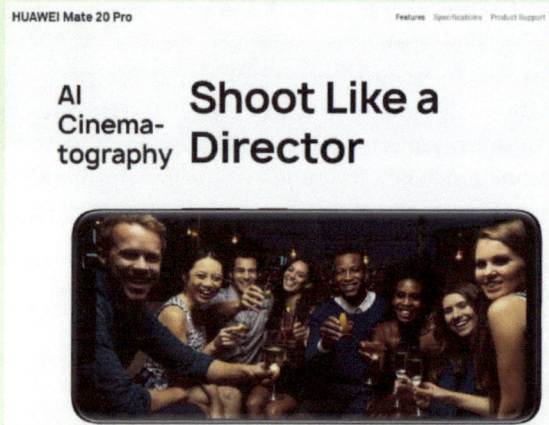

Source: https://consumer.huawei.com/en/phones/mate20-pro/

The Mate20 Pro features a Kirin 980-based leading computing system, a

---

[6] Cost Comparison – Apple iPhone X, Apple iPhone 8, Huawei Mate 10, Samsung Galaxy S8, TechInsights, https://techinsights.com/about-techinsights/overview/blog/cost-comparison-apple-iphone-x-apple-iphone-8-huawei-mate-10-samsung-galaxy-s8/

[7] Mate P20 Pro, consumer.huawei.com, https://consumer.huawei.com/au/phones/mate20-pro/

unique 4200mah battery + 40W super-fast charge + 15W wireless fast charge function. The 2K hyperbolic OLED screen puts Huawei at the top of the mobile screen manufacturers for the first time. In addition, the product also has a structured light-based face ID, under-screen fingerprint recognition, dual-frequency GPS positioning, fully symmetrical design, and back cover anti-fingerprint. With these features, Mate20 pro has become one of the benchmarks for smartphones worldwide.

Regarding the pricing of the Chinese market, the price of Samsung note9 starts from RMB 6,999, the price of iPhone Xs MAX starts from RMB 9,599, and the price of mate20 pro starts from RMB 5,399. In addition, the price of mate20 pro in Europe is 1,049 euros, equivalent to about RMB 8,300. Overall, following the technology improvements, Huawei has moved upward on pricing so the gap with its competitors was also narrowing. In recent years, Huawei has been continuously enhancing its technical strength and gaining the brand awareness, and its market share has continued to increase.

The Mate20 series leads the innovation of the mobile phone industry in terms of AI, performance, battery life, charging, camera, and design. The global shipments exceeded 5 million units in two months, and Mate20 Pro also achieved a historic breakthrough in pricing in Europe.

No. 1 5G foldable phone: Product Mate X

On February 24, 2019, Huawei released the world's first 5G foldable screen phone Mate X[8]. Ushering in the 5G revolution with the Huawei Balong 5000, the world's first 7nm multi-mode 5G chipset achieves the industry-leading 5G download speed. The Mate X with Balong 5000 officially unlocks a new experience in the 5G era. It takes only 3 seconds to download a 1G movie, and the dual card supports 4G and 5G respectively. The Mate X is engineered to be impressively thin with the Falcon Wing design. This unique stretchable hinge is artistically crafted to dissolve into the device for a smooth and flat finish on both sides of the device.

The Mate X is declaring a new epoch for screen design that is now edge-to-edge for a real HUAWEI Full View.

The Mate X is equipped with a 4500mAh high-capacity battery and the world's fastest 55W super-fast charge, which can charge to 85% in 30 minutes, and also has AI smart power-saving technology. The Mate X 8GB+512GB is priced at EUR 2,299, which is far more than the Samsung's Galaxy Fold's price of USD 1,980.

Since Apple first set the price of smartphones at more than USD 1K, Samsung and Huawei have also launched mobile phones with more than USD 1K and even released folding phones with more than USD 2K. According to

---

[8] HUAWEI Mate X, consumer.huawei.com, https://www.huawei.com/en/

IDC, the average selling price of smartphones rose from USD 542 a year ago to USD 575 in the fourth quarter of 2018.[9]

HUAWEI Mate X
CO-ENGINEERED WITH *leica*

Meet the Unprecedented

Explore More →

Source： https://www.huawei.com/en/

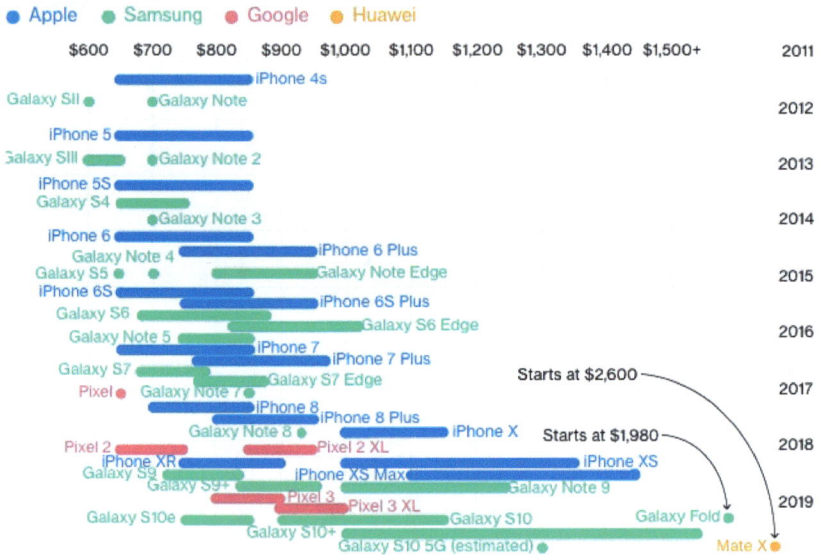

Major Smartphone Prices Over Time
Prices have skyrocketed since 2017

● Apple ● Samsung ● Google ● Huawei

Source: Bloomberg data

Samsung and Huawei are hooked on Apple's high-priced mobile phone strategy

Source： http://tech2ipo.com/10038954

[9] Samsung and Huawei are hooked on Apple's high-priced mobile phone strategy, tech2ipo, http://tech2ipo.com/10038954

Investment in Innovation: More Value to Customer, Higher Price

In recent years, Huawei mobile phone products have been shifted strategically to the high-end market. In this development, innovation has played a key role.[10] Huawei has invested more than 10% of its sales revenue each year in research and development. In the past ten years, Huawei has invested a total of 485 billion Yuan in research and development. At present, Huawei has more than 80 thousand R&D personnel. In 2018 alone, Huawei's R&D investment reached a record 101.5 billion Yuan (about 14.8 billion US dollars), accounting for 14.1% of Huawei's total revenue. By the end of 2018, Huawei had acquired more than 87,800 patents worldwide. According to the World Intellectual Property Organization (WIPO) data, Huawei submitted 5,405 patent applications in 2018, ranking the first in the world.

Summarizing the developments of recent years, thanks to the results of the substantial investments in R&D, Huawei has continuously improved its competitive advantage, has provided more customer value while progressively increased its prices.

Questions:

1. Evaluate the impact of technological innovation on mobile phone pricing.

2. Discuss the impact of pricing on the revenues and profits of mobile phone companies.

3. Analyse the relationship between technological innovation and customer value in the context of Industry 4.0.

---

[10] 2018 Annual Report, Huawei Investment Holdings Co., Ltd., https://www.huawei.com/en/press-events/annual-report/2018?ic_medium=hwdc&ic_source=corp_banner1_annualreport.

PART III

MANAGING THE VALUE

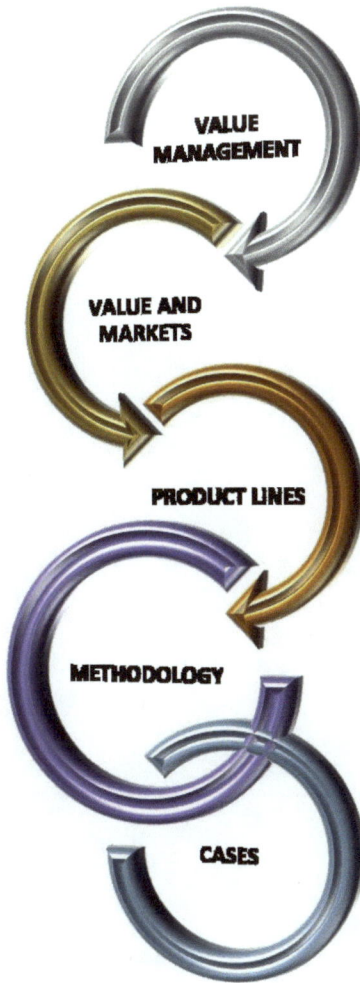

CHAPTER 8

CORPORATE VALUE MANAGEMENT

Given the decisive role of value, the notion of value management appears more and more often in corporate practices and the literature of the 21st century. The notion of value management is very similar to that of product policy, but it is different in that conscious value management makes decisions by always focusing on customer value. The notion of value management can be interpreted in different ways:

- The concept of value management originates from the middle of the 20th century when it was analogue with the value analysis or value engineering developed by Lawrence D Miles and tested successfully at the General Electric Company.

- The notion of value management had been widened by the turn of the century, expressed adequately in the definition of Dumond (2000). According to him, value management includes the organisation of processes within a company – like organization of work, communication, information, customer service and the whole company culture – in such a way that focuses on value creation and continuous modernization (Dumond, 2000).

- Another definition from the same time: "A value creating process means the purchasing, handling and use of resources with the aim of creating value for the consumers" (Chikán and Demeter, 1999, p.3.).

According to our definition, value management is a combination of the approaches quoted above. It starts by planning the value of the elements of products and their aggregates, but it also includes the analysis of how the company's competitiveness compares to that of other organizations on the markets and takes the internal (and external) measures which are necessary for efficiently producing value.

8.1. THE LEVELS AND FUNDAMENTAL CONCEPTS OF VALUE MANAGEMENT

The marketing side of value management has three levels, just as in the case of traditional product policy (Figure 8.1.).

Figure 8.1. The levels of value management

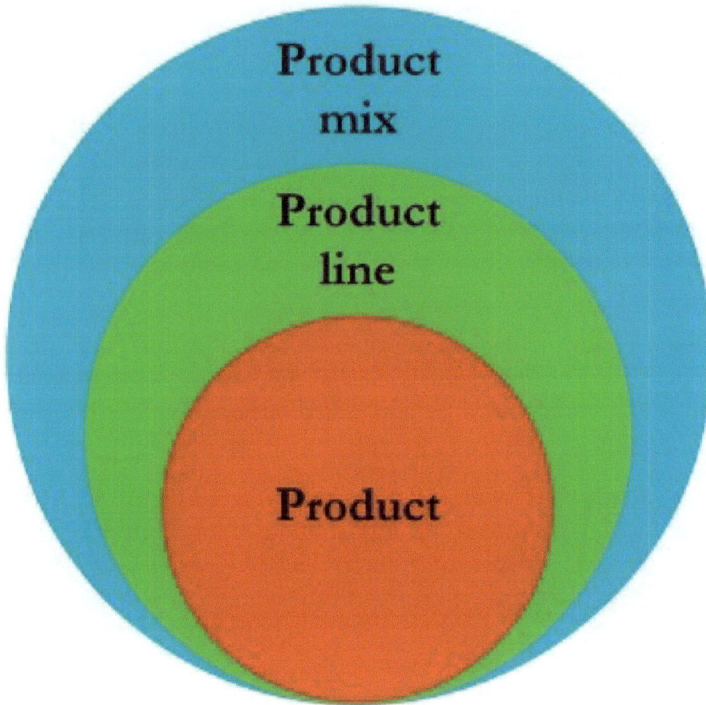

• The management of individual products and services,

• The management of product lines, and

• The management of the companies' total offer that is, the management of the product mix.

Integrated value management cannot interpret these levels separately, in isolation. The relationship is evident: a product line is made up of products which satisfy the same need, are well-designed, represent a differentiated value and are well-positioned, and these well-composed and well-positioned product lines together constitute the company's (or corporate division's) product structure, which determined the successful market position of the whole organization. How closely these levels are connected largely depends on the *brand policy* chosen by the company. From market position point of view, the connection is smaller if the company uses so-called individual branding: as products and product lines are not linked in the minds of customers. Naturally, the integration of value management within the company persists here as well. (Nothing illustrates this better than the organisational system of Procter & Gamble, which has traditionally been practising individual branding: managers in charge of the individual brands in a product line are subordinated to a manager in charge of a whole product line. This manager coordinates the product line's marketing.) It is explicitly important from the point of view of corporate or corporate line brands to carefully plan value, which allows brands to complement each other and enhance each other's value through synergy. Marketing literature usually illustrates the presence of the three levels of products (value) management in the company with the following diagram (Figure 8.2.).

Figure 8.2. Illustration of the company's product portfolio

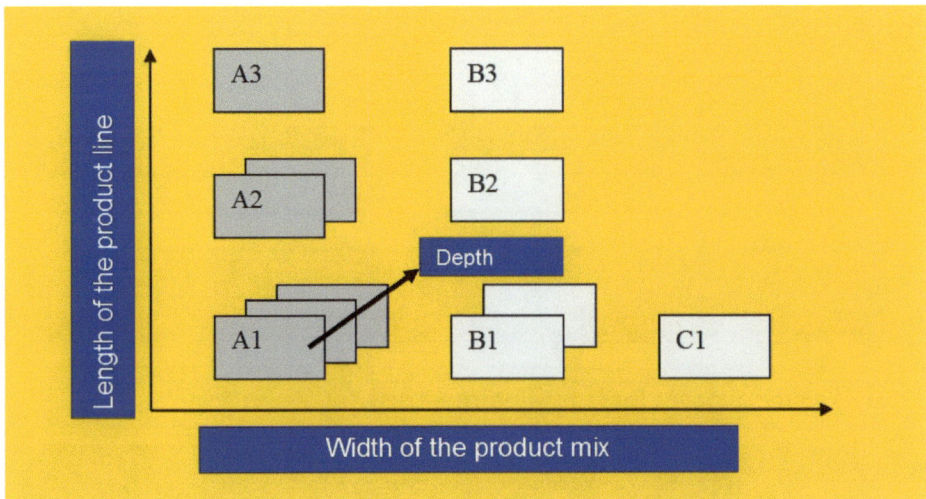

Characteristics:

1. *Width*: the number of products lines

2. *Length*: the average number of products belonging to the product lines

3. *Depth:* the average number of product varieties

4. *Consistency:* the extent of similarity among products and product lines

The offerings of larger companies or company groups cannot really fit into this structure. These interlocking company conglomerates are called company groups or holding companies in Western countries, keiretsus in Japan and chaebols in Korea. Figure 8.3. presents the Samsung company group.

Figure 8.3. The product hierarchy of Samsung

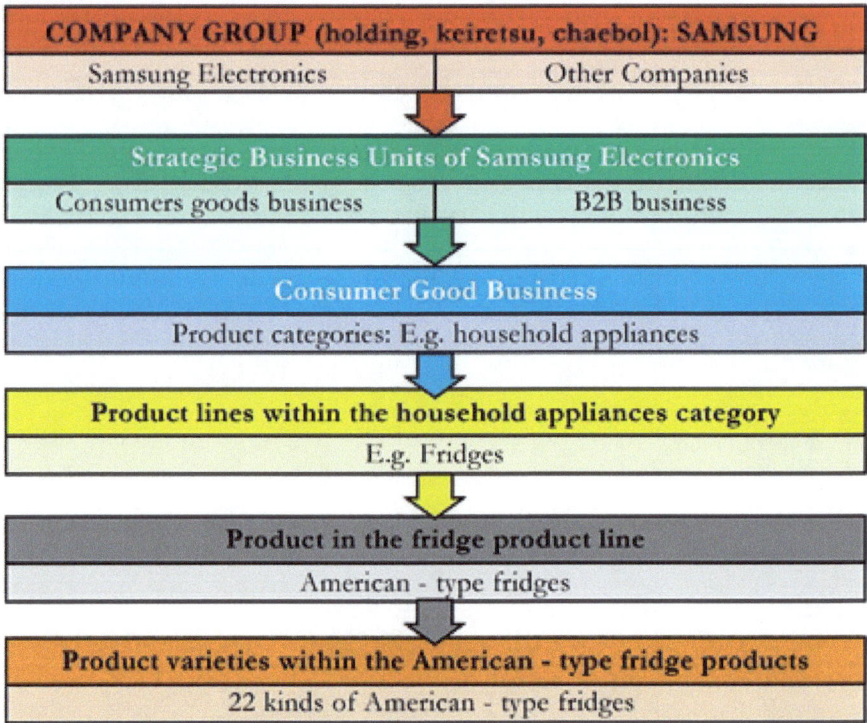

COMPANY GROUP (holding, keiretsu, chaebol): SAMSUNG	
Samsung Electronics	Other Companies

⬇

Strategic Business Units of Samsung Electronics	
Consumers goods business	B2B business

⬇

Consumer Good Business
Product categories: E.g. household appliances

⬇

Product lines within the household appliances category
E.g. Fridges

⬇

Product in the fridge product line
American - type fridges

⬇

Product varieties within the American - type fridge products
22 kinds of American - type fridges

Let's take a closer look at the terms used.

> *The totality of products and services offered by the company is called product mix or* **product portfolio**.
> *The term* **"assortment"** *is similar to product mix, but it is more often used in retail, while product mix is is rather used by producers.*

> The *strategic business unit* (SBU) is the part of the company, which can be clearly distinguished from the others in that it caters for a different, well-determined market, and for which the company prepares separate plans regarding its products and markets.

A *product category* designates the groups of products which satisfy the same or similar kind of needs. Fanta, for example, is a brand that belongs to the *product category* of soft drinks.

The term *product line* is used to describe the group of products offered by the company on the market which can be considered related to each other based on certain characteristics (e.g. same customers, same methods of use, similar production technology, same distribution channels, etc.).

The company function referred to as value management is typically called product portfolio management (PPM) by the non-marketing literature. The literature on production management abounds in articles dealing with product portfolio and new product portfolio management. Many of them investigate, often using complicated mathematical and statistical instruments, how to create an optimal portfolio that can generate the highest profit for the organization.

It is a generally held view in the field that a highly diversified product portfolio which satisfies a wide variety of customer needs can contribute to increasing not only the sales revenues of the company but its performance as well (Van et al., 2012). This general view led to product proliferation, which we mentioned earlier among the megatrends (Tolonen et al., 2014). Masses of new or modernized products appear on the market, while the number of those withdrawn is much more limited. According to estimations, 1.8 new products emerge for 1 product withdrawn from the market. It should also be noted, however, that the higher number of products offered can lead to a decrease in the sales per product and can also increase the uncertainty of customers.

Van et al. (2012) describe, for example, how Procter & Gamble managed to increase the sale of Head and Shoulders by 10% while decreasing the number of varieties offered from 26 to 15.

8.2. THE STRATEGIC AREAS OF VALUE MANAGEMENT

Companies can become successful if they manage their offerings, that is, their product portfolio, in line with the prevailing market conditions and the skills, competences, opportunities and resources of the company. Let's have a look at the most important decision points:

1. The most important strategic question is to decide which market segment (lower, middle, or upper) the company intends to target with its product range. To make this decision, the company must know the structure of the given market, the needs of the customers belonging to the given market segment, as well as its own abilities.

2. It is a strategic task that the company should always be able to shape the profit-generating ability of certain parts of its offering, from its strategic business line to certain products.

3. It is also a strategic question with how wide and deep an offering the company appears on the market. The management of product lines plays a pivotal role in this area.

4. Another strategic question concerns how innovation-sensitive the company is; to what extent it is capable of development, designing new products and launching them on the market.

5. It is a strategic issue how to create sustainability and continuous maintenance along the full length of the company's supply chain, from the purchasing of raw materials to the use of finished goods.

EXHIBIT 8.1. HENKEL'S STRATEGIC BUSINESS UNITS

The Chairman of Henkel, the company which generated 18.7 billion Euro turnover in 2016, summarized the long-term strategy of the company in his presentation entitled **HENKEL 2020+** at the investors' conference in November 2016 as follows:

OBJECTIVE: creating sustainable value.

VISION: leading with innovations, brands and technology.

MISSION: serving our customers and consumers worldwide as the most trusted partner with leading positions in all relevant markets and categories - as a passionate team united by shared values.

VALUES: Customers, people, financial performance, sustainability, family business.

All this is based on a strongly founded and well-balanced, coherent portfolio, which includes three strategic business lines:

Adhesive technology

Beauty care and laundry

Home products

The leading brands of the company include BONERIT, Dial, LOCTITE, Persil, Pril, Purex, Schwarzkopf, Syoss, Technomelt.

The distribution of SBU sales, 2015

- Adhesive technology
- Body care
- Home products

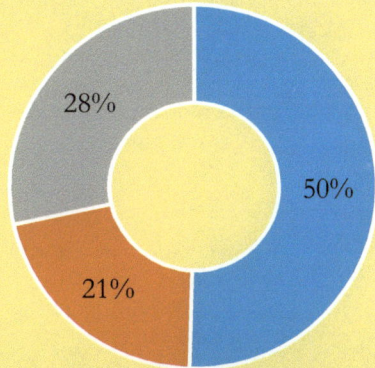

28%

50%

21%

Financial indicators of the three business units (First half of 2017)

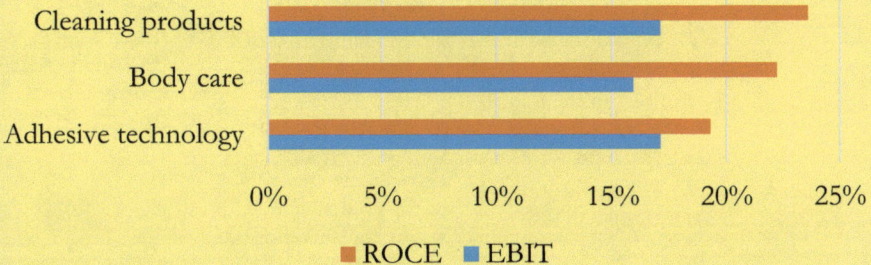

Cleaning products

Body care

Adhesive technology

0%   5%   10%   15%   20%   25%

■ ROCE   ■ EBIT

<u>NOTE</u>: ROCE = Return on Capital Employed; EBIT (Earnings Before Interest and Tax)

Source: Van Bylen and Knobel (2016) Henkel 2020, Investor & Analyst Conference and Henkel.com and **HENKEL 2020+** Henkel.hu

8.3. THE EXECUTORS OF VALUE MANAGEMENT IN THE COMPANY

To be able to put value on the market, a company must have an appropriate organization. This organization is called product management, or according to the given level, product line management and product portfolio management. The tasks of the managers working on these levels are summarized in Table 8.1.

Table 8.1. The levels and tasks of product management

	PRODUCT (BRAND)	PRODUCT-LINE	PRODUCT-STRUCTURE
	Product or brand management	**Product line management**	**Business unit (division) or company management**
Decisions and tasks	• Selection of target market (segment) • Positioning of product • Creation and development of product quality, functions and design • Product differentiation • Packaging • Branding decisions • Price setting • Selection of distribution channels • Market manipulation • Management of the product in the different stages of its life cycle • Etc.	• Selection of target market (segment) • Positioning of product line • Extension or contraction of product lines • Brand policy decisions • Allocation of marketing resources among the products • Modernization of the product line and timing thereof • Establishing the price relationships between the members of the product line • Other marketing-mix decisions • Etc.	• Allocation of resources among product lines • Introduction of new product lines • Elimination of existing product lines • Decisions concerning the modernization and development of product lines • Development of product and product line portfolios • Etc.

Main methods	• Analysis of product life-cycle • Preference and perceptual mapping • Brand awareness and preference studies • Competition monitoring • Price analyses • Measurement of advertisement efficiency • etc.	• Analysis of product line life-cycle • Positioning analysis • Portfolio analysis • Competition monitoring • Brand awareness and preference studies • Price analyses • Measurement of advertisement efficiency • etc.	• Portfolio analysis • Competition analysis • etc.
Planning	Programs	Marketing plans	Strategies, corporate-level marketing plans

The table clearly illustrates how complex the tasks of product managers and product-line managers are, and that they involve a variety of corporate functions. A common criticism of the role of product managers' position is that their role is relatively limited. It is after all the sales department that decides which products should be eliminated and which ones should be kept, R&D decides which new products or productvarieties are ready to be launched on the market, and finally, production decides how many of these products they can produce and at what cost. This fragmentation of decisions can lead to gaps and contradictions between corporate strategy and execution causing damage to the image of the product line and that of the company.

Jaruzelski et al. (2013) argue for a strong product and product line management. They named this model strong-form product management, which according to them guarantees the success of product lines and the execution of the product strategy. In the strong-form product management, the product manager is elevated to the level of "managing director", who can squeeze the results from the business units he/she oversees through a clear understanding of customer needs and leveraging the resources available. To achieve this, several conditions must be satisfied:

- a person with the necessary skills must be found for the task,

- the product manager must be allowed to see the financial indicators even for one specific product,

- the product manager must establish deep customer relations,

- the product manager should have the authority to make decisions even regarding production,

- must be able to cross functional boundaries.

Jaruzelki et al. mention as a good example the chief engineer of Toyota Prius (that's what they called the product manager there), who was given broad decision rights, which led the company to launch their hybrid car two years ahead of the competitors.

8.4. THE RELATIONSHIP BETWEEN VALUE MANAGEMENT AND COST MANAGEMENT

The analysis of the costs of value management, or more precisely of the value/cost ratio and its comparison with the competitors' indicators form an integral part of value management. The process of comparison is practically the same as the activity of *benchmarking* which is given much attention in management literature. There are two ways to analyze cost/value (in addition to benchmarking): either to analyse the most important product characteristics separately or to perform an overall analysis of these characteristics for the whole product. We will focus on the latter one, the overall analysis.

If we represent customer value on the horizontal axis and costs on the vertical axis of a coordinate system, in parallel to the range corresponding to value we can draw the so-called *cost band* too (Shapiro and Dolan, 1989), within which the products having the same function are located (Figure 8.4.). Products and companies found in the lower segment of the band are able to generate more profit, more shareholder value than those in the upper part.

Figure 8.4. Presentation of the cost band

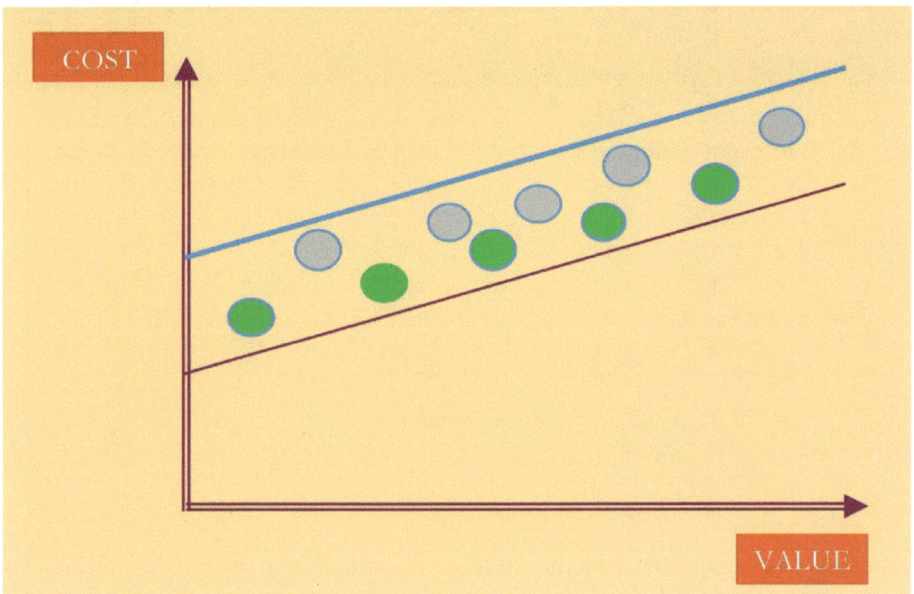

It is the relative technological development of the company, as well as the length of the product lines that determine where the company's products will be located within the cost range. A company having more advanced technology and focusing on fewer products will probably be located close to the lower threshold of the range (these are indicated in green shaded circles). The analysis of the cost band can highlight what changes are necessary and can also provide information about the strategic opportunities of the company. These can include:

- *Creating new value/cost positions (Figure 8.5.)*. Special attention must be paid to selecting the place of the new products because a badly chosen position can lead to cannibalisation, which means that the new products can eat up the market share of the old ones. Positioning by taking into consideration the positions of competing products, however, can significantly improve the competitiveness of the company.

Figure 8.5. Developing new value/cost points

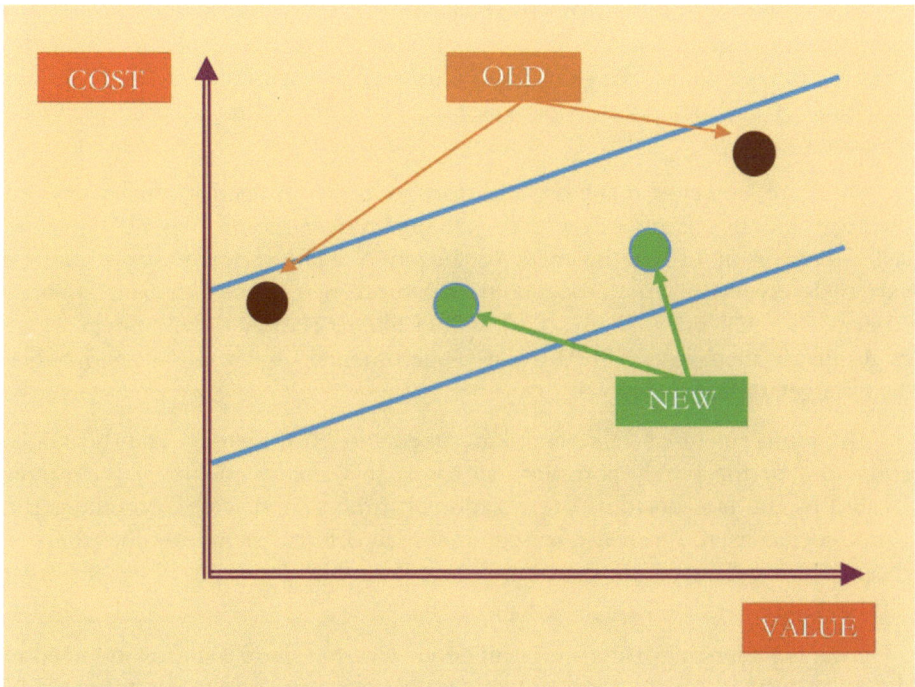

- Another possible solution is that the company decreases the costs of its existing products and/or increases their value, in other words, *it modernizes its products* and shifts them from their original positional.

- A third possibility is for the company is to *try leaving the cost range*. It can be done in small steps, by increasing the value of the company's product while decreasing the costs. Because of these small steps the cost range will slowly move to the right and down because most of the competitors will probably follow this movement too. The first company to start modernization usually enjoys a competitive advantage. Those who cannot keep up with the trend will lag, demand for their products will decrease, and they will be able to generate less profit.

- The fourth option is a technological leap, that is a real innovation. The company initiating innovation will take the lead; its product will create a new cost/value range. If the competitors follow in the footsteps of the pioneer company, the original cost range will make a big shift to the right and down. Those who cannot keep up with the change will probably be forced out of the market.

8.5. A DETOUR: VALUE MANAGEMENT IN THE NONBUSINESS SPHERE

Our book is principally concerned with the value creation activities of profit-oriented organizations. Profit-oriented value creation means that the organization recognizes the value expectations of its customers or other relevant stakeholders and organizes its activities around the need to satisfy these value expectations.

There are, however, many organizations in modern societies which carry out their activities not necessarily with the direct aim of economic benefit. These are called non-profit or non-business organizations. These organizations can be extremely diverse and heterogeneous (for more details see Drucker, 2006 or Andreasen and Kotler, 2008). If we would like to classify them somehow, we could divide them into NGOs (Non-Governmental Organization), and public (i.e., budgetary) organizations.

The requirement of value creation appears in both sectors. The difference compared to the purely corporate sector is that the recipients of the values created by the non-business organizations can be very diverse, sometimes the whole society itself. It can also happen that their offering includes values that the recipients have not even recognized (for example the promotion of breast screening).

What is interesting from our point of view is that there is a growing need in the non-profit sector to carry out business-like activities and to use the tools of value management.

It is especially true in areas where private capital is already present, unintentionally creating competition for the budgetary organization. A typical example is the area of education, particularly higher education. Today, a public university can use the same marketing tools as the profit-oriented and more and more internationalized private universities.

CHAPTER 9

WHICH PART OF THE MARKET DO WE WANT TO CREATE VALUE FOR?

9.1. VALUE LEVELS IN PRODUCT MARKETS

The market of any product is a complicated and complex structure, therefore, it is important which part of the market the company is active in. By complexity of the market we do not mean the different forms of market discussed by economics (perfect market, monopoly, oligopoly, monopolistic competition), but the segmentation of the product market into different parts according to their quality and price level. The structure of the market interpreted in this way can also be defined as the architecture of product groups which are in competition on the market and can be distinguished according to price and quality. This architecture can usually be broken down into three levels (Figure 9.1.). Analysts and practitioners use sometimes more, sometimes less than three levels. Baker (2018) for example analyzing the global beer market distinguished four categories: discount, mainstream, premium and super premium. The British Rail uses only two levels: standard and first class.

Figure 9.1. Typical structure of a product market

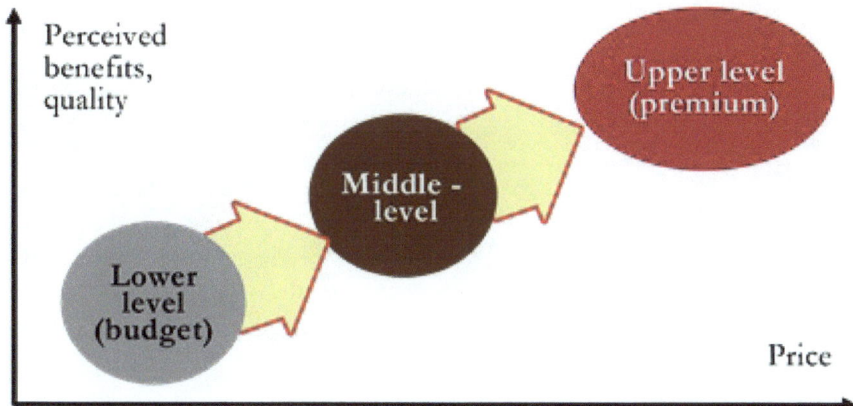

These levels do not necessarily mean similar quality or price: they can be broken down into further sublevels most of the times. As a matter of fact, Figure 9.1. could also be drawn the following way (Figure 9.2.).

Figure 9.2. Structures within the levels

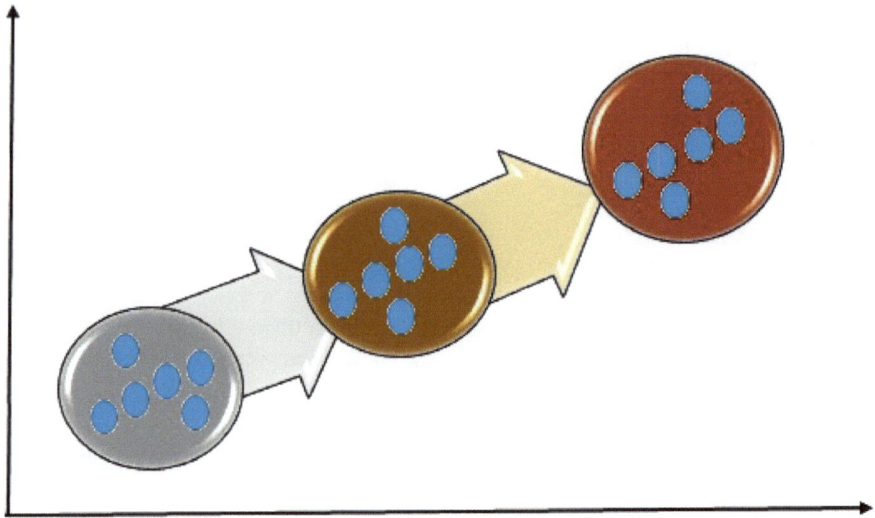

In an earlier paper, the author of this book analysed the market of Canadian leather gloves (Rekettye, 1994: 203–204.) from the point of view of price (quality) and marketable quantities and concluded that the market structure showed a pyramid-like structure, in which lower prices were accompanied by higher quantities and vice versa. New market entrants, for the most part, developing countries with cheap labour, intended to break into the lower segments of the sector characterized by a high labour ratio. This attack from below pushed the whole structure upwards and forced the countries and manufacturers having higher production costs to reorient towards higher market segments with higher quality and better marketing. If they were unable to reach a higher quality level and create more value for the customers of that market segment, they were forced out of the market. Besides the pyramid-shaped market structure, there are inverted pyramid-, barrel- and hourglass-shaped market structures (Figure 9.3.).

> The market of most products are characterized by a trichotomy:
> Economic
> Middle-level
> Premium

Figure 9.3. Possible market structures

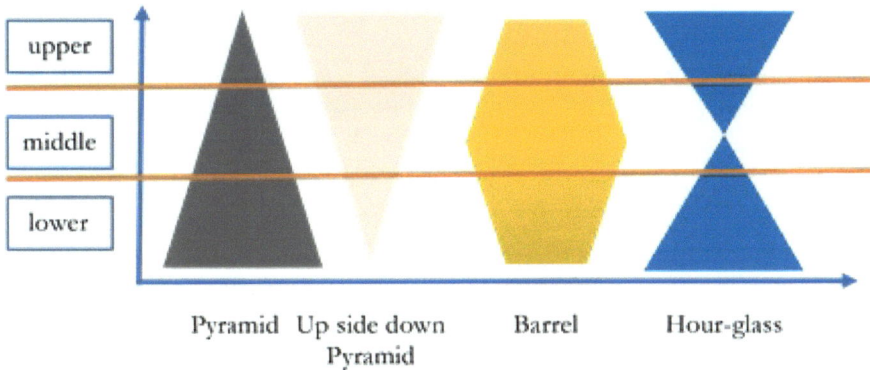

| | Pyramid | Up side down Pyramid | Barrel | Hour-glass |

It is of course not a spur-of-the-moment decision that the company steps up the ladder. It requires long, hard and well-planned work to do so. It took several decades even for the methodically working Japanese to change the perception of their Western European and North American customers about their products from cheap, mass products, to middle level and slowly to premium quality products. Today, the South Korean manufacturers are going down the same road.

There are however companies which are satisfied with a lower position. Such is the case of Snow, for example (See it in Exhibit 9.1.). The biggest advantage of this position is that "economies of scale" can be fully exploited: Big turnover results in low unit costs, which in return can lead to high profits.

EXHIBIT 9.1. YOU HAVE PROBABLY NEVER HEARD OF THE MOST POPULAR BEER IN THE WORLD

Neither Heineken nor Budweiser managed to obtain the title of the most popular brand in the world. The title was awarded again to the Chinese Snow.

We may not even have heard about this brand, but as far as sales are concerned, this brand already dethroned Bud Light in 2008, at least according to Reuter. Based on the report by Business Insider the brand already has 5.5 % of the global market share. Although the report notes that the brand is mainly distributed in China, real foodies can bump into the brand from time to time in some American specialty stores.

So what does it taste like? Fortune magazine described this liquid earlier as a forgettable light lager beer with a not too characteristic flavour. Even with these "weak" qualities, the beer managed to scoop 68 points from the prestigious Beer Advocate website.

"There are beers we buy for their excellent taste, and others we buy because of their low price. Snow fits very well into the latter category" – read one of the comments. It seems that Snow does not intend to look more than what it is: popular beer. And as such, it is a very thought after drink which cannot be considered terrible in its category.

Source: An article by Ádám Zamaróczy published in the online paper Élelmiszer on August 7th 2017. Photo: By Yoshi Canopus - Own work (My own photo), CC BY-SA 3.0, https://commons.wikimedia.org/w/index.php?curid=9409504

These market tiers are clearly visible in the case of most products. Let's take the example of the car tyre market. According to the classification by Gumibisznisz tire and car repair service, car tyre brands can be grouped into three categories (Figure 9.4.).

Figure 9.4. The quality levels of car tyres

Low-range (economic) brands
Barum
Ceat
Dayton
Debica
Kormoran
Marangoni
Matador
Sava
Commercial brands

Mid-range brands
Goodrich
Hankook
Firestone
Fulda
Kleber
Uniroyal
Vredestein
Yokohama

Premium brands
Michelin
Bridgestone
Goodyear
Continental
Dunlop
Pirelli

Source: adapted from http://gumibisznisz.hu/content/28-hogyan-valasszak-autogumit

Michelin states that the tires of the new Pilot Sport 4S UHP solve the pleasure and safety equation for performance enthusiasts, offering unprecedented driving pleasure, exceptional steering precision and tremendous directional stability, while also providing maximum grip on wet or dry roads.

Source: http://www.moderntiredealer.com/news/719480/michelin-adds-new-uhp-tire-to-pilot-line

9.2. COMPETITION BETWEEN AND WITHIN THE MARKET LEVELS

Competition can prevail both between the different value levels of the market and within them. Well, our everyday experiences confirm that the competition within the one market level is much stronger than that between the levels. Looking at the Eastern European countries' car market for example, we can agree that Dacia and Lada belonging to the lower end of the market (where prices started below 7-8 thousand USD in 2017) are not really in competition with Mercedes, Lexus or BMW belonging to the premium category (where prices started at around USD 28-30 thousand in 2017). Competition between the market tiers is therefore limited to the ones close to each other: Dacia is using aggressive price policy to seduce the highly price-sensitive customers of the middle-level market (Suzuki, Hyundai, Kia, etc.). Similarly, those belonging to the upper levels try to win over the less price-sensitive customers belonging to the levels directly below them, but not so much with lower prices but rather by using qualitative, technical and marketing tools.

The competition within the tiers can be much fiercer than between them. Let's have two examples from different industries. Aldi versus Lidl is a competition at the lower end of the market, while Adidas and Nike illustrate the competition between companies at the upper end of the market.

Competition within the levels of the market is much stronger than competition between the levels of the market.

If we look at the car market, we can see an interesting duality in the interpretation of market levels. The traditional classification into mini — small — lower-middle — middle — upper medium — luxury refers to the physical parameters (size, etc.) of the cars, rather than to the quality levels. Nowadays, most manufacturers offer the full range of products and the manufacturers belonging to the lower, mid and upper levels of the market are present in all of the above categories. Just as Mercedes has a small car, Kia has a luxury car. The difference is however huge: Kia offered its products in the price range of USD 10 to 50 thousand in 2017, while Mercedes offered them in the price range of USD 25 and 300 thousand.

EXHIBIT 9.2. ALDI VS LIDL: GLOBAL DISCOUNT RACE

Who will win the discount war?

The traditional markets of Aldi, the „father" of the hard-discount concept, have come close to saturation in Austria, Germany and the Benelux countries. Does it mean that Aldi must give up Europe to Lidl?

When a retail company realizes that the market is getting saturated, it usually responds by expanding the range of its products and services or by diversifying its activities. But what can it do, if all this goes against its basic concept, as in the case of Aldi? One solution could be to expand abroad, but what if the retailer sees that wherever it appears with its concept, others have already implemented it with success?

Everywhere Aldi opened markets in recent years, it had to face exceptionally tough competition, especially from Lidl. This latter got ahead of its rival in many countries due to its flexibility and because when the circumstances required it, it changed its colour like a chameleon and went from a hard discount store to a discount supermarket.

Source: Part of the article by Matthias Queek, the journalist of Planet Retail published in Élelmiszer online in October 2010 http://elelmiszer.hu/kereskedelem/cikk/aldilidl__globalis_versenyfutas. Source of the logos: Wikipedia, public domain

EXHIBIT 9.3. ADIDAS VERSUS NIKE

The Three Stripes are winning against Swoosh, or aren't they?

Adidas Superstar is a street footwear brand that goes way back to 1969, everybody recognizes it from the three stripes and iconic shell-like toe cap.

Its price is not drastically high, so children, teens, young men, even older men keep wearing it as a reminder of the time when the legendary rap band, Run-DMC wore it without shoestrings in the 1980s. It seems that retro and casual fashion trends favour this shoe brand.

Adidas has become the favourite of investors because the company is beating Nike at their own game: it achieved a growth of 20% in North America, Western Europe and China.

"Adidas continues to clearly outgrow Nike globally" — said Chiara Battistini, the retail analyst of J.P. "This has been a key revenue and profit driver for Adidas."

However, even if Superstar is topping the sneaker list symbolizing the marketing success and increasing popularity of Adidas, it must

be noted that that Nike dominates the top 10 list; not only dominates it,but the list includes only Nike shoes. The Jordan brand generated a turnover of 2.8 bn dollars last year with 18% growth, which is two times higher than that of Nike Basketball backed by Lebron James and Kevin Duran. It's no coincidence that Nike expects the turnover from the Jordan brand to reach 4.5 bn dollars by 2020.

These two big companies, as they are primarily sports apparel manufacturers, are in competition not only with their products, but in sponsoring big events and famous sportspeople too. In 2016 in European soccer, Nike was promoted by Ronaldo, Rooney and Ibrahimovic, while Adidas was promoted by Bale, Pogba and Özil.

Sources: Jonathan Ratner: Nike vs. Adidas http://business.financialpost.com/investing/trading-desk/nike-vs-adidas-the-three-stripes-is-making-gains-on-the-swoosh-but-that-doesnt-tell-the-whole-story/wcm/b17466db-1abd-4a7f-92c7-058497dba9d.

9.3. MIGRATION BETWEEN THE MARKET TIERS

Brands on the upper part of the market guarantee higher prices and higher margins (profit) to the supplier than the brands on the lower levels. It is because they offer higher perceived value for customers. This higher value can be functional or emotional. (A Vuitton bag is probably not in the least more functional than any other brands, however, owning one represents a higher value for certain groups of customers.)

In the interest of higher profit and image, many companies are making efforts to move higher up the imaginary ladder of the market. They do not always succeed. Moving up the ladder can be called premiumization while moving down is called *commoditization* (see Shapiro's thoughts in the Box).

> According to Ben Shapiro, a professor of the Harvard Business School (Shapiro, 2002), there are specialties, commodities and the great in-between. He says that every new product starts as a specialty because customers do not recognize it yet, and it presents some mystic novelty to them. Then come the imitations, the competitors, and the sense of newness wears off and the specialty is degraded to a commodity.

If this two-way movement takes place at the same time, we can talk about *polarization*. According to the surveys by McKinsey we have been witnessing a very strong polarization at the beginning of the 21st century. The revenues in the car, clothing, computer and retail sectors have been growing faster in the upper and lower levels of the market than in the middle, the authors (Kunsen et al., 2005) go so far as to talk about "the vanishing middle". „Staying in the middle is tantamount to a death sentence" — they write.

Examining the typical shopping habits of people, it can be concluded that people's aspirations are characterized by upward movement under normal, recession-free economic circumstances. Most people thrive for a bigger flat to move in, for a bigger car to drive and for better products to buy. And once they have reached this goal, they try to stay there or move even higher up but try to avoid moving back down at all costs. The migration of consumers' demand between the levels of the market is somewhat asymmetric (Figure 9.5.).

It should be noted that in situations of declining income, as was convincingly proven by the financial crisis started in 2008, movement upwards was made impossible *by the income barrier*, and people were even forced to move downwards by breaking the psychological barrier of downwards movement and allowing price to take over the decisive role of quality.

Figure 9.5. The asymmetric movement of consumers' demand between the the market tiers

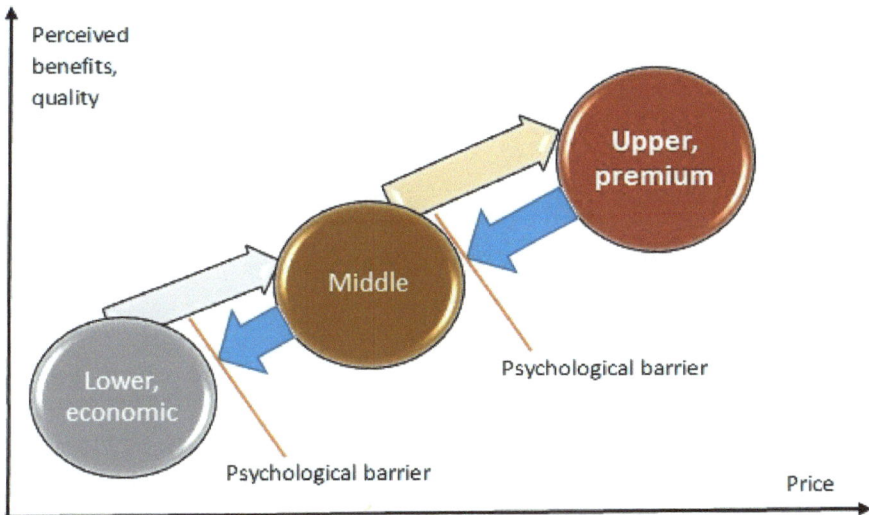

As a result of the financial crisis, even value-conscious customers prefer shops where they can buy their everyday consumer goods at low prices, and this trend is going to continue even after the markets have recovered. Traders, in general, respond to these new needs by launching private label products, and by increasing their weight in the supply of goods and the strategy of the company – was revealed by the global online survey conducted by **Nielsen** in 2010, which included 27 thousand people from 53 countries. More than half of the people polled said that they were buying more private label products during the recession, and 91% of them said that they would continue to do so even if the economy started growing again (Agárdi, 2011:6).

CHAPTER 10

THE KEY ELEMENT OF VALUE
MANAGEMENT - THE PRODUCT LINE

We have already outlined earlier that product or value management has three levels: the level of the *product, the product line and the product structure*. Having reviewed the relevant literature and practice, we have arrived at the conclusion that the *product line has a prominent role* among these three. Looking at the historical development of companies it can be seen that companies place a differentiated product offering on the market in order to stay competitive. They adapt the features, functions and forms of their products to the needs of the different customer groups; they pursue a multi-brand policy, which means they rapidly expand the number of the products and brands offered, even if they started their activity with the development of a *single* product within a category.

By the beginning of the 21st century, the width and the depth of product offering reached unprecedented levels in the world. The "over proliferation" of products very often constituted a disadvantage even for the customers. The abundant supply which has become chaotic can confuse customers and make them uncertain about their choices. There is a vast literature on the information and stimulus overload caused by the ever-growing supply and the resulting "confusion and uncertainty" in consumers (Mitchell – Papavassiliou, 1999, Chryssochoidis, 2000). How to handle this increased product supply is difficult even for companies. There have been numerous reports about big multinational companies, like Unilever (Willman, 1999) or Nestlé, carrying out simplifications by decreasing the number of their products offered and focusing on products that belong to their core competences.

10.1. PRODUCT LINE MANAGEMENT

These changes in the market also confirm that a well-planned *product line management* is gaining more ground in managing the company offer and in communicating with consumers. In most companies, products belonging to the same product line share a lot of common things: e.g., brand name, distribution channel, promotion activities. Besides marketing, they also share common development, manufacturing activities and use the same components, and so on

It can also be said that companies have developed *core competences* over time which allow them to serve the market of the given product line. These are the competences that further developments (product and market development) can be based on (Figure 10.1.).

Figure 10.1. The core competence of the product line

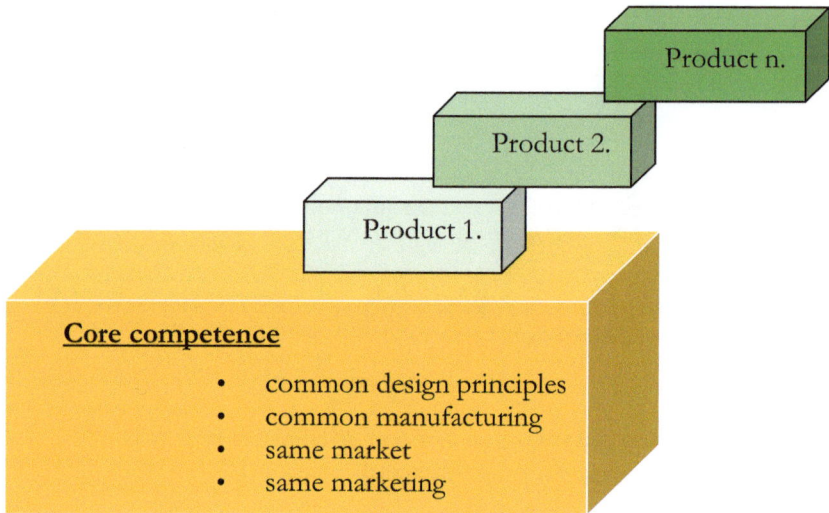

The product line is the main element of product management and corporate value strategy. The main characteristics of the product line will serve as a basis for the developments of individual product items on the one hand, and the modernization of the company's product structure (portfolio) on the other.

The product line can be defined as the group of products created by the company, which are related to each other based on certain criteria. The question is what are the common factors that connect these products. The relationship can be of engineering, technological, design or marketing nature:

- From an engineering point of view, it can be the strong similarity of the basic operational design of the product and a large share of the same parts or components used.
- From a technological point of view, it is the similarity of the manufacturing process;
- From a design point of view, the similar appearance of the product items.
- From a marketing point of view, the similarity of the market, customers, distribution channels and communicational and promotional tools can constitute the common platform based on which we can talk about a product line.

These similarities between products can help improve the operational and marketing efficiency of a company and its competitiveness. It is evident that manufacturing the dozens of products belonging to the product line in a similar fashion or marketing them with the same tools is more efficient than doing it all for each product differently. A good example for this is the strategy of Black & Decker's hand tool business line which involves the construction of many of their products from the same components. See the Exhibit 10.1.

EXHIBIT 10.1. THE EXAMPLE OF BLACK & DECKER

The company had several hundreds of products in 1970. These products included 30 types of engines, more than 60 types of casings, and the company used dozens of operating panels. Furthermore, these hundreds of products each had a different armature. The management decided that to maintain the competitiveness of the company the product costs should be cut by 1/3 in the following decade. Black & Decker drew up plans for the development of product lines which would be based on similar parts and modules. They spent some 20 million dollars on implementing the plan. First, they developed the hexagonal copper winding with the necessary electric plug-in system. The engineers designed a standard motor casing and control system, and even more standardized glued armature. The company then made these modifications on each product line. And the result was dramatic: the product costs decreased by 50%, their 20% market share increased significantly, and the number of competitors dropped from 20 to 3. (Meyer – Utterback, 1993, 113-114 old.)

It must be noted, that Black & Decker merged with Stanley Works in 2010 and was renamed StanleyBlack & Decker. In 2017, the company acquired Sears's Craftman division.

10.2. THE TARGET MARKET AND THE POSITIONING OF THE PRODUCT LINE AND THE NEED TO CREATE A COMMON IMAGE

It is an important question which segment of the market the company intends to target with the given product line. This decision will fundamentally determine the main actions to be taken regarding products and their marketing. Let's see the example of the automobile industry. The differences between the product lines were clearly identifiable in the 1970s and '80s: a part of the manufacturers (the so-called „specialists in high quality", like Mercedes and BMW) targeted the upper segments of the market with a relatively narrow range of offerings through expensive and high-quality dealers, offering high-performance luxury products that were distributed in small quantities. Other manufacturers (mainly Japanese ones, the so-called "volume-manufacturers") marketed a wider range of cheaper, but still good quality products in large quantities (not only sedans or coupes but also minibuses, small vans, sports cars, micro-mini cars, four-wheeler commercial vehicles, etc.). These product lines targeted different segments of the market, and there was real competition between them (Clark and Fujimoto, 1996).

> The common features (e.g. form) are shared by each product in the product line thereby creating the identity and image of the product line and establishing a unified market positioning for it.

However, this clear situation had changed radically by the turn of the century: we will come back to this later. This example from the automobile industry shows how fundamentally the target market determines the features of the product and its marketing. Those targeting the upper segments of the market developed technological and marketing competences that allow them to serve this specific market. And what is even more important: *these common features* (which are exhibited by the products through the luxury, the performance, the form and the design, as well as by the supporting brand, distribution channel and price policies, etc.*) are shared by each product in the product line thereby creating the identity and image of the product line and establishing a unified market positioning for them.*

When there are more active players in the same market segment, it is crucial to distinguish the identity of the product line from the competitors. To illustrate this, we will continue to use the automobile industry as an example.

EXHIBIT 10.2. THE JOURNEY OF HONDA AND BMW UNTIL TODAY

HONDA

Honda used to be a typical product-oriented company in the 1970s and '80s. It launched a series of unique new products targeting a market niche with each of them without paying particular attention to product line philosophy.

As a result, the company had a relatively simple market niche-oriented product line by the end of the 1970s. As far as their global product line strategy, it was very simple too: it targeted the global market. The same simplicity characterized the organization as well. It did not have either a formal product management organization or a product line planning department. Honda's success turned the company into a so-called full-scale manufacturer in the 1980s. The product line became more and more complex, and the company started to develop the distinguishing identity of its products. In the beginning, the company intended to create this identity by the informal coordination of its lead engineers.

However, the product line that the company marketed in the different regions of the world became too complex to let the identity efforts work sufficiently. There was a growing need for the company to restructure its development organization.

The watershed was marked by the launching of the Honda Accord on the Japanese market in 1990. While the Accord enjoyed great success in the United States, its size and conservative form disappointed Japanese customers. It became apparent very soon that Honda's development organization needed severe restructuring. One "global product" was not capable of satisfying the more and more

The Honda Accord of 1990

exigent customers of regional markets. It also became evident that Honda had to find a way to express its corporate identity through its models.

The method according to which developments were driven by unique products was not viable anymore. The challenge for Honda was to use its engineering and design strengths to create a platform for the common features based on which it could develop the regional differences of its models. It was the objective that the restructured development organization of Honda set for itself from 1991. As a result of this development, the company today involves the experts of the target markets to assist in designing the product lines of passenger cars, which were given a common identity in 2017.

Fit-Jazz
B-Segment Exterior.
C-Segment Interior.

CIVIC
Fuel Efficiency coupled with Style

ACCORD
Honda's Best-Selling Vehicle

HR-V

CR-V
Go anywhere in the versatile CR-V

NSX

Clarity Fuel Cell
World's First Five-passenger Sedan-type FCV

Hybrid Cars

Source: CC BY 2.0, https://commons.wikimedia.org/w/index.php?curid=950136. By BMW - http://brandsoftheworld.com, https://commons.wikimedia.org/w/index. php? curid=22309422

BMW

BMW was in a completely different situation at the end of the 20th century. Product development was governed by the strict traditions of BMW's precise and clear image. The continuity of the form and the basic concept which was established at the end of the 20th century and the beginning of the 21st century is remarkable.

This technical-technological and conceptual continuity stemmed from the meticulous approach and functional organization of BMW's engineers. However, when the competition became much fiercer at the end of the 20th century, BMW was forced to turn towards unique developments very quickly and efficiently by keeping the characteristics of its products. The acquisition of Rover in 1994 made this transformation process more dramatic and turned BMW into the manufacturer of a complete product line. BMW started the extension of its product line by introducing the small coupes belonging to 3 Series and maintaining the Rover brand (which was abandoned later) and continued with the introduction of 2 Series and 1 Series until the company became ready to compete in the different

segments of the market in a way that the new products maintained the "BMW-character".

The kidney-shaped radiator grilles figured in the photo are characteristics of the iconic BMW brand.

Despite their different historical backgrounds, Honda and BMW are direct competitors in certain areas today. With its Acura brand, Honda is attacking BMW in its original market, in the United States, while BMW is directly competing in Europe, in Honda's mass market first with the Rover line, and with 1, 2 and 3 Series. *The competition between the two companies is not primarily the battle of products but rather the battle of the product lines.* The individual products must, of course, adapt to the needs of the given market segments, but the developers, who create these products, must develop the distinguishing character of the product line. They must do so by not making the products similar to each other, so they can keep their individual character. This is a very delicate equilibrium, an equilibrium which determines the competition.

Sources: Clark and Fujimoto (1996, 316-321 old.). http://www.honda.com/

10.3. DECISIONS TO MODIFY THE PRODUCT LINE

A product line, as the first and most important aggregate of the offering, has two quantifiable dimensions from a market point of view:

- The *length* of the product line, i.e., the number of different products offered in a product line, which can be distinguished from each other, but which are related in the sense mentioned earlier.

- The *depth of the product line*, which refers to the average number of varieties (size, etc.) of the product item in a product line put on the market by the company.

The first set of decisions to modify the product line concerns the changing of these two dimensions. The number of products or the number of varieties of specific products offered to the market can be decreased or increased. (The attention is focused on the change in the number of products offered, that is the extension or narrowing of the product line.) The other important set of decisions concern the modernization of the individual elements of the product line or the whole product line. The present book addresses two of the potential decisions, the extension of the product lines and the modernization thereof.

The extension of product lines

The length of the product lines is the result of strategic considerations in most cases. Due to their different value/price positions, the products in the line satisfy different consumer needs forming a peculiar order starting from the lower value/price relation and going into the direction of the higher value/price relation (see Figure 10.2.). It is especially true for so-called shopping and specialty consumer goods. In real life, the members of the line never form such a regular order. Let us illustrate this with the presentation of BMW's American price list showing the starting price and the price of the most expensive variety of the given product (Figure 10.3.).

Figure 10.2. Price-value ratios within the product line

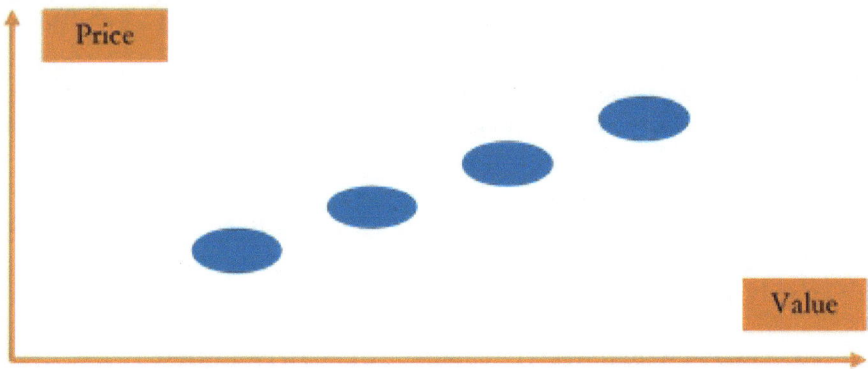

Figure 10.3. The starting and maximum prices of BMW's 1 to 7 series (2017, in dollars)

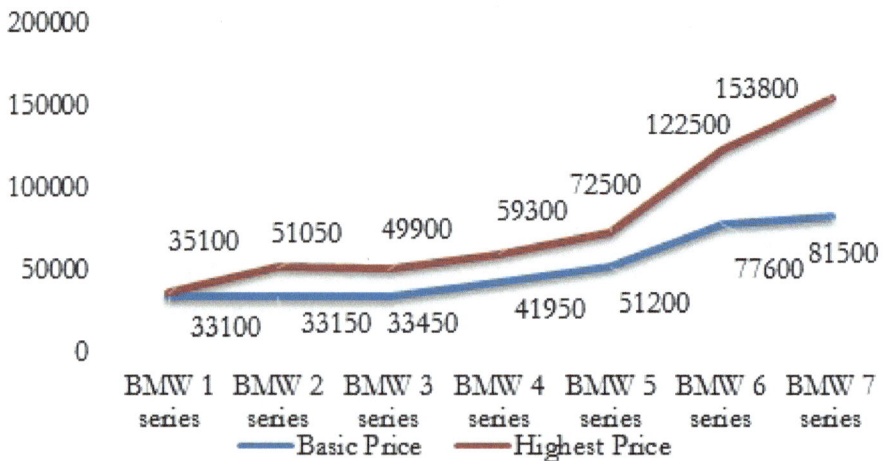

Source: www.autoguide.com/new cars/bmw/. Note: BMW 8 series was introduced in 2018 first with one model priced at USD 111 200.

There are, of course, product lines in which the products do not differ in their price or quality, only in their design (flavouring). A good example is one of Danone's most well-known product line, the Light and Fit. The "Light and Fit" product line with its wide variety of fruit flavours, high quality and affordable price can become the favourite of both children and adults. The Light and Fit brand is a real family yoghurt; its products can be bought in a variety of sizes." – writes its homepage).

Extension can be done in four directions: (1) downward (2) upward (3) in both directions simultaneously (up and down) as well as (4) such an extension, which does not mean a change in the current price/value position, i.e., the company continues to offer several products in the same position. This latter practice is called line filling.

It can be seen through our example of the automobile industry that while the German manufacturers (Mercedes, BMW, Audi) specialized in the higher segments of the market started to extend their product lines downward, the Japanese manufacturers (Toyota, Honda, Nissan, etc.) belonging to the lower-middle category extended their passenger car product lines upward.

The modification of the length of the product line and the extension of the product line are typically provoked by the competition and the fight for the highest market share possible.

Quelch and Kenny (1994), who already warn of the risks of hasty product line extension in the title of their book „Extend Profits, Not Product Lines" – enumerate the following reasons:

(1) market segmentation (meeting the needs of various customer segments),

(2) customer desires („customers are always on the lookout for something different"),

(3) pricing breadth,

(4) channelling of excess capacities,

(5) short-term gain,

(6) competitive intensity and

(7) trade pressure.

Examining the fast-moving consumer goods Nijssen (1999) highlighted three factors:

(1) competitive intensity,

(2) trade pressure from retailers and

(3) consumer behaviour of always looking for something different.

Attention must be drawn to the risks of product line extension (Quelch and Kenny, op.cit). The majority of product line extensions do not contribute to increased sales, because they are not intended to satisfy new needs, they only differentiate the supply, unnecessarily in many cases.

However, the overextension of the product lines (product proliferation) can involve a lot of risks (Buday, 1989; Wan, et al., 2012; Tolonen et al., 2014). From a market point of view the most important of these include:

- The excessive size of the product line obviously weakens the market identity of the product line, which is fundamental in the context of increased competition, as was pointed out earlier.

- It can decrease brand loyalty. Customers may lose faith in the former (core) brand with the appearance of every new product element, and their uncertainty may increase.

- The company needs to focus its marketing resources to more areas.

- The more products a company has the better target it becomes for its competitors.

We will demonstrate this latter by continuing our discussion of the price/value range (Figure 10.4.). Let's consider a long (Products "A") and a shorter product line (Products "B"). Assuming these two product lines are at the same technological level, the products of the company producing the shorter product line enjoy a more favourable cost position, and as a result, can appear on the market with relatively lower prices. As shown in the figure, product 1 of the product line "B" covers products 1 to 4 of the product line "A" from value and price point of view. Product 2 of the product line "B", on the other hand, covers products 4 to 7 of the product line "A" (and so on), and therefore offers a better alternative for the customers.

Highlighting the risks of product line extension does not mean that there is no need for extension. It merely suggests that a product line should only be extended after taking into account the aspects of value management and carefully planning the decision based on thorough market and economic analysis.

Modernization of product lines

The modernization of the product line is a fundamental product policy decision, the purpose of which is to maintain the company's competitive position from both technological and market point of view. Product line modernization means more than the modernization of the individual products belonging to the product line: it concerns the dynamics of the core competence which defines the production, development and sales philosophy of the whole product line. Our example taken from the automobile industry also intended to prove that the core competence behind the product line concept is more than just the common design and technological platform of the related products.

Figure 10.4. Comparison of the price/value ratio of longer and shorter product lines

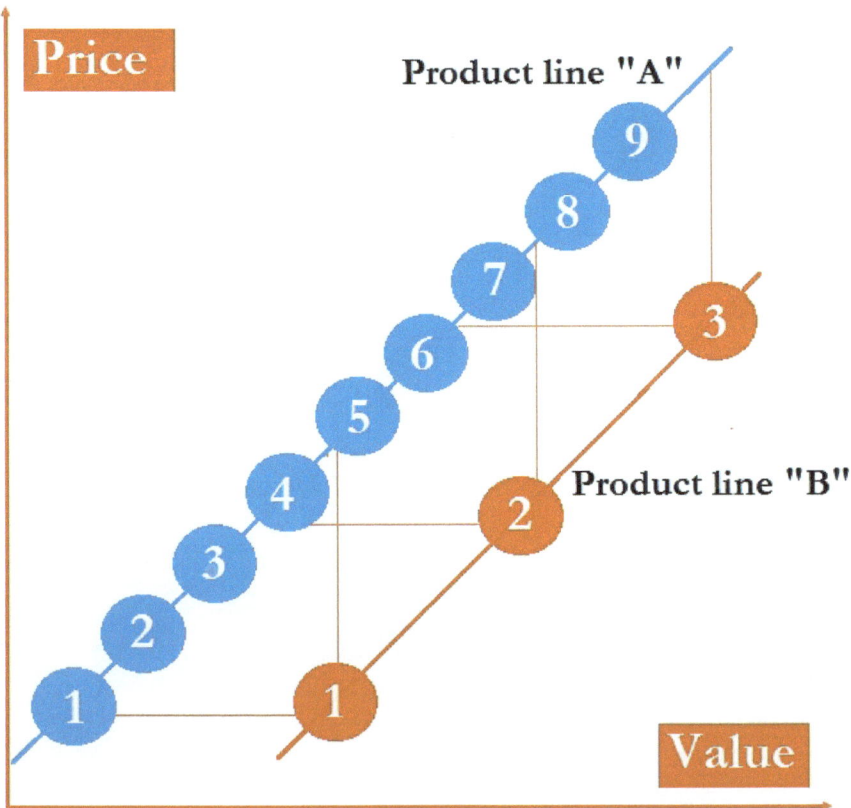

To have a successful product line, it is necessary to get to know the customers of the target market, understand how their needs change, how they use the product, and how the product fits into their consumer infrastructure. Modernizing a product line also involves the revision of the latter aspects. The results of developing the core competence of the product line are visible in the *new generation* of products. The new generation is the integral however a more advanced continuation of the earlier product group. The successive product line generations contribute to maintaining and improving the competitiveness of the business line and the company in the market.

The development of the product line's core competence can often identify new areas, which can serve not only as a basis for the new generation of the existing product line but for a new business line and a new product line as well. This process is shown in Figure 10.5.

Figure 10.5. The evolution of product lines

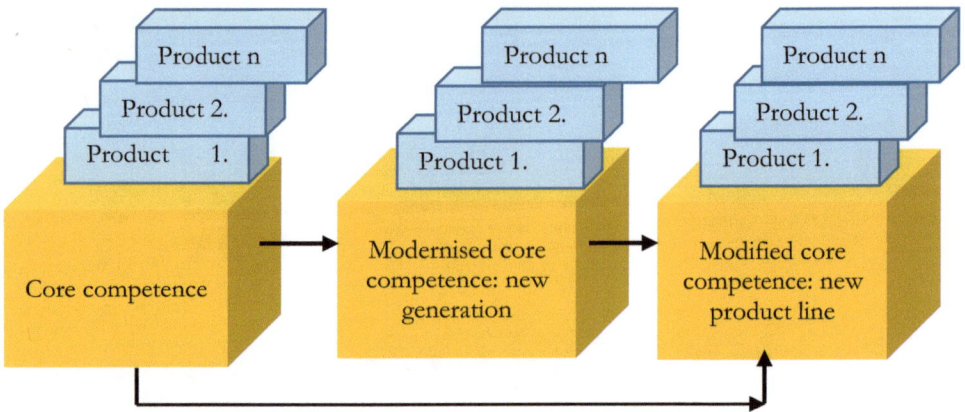

Wheelwright and Sasser Jr. (1989) suggest the drawing of a product development map for the systematic development of each element in the product line and for designing the modernized product generations. Their work takes us through the development concept of the first three generations of the Coolidge vacuum cleaner (1952-1968, 1967-1978 and 1977-1985).

The discussion of product line extension, the modernization of products and product lines, as well as the development of new product lines has taken us to the next stop of our train of thought, the broad field of new products, innovations and product development.

CHAPTER 11

POSITIONING THE VALUE - METHODOLOGICAL TOOLS

In this chapter, we will combine planning the value of the products with *their positioning*. This combination is based on the logic that these two activities require the same kind of preparations and on the consideration that it is not enough to create a value proposition; it must be communicated to the consumers of the target market. This latter is called positioning. The method will be presented through the example of empirical research; but let us first clarify the methodological bases.

> It is not enough to create a value proposition; it must be communicated to the consumers of the target market.

11.1. TYPES OF PRODUCT-MARKET MAPS AND THE METHODOLOGIES USED IN THEIR PREPARATION

In value management, companies should first understand what place *their products (brands) and product lines compared to the other competing products occupy in the minds of the target market's consumers*. To do this, they should find out how consumers choose from competing products, what their preferences are, and what they like about the products. To do this successfully, companies should find the answers to the following questions:

- On which dimensions (features, components) do customers differentiate the products competing in the market?

- What are the relative weights of the different dimensions in the purchase decisions?

- How customers compare these dimensions in case of the company's own and competitors' products; in other words, how do customers "perceive" these attributes?

- How satisfied are the customers?

- What do customers want, i.e., what are their preferences concerning these dimensions in the different market segments??

Preparing and analyzing the different maps about the market positions of the products can help a lot in answering these questions. The mainstream literature distinguishes five basic maps (see Figure 11.1).

Figure 11.1. Product positioning maps in marketing

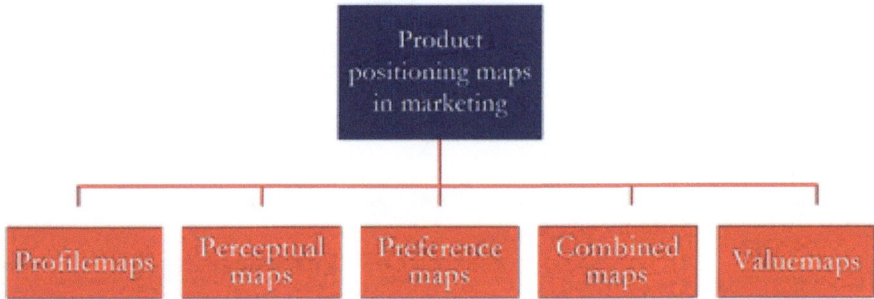

11.2. CONVENTIONAL PROFILE MAPPING

Profile mapping is used to compare how experts and/or consumers rate the company's product or service in relation to similar offerings of the competitor(s). It is also referred to as a snake-chart, because of its form. A semantic differential scale is applied in this case. Let's suppose that a bank would like to see how one of its branches in the town compares to the branch of its main competitor (Figure 11.2.). The first task is to determine the most important attributes of the bank branch. This can be done by asking the opinion of experts or by doing focus group surveys with existing clients. The respondents of the main survey can also be experts or customers.

Figure 11.2. clearly shows the differences between the given attributes. If we added up the average scores, we would get a very misleading result: both branches obtained the same score (28.9) in our example. It would be more useful to measure the importance of each attribute and to weigh the scores according to their importance. Let's assume that the respondents assign importance to the attributes listed in the first column on a scale of 1 to 10. If the scores were weighed accordingly there would be significant differences in favour of the competitor (158.2 versus 184.9). It reveals that the bank's own branch performs poorly in the key areas (price and the expertise of the staff). It also gives an indication to the company in which areas they should improve to provide better value to their customers and to increase their competitiveness.

Figure 11.2. Comparison of two bank branches

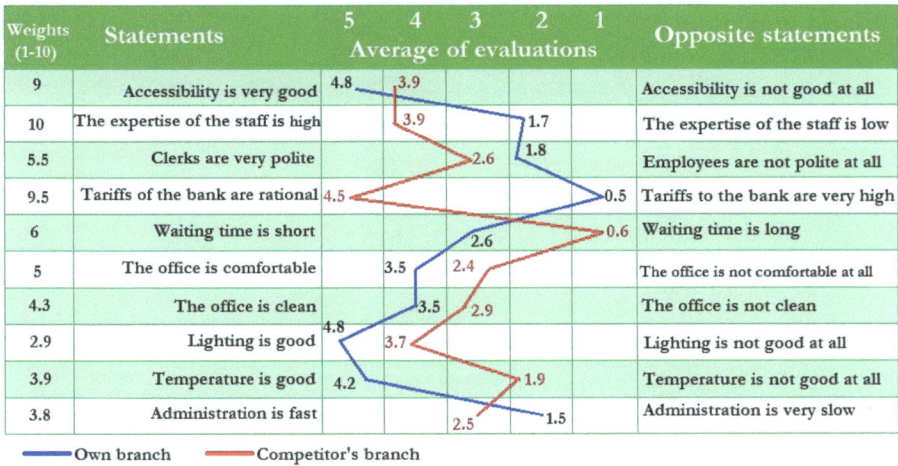

Weights (1-10)	Statements	5	4	3	2	1	Opposite statements
			Average of evaluations				
9	Accessibility is very good	4.8	3.9				Accessibility is not good at all
10	The expertise of the staff is high		3.9		1.7		The expertise of the staff is low
5.5	Clerks are very polite			2.6	1.8		Employees are not polite at all
9.5	Tariffs of the bank are rational	4.5				0.5	Tariffs to the bank are very high
6	Waiting time is short			2.6		0.6	Waiting time is long
5	The office is comfortable		3.5	2.4			The office is not comfortable at all
4.3	The office is clean		3.5	2.9			The office is not clean
2.9	Lighting is good	4.8	3.7				Lighting is not good at all
3.9	Temperature is good	4.2			1.9		Temperature is not good at all
3.8	Administration is fast			2.5	1.5		Administration is very slow

——Own branch   ——Competitor's branch

11.3. PERCEPTUAL AND PREFERENCE MAPS

These maps are very handy tools for the marketing managers because they can visually display the structure of the market in which their products are competing. The maps can be used to indicate the preferences of customers for the given products or product lines, and/or the perceptions of these. Comparing preferences with perceptions can indicate where new products could be launched successfully, and can help to determine the strategic steps, such as how to change the actual value attributes of the products, how to differentiate them, in what direction to position or reposition them.

In most cases, these maps present the market structure in two dimensions. The products are indicated by the points determined by the coordinates of the two dimensions. The perceptual maps can also help to study the image which differentiates competing products; the similarity of two products is in inverse relation to the distance between them. If the two brands are located close to each other on the perceptual map, they are perceived very similar by the consumers. Conversely, if the distance between the products is big, consumers perceive the difference between them significant.

It is a question of methodology how to create these maps. First, researchers need to determine *which competing products or brands to include in the study*. There are two important things to take into consideration:

- Which products should be included in the study largely depends on how the company views the competition. If, for example, the manufacturer Suzuki does not target the premium segment with its cars, than Volvo, BMW, Mercedes and the other luxury brands should not be included in the study.

- Only those products should be included in the study which are relatively well-known by the respondents.

The products in the study delimit to a certain extent *the attributes to be examined* too. Let's stay with the example of Suzuki. The exclusion of the big cars from the study means that the size of the car will not be considered as an important differentiating attribute.

When determining the attributes to be researched it is important that from the point of view of the potential buyers that they are

- important and

- have a differentiating nature in relation to the product.

> In the case of airlines, for example, safety is essential for the customers, yet it is not a differentiating character, because each airline should be assumed safe in scheduled traffic by their very nature, apart from a few extreme examples.

Researchers should therefore first determine the products to be included in the research and the most important attributes based on which customers used to rate these products. The attributes can be selected by asking experts and/or consumers (See for example the most important features of the American smartphones users in Exhibit 11.1.). Then, researchers compile a questionnaire and ask consumers to rate the products based on these attributes.

As was mentioned earlier, these maps typically have two dimensions. It is rare that a product can be assessed based on only two attributes. If it happens, the case is simple, because these two attributes need to be displayed in a coordinate system. If there are more attributes, they need to be displayed either in pairs on successive maps (but this significantly limits the applicability of the perceptual map), or statistical-mathematical methods are needed to derive two dimensions from multiple attributes.

There are two statistical methods used for this purpose: one of them is called *factor analysis*, and the other one is called *multivariate discriminant analysis*.

There are many products whose specific attributes are difficult to define. The consumers themselves are unable to tell, for example, why they prefer one perfume to another. The method based on *general comparison* is used in such cases. When using this method, consumers are usually asked to describe the *similarities perceived* between products and to make a *preference order* of the products included in the survey. The data obtained this way can help to create perceptual/value maps using the so-called *multidimensional scaling method*.

EXHIBIT 11.1. THE MOST WANTED SMARTPHONE FEATURES

While manufacturers day by day augment their phones with new and complicated features, a recent survey by Morning Consult Company has revealed that the basic functions are at the top of the American smartphone users' preference list.

What Smartphone Buyers Really Want

Features considered somewhat/very important when deciding which smartphone to buy

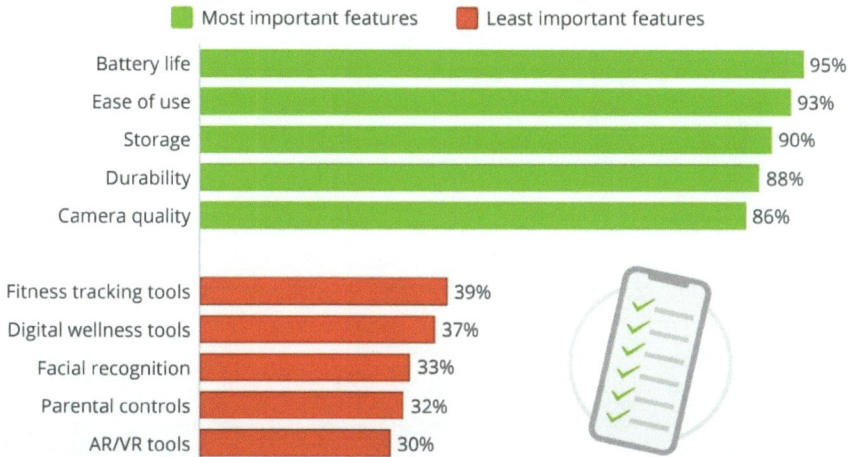

■ Most important features   ■ Least important features

Feature	%
Battery life	95%
Ease of use	93%
Storage	90%
Durability	88%
Camera quality	86%
Fitness tracking tools	39%
Digital wellness tools	37%
Facial recognition	33%
Parental controls	32%
AR/VR tools	30%

Based on a survey among 1,894 U.S. smartphone owners conducted in November 2018
@StatistaCharts Source: Morning Consult

statista

Source: Richter, F. What Smartphone Buyers Really Want. Statista, Feb. 19, 2019 (https://www.statista.com/chart/5995/the-most-wanted-smartphone-features/, accessed 20.02.2019.

EXHIBIT 11.2. SCALES USED IN PERCEPTUAL AND PREFERENCE MAPPING

Scale questions used in attitude surveys are the most appropriate for evaluation. These include among others the *Likert-type scale* or *the semantic differential scale* (Sándorné, 1980; Churchill, 1991). The Likert-type scale is credited to the American psychologist and sociologist Rensis Likert, who developed his method for measuring attitudes in 1932 as part of his doctoral thesis, which is still a popular tool in survey research. The method fundamentally consists of expressing the rate of respondents' agreement with different statements on a scale of, usually, 1 to 5 or 1 to 7.

If the scales are odd-numbered, respondents can have a neutral opinion about the statements (Zerényi, 2016:470).

How much do you agree with the following statements?	Strongly agree	Agree	Neutral (neither agree nor disagree)	Disagree	Strongly disagree
	5	4	3	2	1
The passenger car X is comfortable					
The design of the car X is excellent					

The semantic differential scale offers two contrasting statements, and respondents are asked to choose where their positions about the phenomenon in question lie on a scale between these two statements. This type of scale is widely used for comparing the image of brands, products or companies.

How would you describe hypermarket X?						
Clean						Dirty
Comfortable						Uncomfortable
Light						Dark
Innovative						Conservative

PRESENTATION OF A REAL RESEARCH

We are going to present how the first method is used through a study conducted in Hungary some years ago. The product group chosen included small-medium sized cars which were well-known by people and sold in large quantities in at the time.

The following brands were included in the survey:

Lada Samara

Opel Astra

Skoda Felicia

Suzuki Swift

Toyota Corolla

Volkswagen Golf

The main aim of the research study was to find out which attributes of cars Hungarian people considered important in their purchase decisions and to find out how they perceive these brands.

With the help of focus group discussions, eight attributes were selectedUsing the Likert-type scale respondents were asked to rate these attributes based on the importance they represented to them on a scale of 1 to 10 (with 1 being *not important at all* and 10 being *extremely important)* The following attributes were chosen:

(a) The purchase price of the car (price)

(b) Safety of the vehicle(safety)

(c) Attractiveness, the design of the car (design)

(d) Low running costs of the vehicle (consumption, insurance, etc.) (cost)

(e) Technical parameters of the car's performance (acceleration, speed, and so on) (performance)

(f) Image of the given brand (image)

(g) Expected low level of defects (reliability)

(h) Comfort offered by the car (comfort)

The results of the survey are summarized below (Figure 11.3.).

Figure 11.3. The importance of the different the attributes

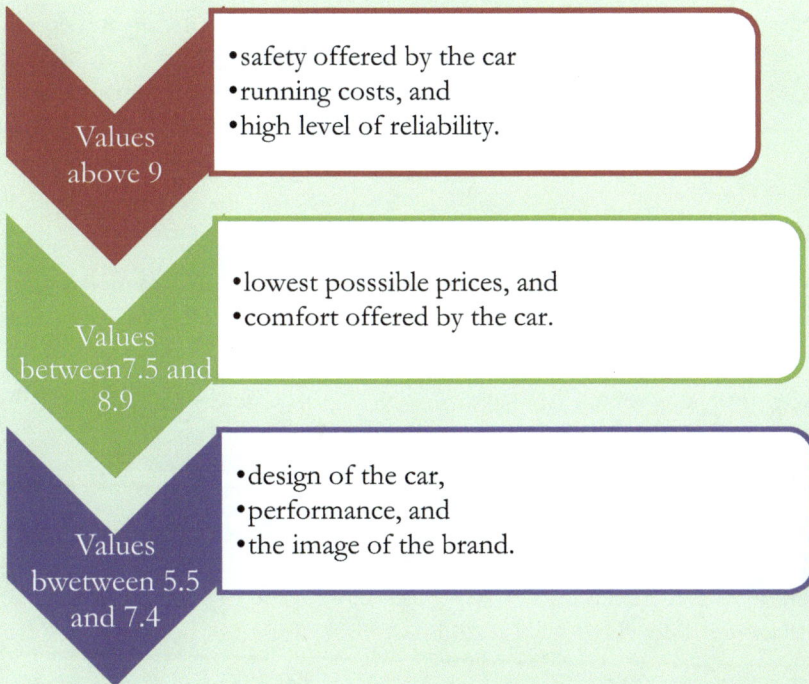

Values above 9	• safety offered by the car • running costs, and • high level of reliability.
Values between 7.5 and 8.9	• lowest posssible prices, and • comfort offered by the car.
Values bwetween 5.5 and 7.4	• design of the car, • performance, and • the image of the brand.

This indicated that the emotional factors (form, brand image, and even the performance of the car) were considered secondary to the more objective factors (safety, costs and price) in Hungary at that time. We would obviously get entirely different results today.

Next, we wanted to examine how the respondents perceived the attributes of the different car brands included in the research. We used the semantic differential scale in this case.

Table 11.1. The average rating of the attributes of different car brands

	Suzuki	Opel	Lada	VW	Toyota	Skoda
Price	5.52	6.66	5.95	7.52	8.04	7.22
Safety	5.81	7.41	5.17	7..78	8.06	6.86
Form	6.24	7.56	4.59	7.79	8.50	7.52
Cost	5.65	6.36	5.80	6.67	7.18	6.64
Performance	5.72	7.29	5.22	7.74	8.10	6.82
Image	6.16	7.58	4.80	8.12	8.27	6.66
Reliability	6.62	7.32	5.25	7.77	7.97	6.86
Comfort	5.92	7.62	5.31	7.73	8.49	7.49

Perceptual maps commonly have two dimensions, as mentioned earlier, because of their visual clarity. The number of variables characterizing the product is usually more than two. In our example, eight variables were considered important in the consumers' perception of cars. As a result, the two axes need to be determined with a method which is capable of compressing the contents of the variables. We have chosen factor analysis from the SPSS software package, more specifically the principal component analysis for this purpose. This method is often used for creating perception maps even according to international literature (Moore, Pessemier 1993, p. 154.).

We will refrain from defining factor analysis because every student or professional of marketing should know all about it.

Based on the variables, the two factors remaining after performing the factor analysis can be called:

First factor: *utility value of the car* (or, its quality, in general), which includes the safety offered by the vehicle, its performance, the low defect rate, the form of the car and the image of the brand.

Second factor: *the price and running costs of the car.*

The following perception map could be created from these data (Figure 11.4.). The perception map could visually display well the structure that consumers involved in the survey developed about the product. Some of the characteristics of the structure are as follows:

Suzuki (which may not fit the structure exactly, because all the other cars in the comparison were bigger than that) was perceived by consumers to be the cheapest (purchase price + running costs),

The least utility value was attributed to *Lada*,

Toyota was perceived to have the highest utility value, and the perception of the car's price and costs were perceived accordingly too.

Each car brand had a very differentiated value image, as they were all located quite far from each other on the perception map (although the image of *Opel Astra*, *VW Golf* and *Toyota Corolla* were slightly similar).

Figure 11.4. The perceptual map

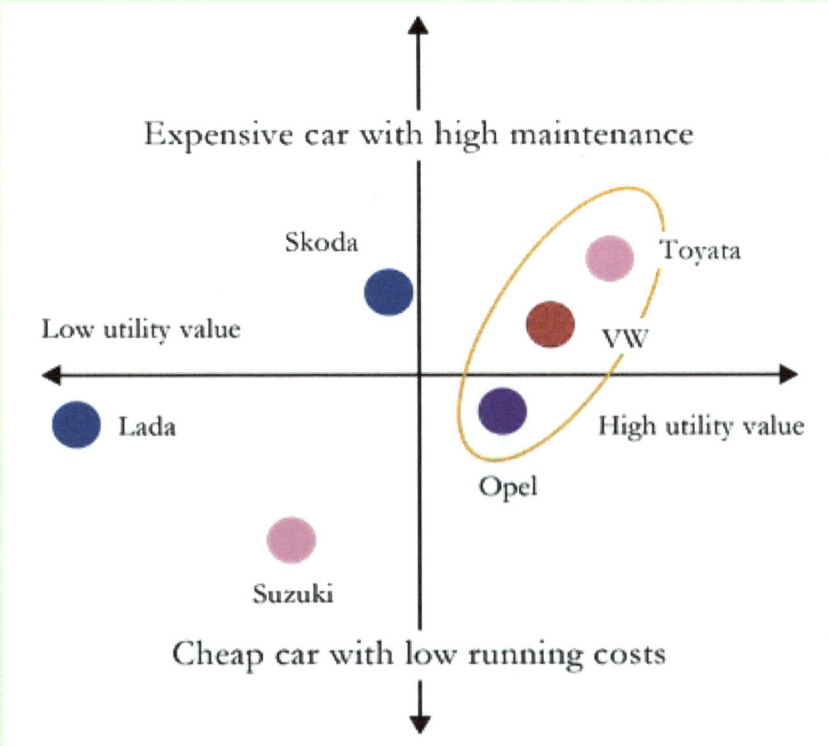

11.4. COMBINATION OF PREFERENCE MAPS WITH PERCEPTUAL MAPS

Preference maps show the company who the potential customers are and what expectations the different segments have towards the product. There are extremely complicated statistical methods to get to know these expectations. The description of these methods and the use of the relevant software are presented by Lilien and Rangaswamy (2004). We will not discuss them in detail but will present the methods and benefits of preference maps through simple and easily understandable examples, and the possible ways of combining the perceptions and preferences.

Two models are typically used in preference surveys:

- the ideal point model for preference, and

- the ideal vector model for preference.

We will present the ideal point model through a simple, imaginary example. Let's assume that a local brewery would like to find out their customers' preferences with regard to cheap versus expensive (premium) beers, and light (low-alcohol content) versus strong (high-alcohol content) beers. Using a semantic differential scale, the company can obtain the representative sample from its customers as in Figure 11.5.

Figure 11.5. The semantic differential scale

WHAT TYPE OF BEER DO YOU LIKE?

Affordable/ cheap beer	-5	-4	-3	-2	-1	0	1	2	3	4	5	Premium, expensive, elegant beer
Light/low-alcohol content beer	-5	-4	-3	-2	-1	0	1	2	3	4	5	Strong/high-alcohol content beer

Well, the distribution of responses will probably form density points, the analysis of which can help determine the ideal segment. Two such points were identified in Figure 11.6, the ideal points indicating the beer preferences of men and women.

Figure 11.6. Ideal points in the market of beers

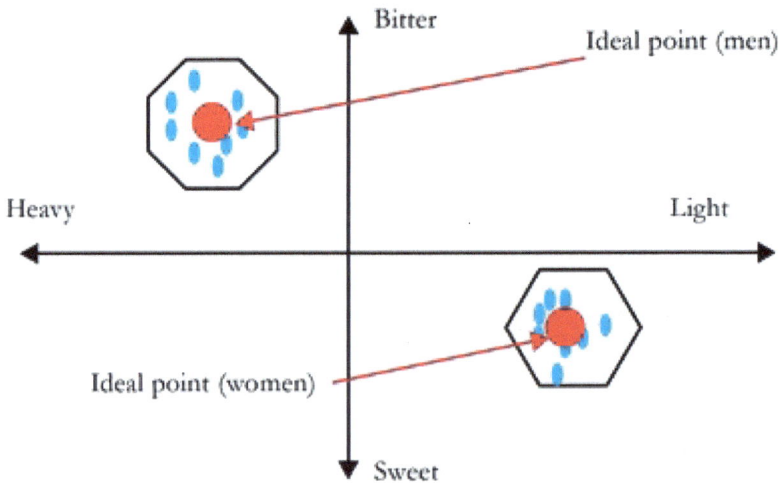

Note: this visual recognition of the density is only possible if the number of respondents is just a few dozens. If the sample is big, more complex statistical methods are needed (e.g., cluster analysis). These methods allow identifying not only two but several segments (and ideal points).

Afterwards, the perceptual and preference maps should be combined, which was done in the virtual example as shown in Figure 11.7.

Figure 11.7. Combination of preference and perceptual maps

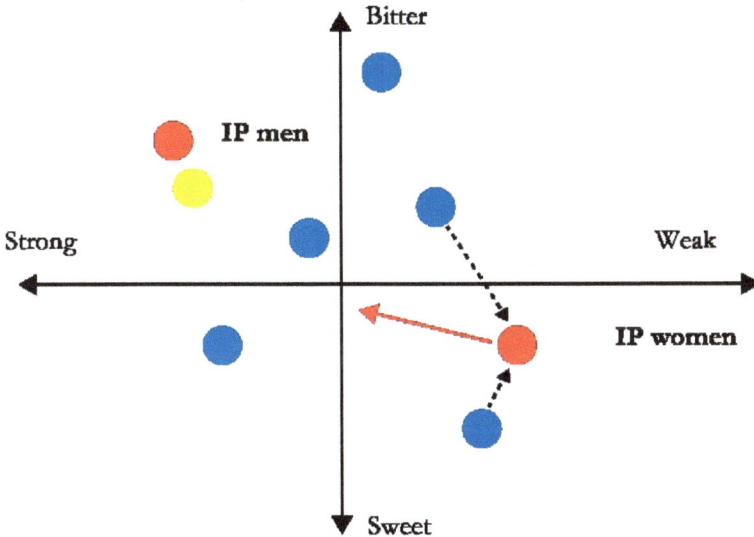

The figure clearly shows what needs to be done. Since the needs of men are covered by the product visualized in yellow, the task is to satisfy the needs of women better. There are two possibilities for this:

- the company should either develop a product specially designed for this segment, or

- should try to reposition a product which is close enough. This can be done through creative marketing communication, but care should be taken that preferences tend to change as well (see red arrow).

The ideal vector model is often used in combination with the perceptual maps. In this case, researchers use the positioning technique to determine the most important attributes of the product. Then they perform a regression analysis where the data from the survey constitute the independent variables and the preference data present the dependent variables (Figure 11.8.).

Performing a regression analysis of all the data obtained from the survey can lead to an ideal vector, which can be a difficult starting point. Researchers therefore first determine the potential segments and their ideal vectors using the method of cluster analysis. As an example (an imaginary one again), let's have a look at the potential preference vectors of beverages (Figure 11.9.).

Figure 11.8. Preference vectors

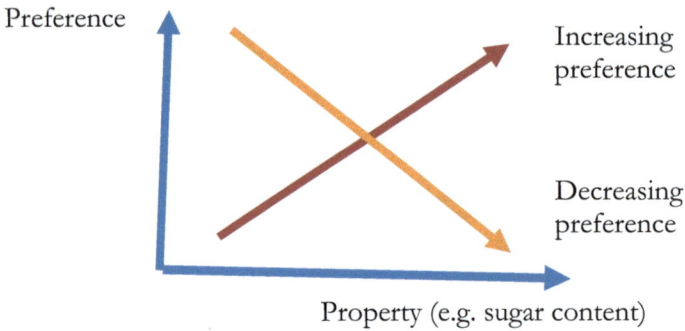

Figure 11.9. The possible preference vectors of beverages

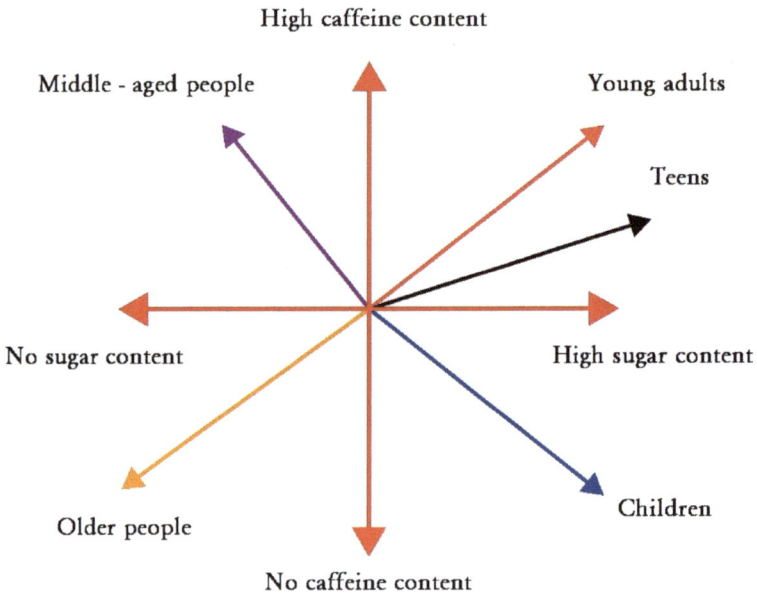

11.5. THE ROLE OF VALUE MAPS IN VALUE MANAGEMENT

The perceptual map presented in Figure 11.4. can also function as a *value map*. The horizontal axis, which we called the utility, indicates the perceived value of the brands included in the research. The vertical axis, on the other hand, indicates the price perceived. If we accept this, a 45-degree line can be drawn in the coordinate system which illustrates the equilibrium of perceived value and perceived price. This line referred to as *value equivalence line* (Garda and Marn, 1993) or *indifference curve* (Golub and Henry, 2000) in the literature. According to the definition of the line, if the perceived position of the product falls on this line, customers feel the value of the product is in balance with the price paid for it. It is clear, however, that the measurement of perceived value (utility) and perceived price are never accurate, so the fair value line should be interpreted more *as a fair-value corridor*. Those brands that fall below the value equivalence line in the coordinate system have a competitive advantage over the products that fall above the line. To illustrate the above, let's return to our example of the perception of medium-sized cars (Figure 11.10.).

The perceived value positions can vary across customers. The perceptual or value map can only present the position of the company's products adequately if it reflects the perceptions of the target segment.

A survey based on a representative sample, such as our example of cars, is also suitable to show the varying value sets of the different market segments. This is illustrated by Figure 11.11, which presents the varying value positions of two brands, Suzuki and Toyota, as perceived by two demographic segments according to the survey.

Figure 11.10. The value map with fair-value reference line

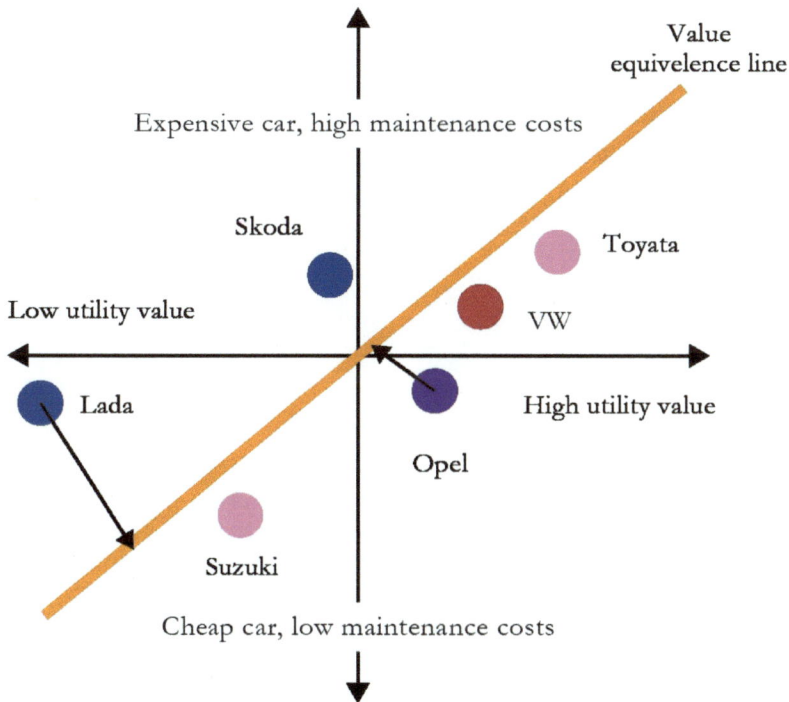

Figure 11.11. The perception value of Suzuki and Toyota in two different age groups

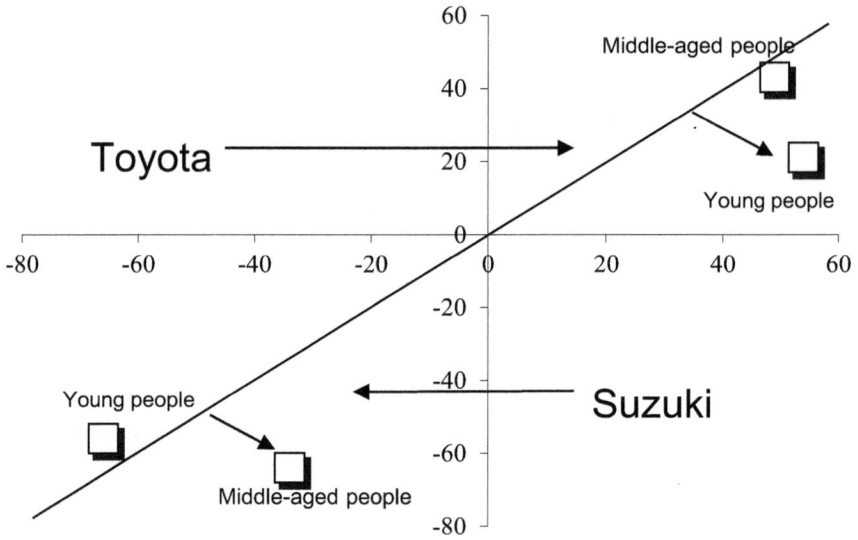

CASE III-1. IS SUSTAINABILITY A VALUE ELEMENT OF HIGHER EDUCATION?

Á. Papp-Váry and R. Lukács

Universities play an outstanding role in sustainable development. On the one hand, they seek to manage their direct social, economic and environmental impacts as a service firm. On the other hand, they are able to shape social attitudes through the educational services provided by them as they educate the next generation of decision-makers. Moreover, they may contribute to the solution of global problems serving as scientific workshops. However, we may wonder if this is important for their key stakeholders: university students. What can we learn from the example of British universities in this context?

The special status of universities

In terms of sustainable development, the mission of higher education institutions is more complex and long-term compared to other companies, and their motivation is also somewhat different. Jennifer McMillin and Rob Dyball distinguish three major dimensions of institutional sustainability through the example of Australian National University, Canberra: Campus Operations, Curriculum and Research. In an ideal case, research and education, operations and areas of research also interact, utilizing a mutually beneficial framework of information exchange and cooperation (Mcmillin & Dyball, 2009).

University sustainability ranking

People & Planet's University League is a league table of higher education institutions operating in the United Kingdom ranked by environmental and ethical performance. It has been published for ten years. People & Planet is the largest student network campaigning for social and environmental justice. In addition to public information available online, they also use the database of the Higher Education Statistics Agency (HESA) to compile the rankings. The ranking compares more than 150 UK universities according to 13 major criteria (People & Planet University League, 2017):

- Policy and Strategy

- Staff

- Environmental Auditing & Management Systems

- Ethical Investment & Banking

- Managing Carbon

- Workers' Rights

- Sustainable Food

- Staff and Student Engagement

- Education for Sustainable Development

- Energy Sources

- Waste and Recycling

- Carbon Reduction

- Water Reduction

In 2019, University of Gloucestershire, Manchester Metropolitan University and Nottingham Trent University ranked top. They obtained the maximum score in several indicators and achieved the weakest results in staff rights. The 2019 chapter of the traditional Cambridge-Oxford rivalry was won by the University of Oxford, although it was only ranked 45th, 22 places ahead of the University of Cambridge, ranked 67th (People & Planet University League, 2019).

The development experienced in the past decade is characterized by the fact that in 2007 only five of the examined institutions recycled more than half of their waste, but the number was 85 in 2017, demonstrating that sustainability is becoming increasingly important. University students also pay more and more attention to "green" issues; Manchester Metropolitan University, which ranked 2nd in the list, provides several recycling opportunities including the rental of electric cars, the introduction of table bins for waste sorting, and water recycling (Lightfoot, 2017). But let us examine in more detail what makes a sustainable university in the UK.

Best practices in sustainability in the United Kingdom

Besides the initiatives mentioned in the previous part, *Manchester Metropolitan University* also runs a contest between residence halls for the sorting of their waste; each student may participate in sustainability training programmes free of charge, and both students and university staff may order weekly vegetable boxes from producers. A subpage for the communication of becoming sustainable was created on the university website, visitors may sign up for a regular newsletter on sustainability, and sustainability ambassadors selected from university students also facilitate this change of attitude (Manchester Metropolitan University, 2018).

All these aspects are included in the environmental sustainability policy, the six-year environmental sustainability strategy, and the related action plans. To create their strategy, they took in account the 17 sustainable development goals defined by the United Nations. The most important objectives set out for the period until 2020 are: the reduction of carbon emissions and water and energy consumption, the maintenance of the environmental management system and compliance with the ethical investment policy, increasing the sustainability of buildings and procurement, and minimizing the impact of travel (Manchester Metropolitan University, 2018).

The *University of Gloucestershire* was only 0.7% ahead the result of Manchester Metropolitan University. Their university website also has a subpage dedicated to sustainability; the institution has operated a community garden for ten years, and the number of people participating in the university's sustainability internship programme increases each year. The aim of the Learning Innovation for Tomorrow (LIFT) programme is to include sustainability in education and connect the sustainability team with the academic development field. This included the students' pop-up activities and arts and crafts activities presenting the UN's sustainability goals at the Cheltenham Jazz festival. (University of Gloucestershire, 2018)

The sustainability report of the University of Gloucestershire also focuses on the United Nations' sustainability goals and reports on the implementation status of the five key objectives set out in the institution's sustainability strategy. These are the principles and aspects of sustainability in organizational direction and culture, in student experience as part of education, as part of the academic strategy within teaching, research and learning, in the area of business operation and development, and as an added value of collaborations (University of Gloucestershire, 2018).

Nottingham Trent University also has a website subpage focusing on sustainability, and the sustainability team also operates its own social media channels. Students starting their studies are informed about the efforts of the university and their opportunities to take part in the programmes. Staff discussions introducing the members of the sustainable development team are held regularly. They aim to get students and colleagues involved in the university's efforts to reduce carbon emissions with the help of the Carbon Elephant programme – this includes a scheme offering bike hire from the university at a discounted price (Nottingham Trent University, 2018).

The sustainability report of the university is also based on the United Nation's sustainability goals, and introduces several initiatives. For example, we are informed that there are ten beehives on the four campuses of the university, and a small producers' market is organized regularly to connect students with local small businesses. In the previous academic year, 314 students completed their professional traineeship in the field of sustainability, and the Green Leaders scheme has facilitated the implementation of four student projects that contributed to the university's sustainability. Ten research teams focusing on sustainability are active within the institution, and the Sustainability Action Forum brings together staff working in different fields (Nottingham Trent University, 2018).

The ranking of green universities

The UI GreenMetric World University Ranking created by Universitas Indonesia ranks universities according to Setting & Infrastructure, Energy & Climate Change, Waste, Water, Transportation, and Education & Research. Interestingly, the list only includes one of the UK universities presented above, Notthingham Trent University, ranked fifth - just behind of the University of Oxford (UI Green Metric World University Ranking, 2019).

Do green/responsible university students exist at all?

Based on their research in Australia, Butt et al. questioned the existence of "green student" as a phenomenon and their possible influence on the sustainability schemes of universities. Although the institutions in question provide opportunities for involvement in programmes and decision making, the students' willingness to participate was low. It was also found that universities should seek to achieve a higher engagement of students as important stakeholders – both in the development of the sustainability strategy and its implementation (Butt et al., 2014).

It is interesting to see that this aspect has not been examined by the People & Planet University League ranking in the UK and the global UI Green Metric World University Ranking, although in other industries it has become a best (and required) practice that companies identify the stakeholders' expectations and involve them in their decisions regarding sustainability.

The question is what specific topic (a positive issue or possibly a scandal) will make future university students more conscious stakeholders and motivate universities to implement social responsibility practices that are more strategic than today, considering most important stakeholder expectations and the influence of their core activities? That is, can future competition in the market of higher education institutions embrace the universities' social responsibility as an important factor in addition to the acquired knowledge and employment opportunities?

Summary

Although the presence of "green students" can hardly be noticed, it has become apparent that universities have a great responsibility in the field of sustainability as a result of their particular function (that is, educating the next generation of leaders), substantial toolbox and wide range of opportunities (research and collaborations).

In this regard, the competition for consumers has not yet been as intense as in the case of car or food brands. As a result standardized frameworks and indicators have not yet been defined. An industry policy established in addition to individual sustainability programmes realized locally would not only make the market transparent for consumers investing into their future (that is, future university students) but also facilitate the sharing of best practices and the development of further programmes. Therefore, sustainability would become an even more important and valuable element of higher education.

Questions and tasks:

1. What trends and events could facilitate the appearance of a large number of green university students in higher education institutions? When and how could the sustainability of a university become a criteria in choosing a university?

2. What criteria and dimensions should a university consider in the development of its sustainability strategy?

3. What could universities do in order to better engage their key stakeholders (university students) in their sustainability programmes and decision-making regarding sustainability?

References

Butt, L. – More, E. – Avery, G.C. (2014): The myth of the 'green student' involvement in Australian university sustainable programmes. Studies in Higher Education. Vol. 39, No. 5, pp. 786-804.

Lightfoot, Liz (2017): New university tops green table as Oxbridge lags behind. The Guardian. Link: https://www.theguardian.com/education/2017/nov/14/university-green-table-oxbridge-people-planet, Published: 14 November 2017, downloaded: 2 November 2018

Manchester Metropolitan University (2018): https://www.mmu.ac.uk/ environment/, downloaded: 2 November 2018

Mcmillin, Jennifer – Dyball, Rob (2009): Developing a Whole-of-University Approach to Educating for Sustainability: Linking Curriculum, Resarch and Sustainable Campus Operations. Journal of Education for Sustainable Development. Vol. 3, No. 55, pp. 55-64.

Nottingham Trent University (2019): http://www4.ntu.ac.uk/sustainability/ index.html, downloaded: 25 July 2019

People & Planet University League (2019): link: https://peopleandplanet.org, downloaded: 25 July 2019

Ui Green Metric World University Ranking (2019): link: http://greenmetric. ui.ac.id, downloaded: 25 July 2019

University Of Gloucestershire (2018): https://sustainability.glos.ac.uk, downloaded: 2 November 2018.

CASE III-2. HOW CAN A LOYALTY PROGRAMME DELIVER VALUE TO CUSTOMERS?

Ahmet Murat Yetkin

Hopi represents a new generation of loyalty programmes; its structure is unique not only in Turkey but also in the entire world. This case study examines the success achieved in the first years of the programme and the methods of how it has provided advantages for both customers and member merchants.

Boyner Group is the largest public clothing and fashion retailer in Turkey. It consists of seven companies, more than 500 stores, eight e-commerce sites, and 10,000 employees. Hopi was created in 2015 by Boyner Group. Hopi is a pioneer in loyalty programmes because of its unique structure. In Turkey, competition is very strong in this sector; profit margins are decreasing daily due to this intense competition. Hopi was able to make a difference, and with its innovative features, Hopi has become a big success.

The technology of Hopi's loyalty programme

Hopi is a mobile application that does not have a physical card but works on mobile devices such as mobile phones and tablets. There is no annual subscription fee. By 2018, Hopi reached six million customers and over 150 member merchants. Hopi does not sell products itself but rather provides significant benefits to its customers for every purchase they make from its member merchants. These 150 member merchants come from very various sectors. The main sectors usually include more than one brand; there are several restaurant chains and clothing chains as part of the Hopi loyalty programme. Therefore, if a customer wants to buy a new suit, for example, he can choose between various clothing member stores. Member merchants are not only large but also small and mid-size companies. Any company can become a member merchant as long as it offers its products across Turkey.

Hopi customers earn points on each purchase made through the app, even for their daily essential spending, such as hypermarket shopping. However, the main difference between Hopi and other rewards systems is that Hopi customers can spend their earned points at different member merchants. In many cases, their points may be worth more than the amount they accumulated. The points' value is based on the customers' spending; on the number of points they have accumulated, and the member merchants' trade preferences.

Benefits for the participating merchants

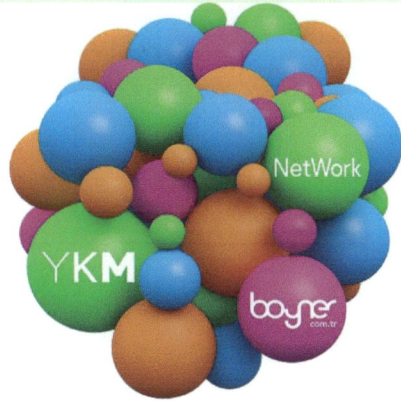

The Hopi logo displaying some member merchants (key players in the clothing and fashion market)

Hopi creates value for its customers and member merchants. Hopi personalizes its merchants' campaigns by taking advantage of big data and artificial intelligence. The special *artificial intelligence* software behind Hopi matches the needs and expectations of its customers with the thousands of offers of its member merchants in the most appropriate way. Thus, Hopi's customers can follow and benefit from the most attractive campaigns and offers that fit their preferences and habits. Similarly, member merchants can increase their productivity by delivering appropriate products and offers to their customers at no additional costs. There are member merchants, who achieved a 20 percent traffic increase and a 50 percent sales increase, thanks to the successful Hopi campaigns. For member merchants, it is a very cost-efficient way to get their special offers to the right customers, increase their traffic and sales, and most importantly, gain new customers continuously.

Benefits for their customers

Customers always receive the right offers thanks to the artificial intelligence behind Hopi. More than half of the Hopi customers consider Hopi as an important part of their shopping, and they actively use it. The total transaction volume of Hopi programme's reached 700 million TL (117 million euros). During the first couple years of the programme, Hopi customers earned 30 million 'points' equivalent to 5 million euros) on their purchases, and with various campaigns they spent their points 1.6 times more valuable as 50 million 'points' (8.3 million euros).

Hopi targets a diverse customer base as illustrated in its advertisement (see the photo): men, women, teenagers middle-aged people, seniors, customers from various professions and lifestyles.

An advertisement for Hopi starring one of the most important theatre performers in Turkey representing different characters.

Currently, 70% of Hopi customers voluntarily share their location information with Hopi. This ratio is very high, and Hopi is the only company in Turkey to have access to such valuable information. For example, GSM operators only know their own customers' location information and are usually not allowed to process this information. Therefore, they are unable to use this information even for their own customers. Customers are willing to share their location information with Hopi because they trust Hopi. Additionally, by sharing their location information with Hopi, customers can earn additional points. However, without trust and seeing the real value, customers would not share their location information and let Hopi process that information for better-personalized offers.

For example, Hopi knows that customer A consumes product B from hypermarket X. With artificial intelligence, Hopi can predict that customer A will need the same product while he is travelling. Because Hopi knows its customers' instant location information, Hopi can send an offer to customer A when he is close to hypermarket X in another city.

Another example can be found when Customer A shops in the member merchant store Store Y. From the location information, Hopi knows the exact moment when Customer A enters Store Y. Additionally, from the big data, Hopi knows that Customer A uses Perfume P and that it is sold in Store Y and it is in stock. Hopi also knows that Customer A's last perfume purchase was a while ago and that he purchases the same perfume regularly. Therefore, Hopi can send a push notification and offer a special discount, additional points, or double Customer A's points' value if he purchases Perfume P in two hours from Store Y.

In the Hopi programme, multiple member merchants operate in the same sector, and it shows the power of this new generation of the loyalty programme. Because there are various member merchants in the same sector, customers become loyal to Hopi programme as a whole, not to a particular member merchant. Customers have the freedom to select products from different member merchants operating in the same sector.

Hopi was selected as the "most popular application", "best shopping application" and "best communicating practice application" by the Popular Mobile Applications of 2015 survey organized by the one of the world's most prestige mobile platforms Mobile Marketing Association Turkey (MMA Turkey) with nearly thousand participants.

Questions and Tasks:

1. Please compare Hopi's technology with the programmes you use or you are familiar with!

2. What are the main advantages of HOPI for customers compared with other loyalty programmes?

3. What do you think about the possible conflicts among member and non-member merchants from the free market policy perspective?

PART IV

PLANNING AND DEVELOPMENT OF VALUE

CHAPTER 12

THE ROLE OF INNOVATION

There is a general consensus in the literature that innovation and the launch of new products are key factors of market success. It is also agreed that these functions have a growing importance in the new market conditions that characterize the turn of the millennium. More than 25 percent of total revenue and profits across industries comes from the launch of new products, according to a McKinsey survey (Buffoni et al., 2017).

designed by freepik.com

There is a further agreement that the economic and technological trends indicate that innovation will play more a prominent role in the future. It will become a means of survival for many companies. Such agreement is, however, far from being unanimous when we come to the definition of the concept, the scope of such an interpretation or the innovation process.

Therefore, this chapter starts presenting the topic by clarifying the basic terms.

Despite the increasing interest in innovation both by academics and practitioners, the term itself has not been defined clearly to this day, and the lack of definition may be the reason behind the problems with measuring innovation (Johannessen et al., 2001).

Some of the scholars go back to the writings of Schumpeter in the 1940s and '50s and point out that Schumpeter made a clear distinction between the notions of *invention* and *innovation*. Hoványi (2000) also refers to Schumpeter when concluding that innovation only occurs if the 'creative idea' is confirmed by market success.

Invention refers to the discovery of ideas and methods related to new products and technologies, while innovation means the application of new inventions, the development and marketing of new products.

According to the message of this book invention (including the inventions of innovators who may not have received formal training) and the practical application are the functions of two different areas. Invention is a concept of science, while innovation is that of business life. The divide between these two areas is not strict or impassable: nowadays, the two areas seem to be more and more interdependent and interconnected. The results of basic research make a faster impact on practice, and the needs of practice determine the directions of basic research to a greater extent.

> More than 25 percent of total revenue and profits across industries comes from the launch of new products, according to a McKinsey survey

As a matter of fact, it is a case of combining the two hypotheses related to innovation: the fusion of 'technological push' and 'demand pull'. Technological push gives priority to the scientific knowledge that creates novelty, while demand pull emphasizes the priority of economic need. These two driving forces behind innovation go comfortably together, and in fact, they depend on each other (Figure 12.1.).

Figure 12.1. Technological push and demand pull

If we agree that innovation is a concept belonging mainly to economic and business life (Drucker, 1985), we should note that the application of new things and innovation play an important role in other spheres of social life too. The analysis in this chapter will continue with the the field of economic application. The starting point of innovation is the introduction of *something new*. It is *novelty* that distinguishes innovation from a simple modification. The Green Paper on Innovation" of the European Commission (1995) defines innovation as being "a synonym for the successful production, assimilation and exploitation of novelty in the economic and social spheres." The concept of novelty, however, immediately raises questions, as do Johannessen et al. (2001) in the title of their paper: 'What is new, how new, new to whom?'.

12.1. HOW NEW? - CONTINUITY AND DISCONTINUITY

Since innovation is closely related to the concept of newness, the analysis starts with the question „how new? It is important to clarify the degree of newness because the concepts used to describe innovation in theory and practice will depend on this. Namings and concepts, concerning newness are however rather overlapping; sometimes even confusing Susan Hart (1996) makes a distinction between development and innovation with regard to the degree of newness (Figure 12.2.).

Figure 12.2. The newness continuum

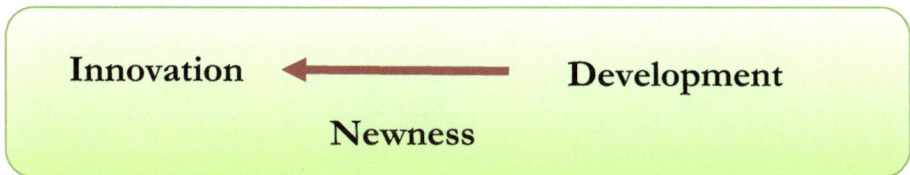

Miller and Morris (1999) distinguish between continuous and discontinuous (non-continuous) forms of innovation. Others use the terms continuous and radical innovation (Cooper, 1988), or incremental and radical innovation (Johannessen, 2001), while some academics speak about continuous and revolutionary innovations. Radical innovation is also frequently referred to as „breakthrough" (Waite et al. 1999). Zairi (1995), using the terms continuous and discontinuous innovation, emphasizing that some in the former category could be differentiated as dynamically continuous innovation. Iványi and Hoffer (1999) argue that, nowadays, the notion of innovation should include not only the basic changes but also smaller improvements or refinements of products and technologies. Nevertheless, they believe that the degrees of newness should be classified, and they suggest using the terms "fundamental innovation", "development innovation" and "appearance innovation".

From a marketing perspective, it seems useful to distinguish between a newness *based on old structures* and a newness breaking with the old structures and *presupposing new ones*. The two types of novelty require different approaches from companies and different attitudes from customers. It is with this consideration in mind that we distinguish continuous and non-continuous (discontinuous) innovation in this book.

Innovation can be defined as continuous if it builds on something already existing and creates compatibility between the old and the new. Regarding products, continuous innovation does not require a change in consumers' buying behaviour or user habits, as the function of the product remains the same, except that it better satisfies consumer needs. "Continuous innovation occurs within the boundaries of this known world. It works when the future competitive

193

requirements of customers can be met within existing industry structures, within existing competitive architecture. Continuous innovation is characterized by convergent way of thinking - including progressive modernization, sharper focus, and as a result, increasing specialization" - concludes Miller and Morris (1999, p. 4.).

The most important feature of discontinuous innovation is breaking with the past and leading to radical, revolutionary change. According to Miller and Morris cited earlier, this type of innovation „falls outside" existing markets or market segments, and when successful, it extends and redefines the market, exposing new opportunities. It requires a lateral, divergent, way of thinking overstepping the present boundaries (Op.cit. p.6.). In the case of products, breaking with the past brings about a change in the 'product – consumer' relationship (e.g., the difference between using a typewriter and a word processor). But breaking with the past will change the 'product – other products' relationship as well. The innovative new product will not be compatible with the existing structure (think of the differences between floppy discs and compacts discs). Referring to the new, information age, Dhebar (1994) mentions an additional way of 'breaking with the past': the discontinuity of the 'product – database' relationship. (In this case, the newly developed software, operation system, and so on is not able to handle the previously created files, software or database.) In more contemporary terms we can say that radical innovations redefine the market, that is, they change the existing market structure.

Due to the above-described difficulties, the dissemination of entirely new products may be slower than in the case of the novelties which do not break with the past. There is a vast literature about the diffusion of innovations in the marketplace, though most of them are rooted in the book written by Rogers in 1962.

EXHIBIT 12.1. THE INNOVATIONS OF INNOVATIONS: NEW IDEAS THAT APPEARED IN THE PAST TWO DECADES IN THE THEORY AND PRACTICE OF INNOVATION

Disruptive innovation

The Harvard Business Review published an article by Bowen and Christensen in the January-February issue of 1995, which introduced a new concept in the field of innovation, that of disruptive technology or disruptive innovation. It means that the larger companies concentrate on continuously improving their existing technologies in order to retain their customers and to better satisfy their needs, and they fail to notice that new, mostly smaller companies come out with new solutions at the bottom end of the market appealing to the future needs of the customers and gradually transforming or 'disrupting' the existing structure. In an article also published in the HBR twenty years later, Christensen laments that the concept has become so fashionable that it is now used to refer to all kinds of company successes, even ones that do not concern disruption. UBER, for example, is not a disruptive innovation, because it does not make the use of taxis obsolete; uberBLACK or uberSELECT, on the other hand, appear more likely to be that.

An UBER car in Moscow

Source: By Hipsta.space - Own work, CC BY-SA 4.0, ttps://commons.wikimedia.org/ w/index.php?curid=54001056

Open Innovation, open technology

In his book of 2006, Chesbrough, the advocate of open innovation, presents the differences between the two innovation models (closed and open) through the competition between Lucent and Cisco, the manufacturers of telecommunications equipment.

Lucent was established following the breaking up of AT&T, and it took over the lion's share of Bell Laboratories. Lucent achieved much success with its huge research capacity. Cisco, however, was always close behind and even took the lead many times. The two companies pursued completely different innovation models. Lucent put enormous efforts into developing new materials, spare parts and new systems in their own laboratories. Cisco, on the other hand, did not do any in-house research for practical reasons. They had a different type of ammunition: they invested in start-ups which were involved in such kind of research. Cisco ended up acquiring these companies and created one of the best research networks in the world without doing any research themselves.

Frugal Innovation

Frugal innovation is more than a strategy wrote Radjou and Prahbu in the Harvard Business Review in 2014. It is a new frame of mind which sees resource constraints as an opportunity and one that favours agility over efficiency. Frugal organizations do not seek to wow customers with excellent, technically sophisticated products, but instead, thrive to create good-quality solutions that deliver value to the customers at the lowest cost.

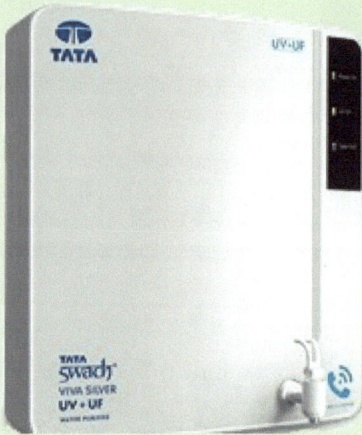

The water purifier Swach, manufactured by Tata Chemicals is a good example of frugal innovation that considered the needs of target customers. The Tatas had figured out that the unavailability of safe drinking water for the economically disadvantaged people had been a worldwide social menace. Research undertaken by the company created the opportunity to develop an affordably-priced water purifier which used rice husk combined with silver nanoparticles for the filtration process

Source: https://iveybusinessjournal.com/publication/frugal-innovation-the-key-to-penetrating-emerging-markets/

12.2. WHAT IS NEW? - THE SCOPE OF MARKETING INNOVATION

The scope of interpretation of innovation as implemented in business is a rather controversial issue. The review of the relevant literature shows that innovation is most frequently mentioned in relation *to products and technologies*. There have recently been lots of discussions about the *innovation of operating processes* too. Process innovation is, for example, the introduction of TQM or the modernization or reengineering of business processes (Cumming, 1998). Marketers believe that one more area could be added to this list, notably *marketing innovation*. Not only products and services, or technologies, or even operating processes can break with the past, but so can marketing too. Existing products and services can be marketed in a completely different way, using radically different marketing tools than before.

EXHIBIT 12.2. INNOVATION IN MARKETING PRACTICE

International examples of successful marketing innovations

Netflix introduced several novelties in the past few years (2016-2017), which turned it into one of the most innovative companies. In December 2016, the company put in place an innovation, which allows any one of its 93 million subscribers to browse the catalogue while an auto-playing trailer specially made for this purpose begins when one scrolls over a title-card. It facilitates the choice instead of tedious searching.

It took the company three years to introduce this innovation and confirms the same kind of commitment to the subscribers that Amazon has shown. Today, Netflix does not only broadcast but also plans to make one thousand hours of original programs in 2017 and invests six billion dollars to increase its library.

"We started [2016] by making Netflix available everywhere," says the vice-president of user-interface now available in130 new countries and "we ended it with making sure you could take it anywhere with you." (Downloading and offline viewing options). The evolution of the number of Netflix subscribers in the past 17 years is shown in the next diagram.

Netflix turns 20: Number of Netflix subscribers, 1999-2017

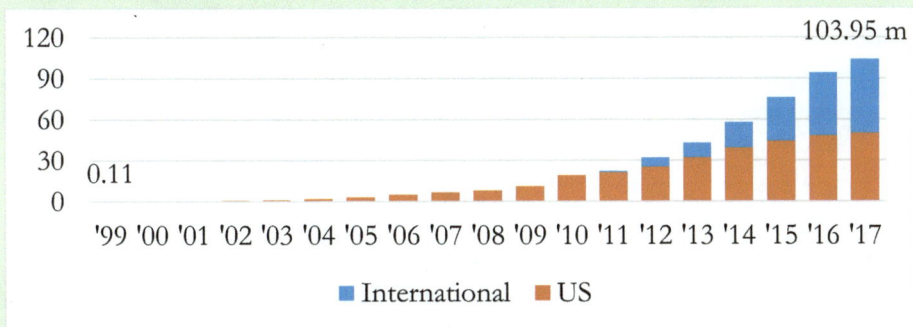

Source: https://www.statista.com and Netflix.

IKEA

IKEA established in 1943 has always been well-known for its innovations. Not only were its products innovative, but also its marketing. The company present in 46 countries focuses its marketing strategy on customer experience, both at the touch points and throughout the whole purchase cycle. The company launched an app on the market (Catalouge app) as early as 2013, which allowed customers to view the furniture in their own surroundings in 3D using the AR tools. The 2018 catalogue of the company was published with the following recommendation:

"Welcome to the brand new 2018 IKEA catalogue. We have redesigned our app and filled it with loads of inspiration, ideas and furnishings knowledge. Discover the pictures, the films the stories; save your favourite pictures and create a mood board; use the 3D function to see how the different furniture would look in your own home. The app will bring the IKEA catalogue closer to your home."

Source: http://onlinecatalogue.ikea.com/hu/hu_HU/IKEA_Catalogue/pages/1?index

NIKE

Trying to find a company with an impeccable presence on social media, take Nike. Its Twitter page @Nike Support provides an excellent example of positive company-customer relations. A quick glance at the tweets and the replies shows how fast, respectful and helpful the replies given to customers are.

Nike made a smart decision to open a separate customer support account because the unity of Nike and Nike store was not disrupted. It is remarkable that a big company like Nike can communicate with its customers in such a fast, careful and customized way. Even with a limited 140 characters, Nike makes it clear that they are there for the people; "If you need something, just yell!", The brand becomes more accessible and friendly with this language.

The lesson that can be drawn is that separating customer support is a model to be followed by other companies too. There's something to be learnt from the language that Nike's support people use. They are interactive, cheerful, and downright playful at times.

Source: https://twitter.com/NikeSupport?ref_src=twsrc%5Etfw&ref_url=http%3A%2F%2F contentmarketinginstitute.com%2F2016%2F07%2Fcontent-marketing-best-brands%2F

It is considered an innovation when book selling (see, for example, the writing of Kim and Mauborgne [1999] about the success of Borderes and B & N book chain) or Internet access are combined with café services, or when florists introduced home delivery. The market can be redefined by well-known products as well; many examples could be enumerated from Japan. The 50 cm^3 small motorbikes have been known for more than 40 years in many markets. Suzuki, however, redefined the market (the American) when it launched its scooters in large volumes, with high quality and at reasonable prices. The same can be said about the four-wheel drive Suzuki Samurai. There are also numerous examples in connection with the Internet: the worldwide web revolutionizes sales, offers personalized communication, and so on. These are all innovations.

Figure 12.3. The multi-dimensional model of innovation

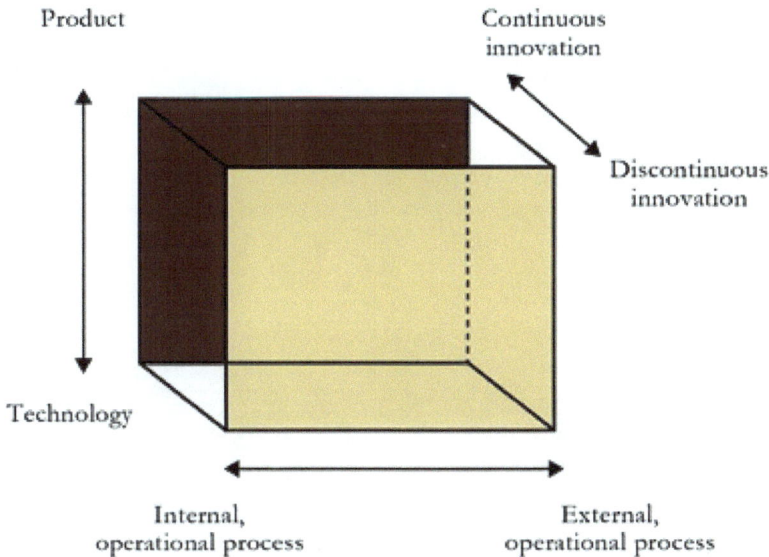

By analogy with Cooper's (1998) multi-dimensional approach, the degrees of newness and the scope of its interpretation can be illustrated in the following diagram (Figure 12.3.). The book primarily focuses on the products and services produced for customers, and the way they are marketed, however, it is important to briefly mention the other areas of innovation, because all aspects of innovations are interrelated and are interdependent in the business life.

12.3. NEW TO WHOM? - TO THE MARKETER OR TO THE MARKET?

When discussing the question "new to whom?" we should always be aware that it can only be understood in connection with the question "how new?". When something is not really new, for example, the cost reduction of a product, it is useless to ask "new to whom?". When the first definitions of innovation were formulated, researchers solved this dilemma in a relatively easy way: „any idea, practice, or material artifact perceived to be new by the relevant unit of adoption" (Zalthalm et al., 1973, p.10.). Later another view began to gain ground regarding new products. A clear-cut distinction should be made between two "relevant units": the company which creates the new product, and the market, which perceives the product or service as new. This approach would seem to be beyond question, although several authors argue (Johannessen et al., 2001) that this answer to the question "new to whom", restricts the interpretation to the level of the products. They believe that in the case of technological or process innovation the market should be replaced by the industry as the second relevant unit.

12.4. CLASSIFICATION OF NEW PRODUCTS

The topic of this book is concerned mainly with new products. The confusion about the concept of "new product" has been gradually cleared in the marketing literature from the beginning of the 1980, since the publication of the research report by Booz, Allen & Hamilton, Inc. (1982), and more and more people accept the categorization of new products as described in this study. (The well-known consulting firm studied 13.000 "new product launches" by 700 companies.) According to them, new products could be classified into the following categories:

- *New to the world* is a product having completely different functions compared to any earlier products, which has entirely new uses, creates new needs, and as such creates new markets. These included at the time television, computer, Rubik's cube, and all sorts of other products. These products are new both to the company and the market.

- *New product lines* include new products which allow the company to enter into an established product market. The product is not new to the world in this case, but new to the company, because they were present in this market earlier.

- *Additions to the existing product lines* with new products. These include products, which add or supplement the company's current product line.

- *Improvement of existing products.* This category of products replace earlier products and offer customer more and/or something different, a higherperceived value.

- *Repositioning.* It concerns products that are intended to be sold in new target markets (market segments), or to be launched for new uses. It means that the physical characteristics of the product remain unchanged, but the communication programme targeting the new market segment focuses on a different function of the product.

- *Cost reductions.* This category includes those "new products" that do not offer any perceivable difference compared to the existing products, but are offered at lower costs.

Figure 12.4. summarizes the results of the BAH study from the point of the market and the companies.

Figure 12.4. Categorization of new products

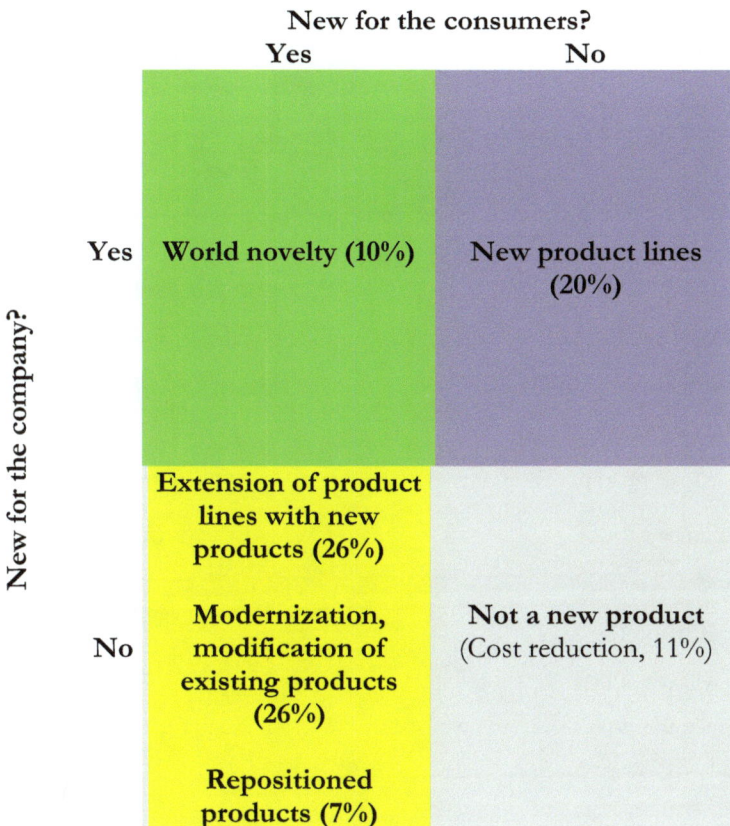

	New for the consumers?	
	Yes	**No**
Yes	World novelty (10%)	New product lines (20%)
No	Extension of product lines with new products (26%)	Not a new product (Cost reduction, 11%)
	Modernization, modification of existing products (26%)	
	Repositioned products (7%)	

New for the company?

EXHIBIT 12.3. THE MOST IMPORTANT INVENTIONS OF THE 21ST CENTURY ACCORDING TO THE TELEGRAPH

Back to image

Bluetooth (2000)	Amazon Kindle (2007)
iPod (2001)	Google Android (2008)
AbiCor artifical heart (2001)	Spotify (2008)
Skype (2003)	4G (2008)
Facebook (2004)	Nissan Leaf (2010)
YouTube (2005)	IBM Watson winning Jeopardy (2011)
Nintendo Wii (2006)	
Apple iPhone (2007)	Google Driverless Car (2012)
BBC iPlayer (2007)	Tinder (2012)

Source: http://www.telegraph.co.uk/technology/2016/03/09/most-important-inventions-of-the-21st-century-in-pictures/

CHAPTER 13

THE REGULARITIES OF INNOVATIONS: THE DOMINANT DESIGN

The historical analysis of innovations implemented in various product categories has allowed researchers to establish a pattern of regularities of innovations, according to which relatively small number of revolutionary and discontinuous innovations are linked with a series of continuous innovations or developments. Utterback (1995) used the examples of photography, lighting and typewriting to present this innovative development. Photography: daguerreotype – ferrotype – glass plate method – dry plate method – Celluloid film – electronic photography. Lighting: candle and oil lamp – gas light – electric light bulb – fluorescent light. Typing: manual typewriter – electric typewriter – word processor – PC with a word processor. Based on the observation of technological evolution researchers (Abernathy-Utterback, 1978; Moore-Pessemier, 1993; Miller-Morris, 1999) identified three stages of innovative development:

- the fluid stage of innovation,
- the emergence of the dominant product form (design), and
- the transitional stage of innovation.

This kind of modelling of industrial innovation became popular with the publication of an article written by Abernathy and Utterback in the Technology Review in 1978. This article can boast of 5.200 citations.

Available at http://teaching.up.edu/bus580/bps/Abernathy%20and%20Utterback,%201978.pdf

13.1. THE "FLUID" STAGE OF INNOVATIONS

The innovations characterizing the first stage are called "fluid type" innovations. This period is the stage of creation of *revolutionary product innovations*. There are numerous examples which prove that revolutionary new products were typically created by individual inventors or smaller companies out of technical inspiration or as a reaction to an unsatisfied market need. These products were based on the needs of a market niche at first, but they later represented the beginning of a new product line's (or product category's) life-cycle. A revolutionary new product often happens to satisfy later a different market than what it was originally planned for (transistors, Xerox, Diesel engine, etc.).

The competition in the fluid phase of innovation is getting strong in the field of product development (the improvement of the product's performance and functions). The fact that the new product is far from complete when it is created has inspired plenty of *follow-on innovations*. Since the expectations of consumers towards revolutionary new products are not yet clear at the time of their emergence, these innovations are often directed at very different versions of the products. These versions are manufactured in small quantities only. The production process, therefore, should be fairly flexible. Production in this phase is more like a "workshop", where general purpose machinery and highly skilled people are employed. Production is carried out by the firms creating the innovation, which are characterized by an "organic" type of organization. If the innovation is created or taken over from the smaller companies by larger companies, a dedicated organization is developed in order to create an "entrepreneurial atmosphere" that is the characteristic of small companies.

13.2. THE EMERGENCE OF THE "DOMINANT DESIGN"

As a result of the experiments and developments that characterized the fluid stage, the *dominant design of the product emerged* in the majority of cases. This is being manifested in an optimal combination of the value elements defining the given product category. This design then becomes the norm whose main features remain unchanged for a long time.

> A dominant design is the one that becomes the accepted norm due to its technical characteristics, the one to which market players must adhere if they hope to command significant market share.
>
> Utterback, 1994

The dominant design is not a direct outcome of the revolutionary innovation, but rather the end product of the evolutionary process that follows. Consider, for example, the Ford Model T; this car had all the characteristics that practically any car manufactured between 1920 and 1970 had: longitudinally front mounted internal combustion engine, rear-wheel drive, a separate body, H type gearbox, water cooled engine, driver's controls. Earlier models already had some of these characteristics, but Model T was the first car that included all of them. Many other examples could be mentioned from the fields of consumer electronics (VHS player), computers (IBM PC, Windows operating system) and other industries. These dominant products will become the starting points for further development and will determine the directions of development for the given product group for decades.

Airbus A380 is the world's largest passenger airliner. Looking at the other popular passenger airliners (e.g., Boeings), one can notice that the basic design is the same.

Photo: By Dmitry A. Mottl - Own work, Public Domain, https://commons.wikimedia. org/w/index.php?curid=2288914

The question arises why a certain model becomes the dominant product. The optimal technological advantage, the favourable reaction of the market to the optimal combination of the value elements or the efforts of the company to freeze any further improvements for the sake of making production more economical can be mentioned as reasons.

EXHIBIT 13.1: THE CASE OF XEROX

It must be noted that good marketing efforts can contribute to directing special attention to certain product designs and making them dominant. An example of this is the case of Xerox: Xerox recognized the importance of product innovation as early as the end of the 1960s and established a research centre in Palo Alto in 1970. Many new products were conceived in this research centre, including among others 'Alto', the robust predecessor of today's personal computer. This product possessed almost all the functions as today's PCs, such as the mouse, Windows, graphical interface, word processor. This company developed later the concept of the local network before anyone else, and the laser printer. All these functions gained huge success in the market, although not for Xerox, but later for IBM, Apple, Novell and Hewlett-Packard. All because Xerox failed to develop a market structure, neglected the marketing function, as was described satirically by Upside magazine. "On the first day PARC (Palo Alto Research Center) created the PC; on the second day the OS (operating system), on the third day, the so-called desktop editor, on the fourth day they developed the foundations of the laser printer. On the fifth day, they realized they did not have any marketing. On the sixth day, they looked into themselves, and on the seventh day, they gave up everything" (Miller – Morris, 1999, p. 57-58).

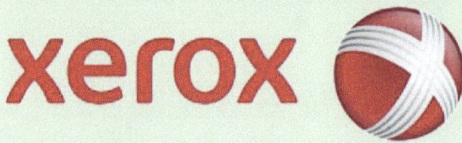

Despite the above example, those who enter the market first usually have an advantage. A good example is the case of video cassette recorders starting from the early eighties: two technologies were fighting for leadership, VHS and Beta. Since VHS gained early success, traders were more willing to buy and stockpile VHS devices, and the software manufacturers preferred to record their programmes on VHS tapes too. This way, more VHS video cassette players could be sold, which increased the economies of scale for these companies. And even though Beta was not in any way inferior technically, and they are still leaders in professional image recording, they had to withdraw from the market of consumer electronics.

The market knowledge of manufacturing companies increases in parallel with the emergence of the dominant design. This can lead them to differentiate their products in order to satisfy the needs of the market segments or market niches. The main features of the new product varieties, however, correspond to the dominant product (cars of different sizes, special vehicles, laptop computer, and so on.).

The good establishment of the dominant product design compels the manufacturers to turn their attention away from product innovation towards *technological and process innovation*. The dominant product has already become popular in the market by that time, can be sold in large quantities, and manufacturers can make higher profits if they rationalize their production processes and develop mass production. The "workshop-style" production is replaced with line production, general-purpose machinery with special tools and special machinery, skilled workers with less skilled ones. This stage is hallmarked by *revolutionary new technological and process innovations*. The interdependence between the *product and the technological/ operating process* is established. The special machinery only allows the manufacturing of certain parts. This makes product changes very inflexible; the basic model becomes very rigid.

13.3. THE "TRANSITION" STAGE OF INNOVATION

Following the emergence of the dominant product design and the development of interdependence between product and technology, a new stage of development begins; the stage of continuous innovation, complementary and additional improvement. This does not affect the basic features of the product. The same is true for technology. Technology becomes large-scale, capital-intensive and inflexible, and provides the opportunity for minor improvements only.

It is difficult to know when a given product design becomes dominant; it can only be decided ex-post. There are several cases when a company misjudged the position of a product and started an investment which was never recovered. This was the case, for example, of Texas Instrument. TI believed that LED display would become dominant in digital watches, and so they carried out huge investments in that field. Soon after, however, the innovations that appeared in LCD technology made these investments redundant [Moore -Pessemier, 1993, p. 60.].

When the relationship between technology and product becomes relatively rigid and interdependent, the competition between the manufacturers takes place at the level of the products that are fundamentally similar; the competition will shift to the prices, the small changes made in the product, and the other areas of marketing, like quality, reliability, image and distribution. Small, additional improvements and changes will appear in the field of technology. The purpose of these is to make the manufacturing of the product cheaper, the product more adaptable to the needs of the market and more differentiated in relation to the products of the competitors. These small changes, if added up, can actually have more impact on the products or the technology than the original innovation.

This stage of innovation is referred to as *"special-type"* innovation in the literature. The minor changes carried out on the product are often perceived by the consumers as a model change, as is illustrated by the automobile industry. Although, some researchers believe that products become more and more similar as they move ahead in the stages of their life cycle, so that a model change can represent a severe market advantage. (The success of the Japanese automobile industry is a good example for this; as result of fast model changes Japanese car manufacturers kept launching newer products in their offering than their North-American competitors.) The innovation development model is illustrated in Figure 13.1.

Figure 13.1. The innovation development model

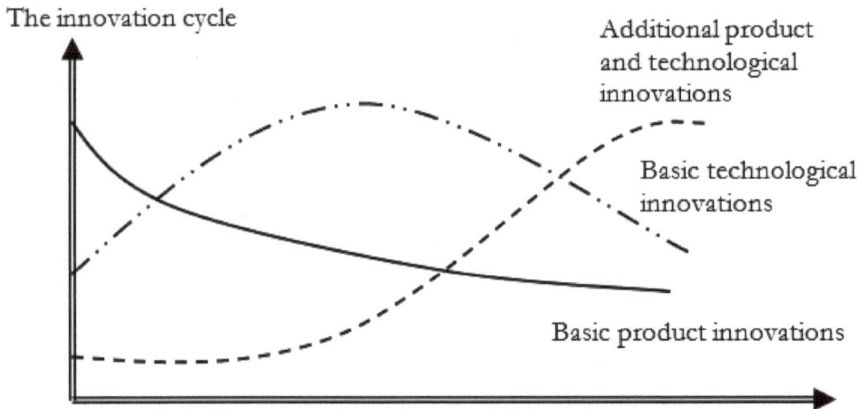

When a new, revolutionary innovation emerges, the innovation cycle starts again. In the field of additional, small-scale developments Japanese management brought revolutionary changes. Mass production made both the product and the technology rigid, as was mentioned earlier, and excluded the initiatives of employees from the process. Japanese management, on the contrary, believed that mass production can be combined with individual initiatives. They set "continuous improvement", "continuous development" as an objective, and gave a big role to individual initiatives in this process. This strategy is very similar to what has been discussed about the third stage of innovation with the only difference, that here the emphasis is on continuous.

The Japanese word for continuous improvement is "*kaizen*", and this is the name that has spread in the management literature as well (Imai, 1991; Wellington, 1995). Figure 13.2 illustrates the combination of innovation- and kaizen-type improvement.

Figure 13.2. The combination of innovation and kaizen

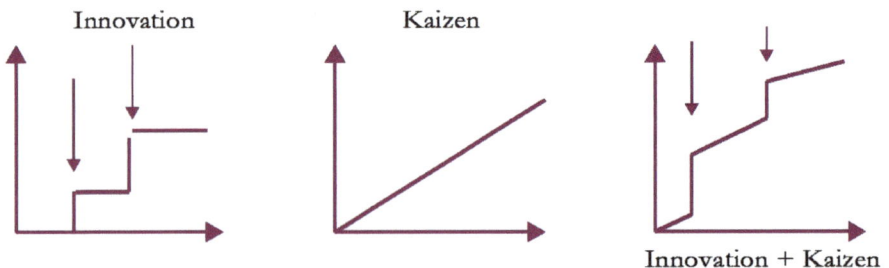

Source: Adapted from Hooley and Sauders, 1993, p. 20.

13.4. LINKING INNOVATION AND MARKETING — THE EMERGENCE OF DOMINANT MARKETING

It was pointed out during the discussion of the evolution of innovation that following the emergence of product innovation (always including service-oriented innovation too) improvements start in several directions using different combinations of the elements of product value. Then in the second stage of innovation emerges the dominant product design, which represents a relatively stable and permanent combination of the value elements. Once the dominant product design is well established, interdependence develops between the product and the technology, the technology applied becomes capital-intensive and relatively rigid. The basic innovation relative to the product is replaced by so-called additional improvement, which differentiates and modernizes the product in order to satisfy the different needs of the various market segments through continuous improvement of the elements of value.

It was concluded in the previous chapter that the concept of innovation is not related to the product and the technology, but is intrinsically linked to the operating processes and the marketing activities of the company too.

The author strongly believes that the evolution of marketing activities follow the same regularities as product innovation.

When a product innovation emerges which "breaks with the past", the task of marketing becomes very complex. How can something be marketed and sold, that has not been known by anyone before? — that is the main question for marketing in this situation. There are no previous experiences of successful marketing available at that time. The revolutionary new product is not clearly related to the previously known needs and expectations of the customers, and consequently, the marketing actions applied with success earlier may not necessarily work.

Nowadays, new Internet-based companies are facing similar problems. Waite et al. (1999) describe, for example, that when the concept of Internet-based television emerged in 1996, the market promised huge opportunities in the United States; everybody had a television and the use of Internet way spreading explosively. Web TV, a subsidiary of Microsoft, launched a massive advertising campaign with the support and the marketing experience of their parent company. The result was very disappointing despite the huge marketing investments. Philips, however, successfully introduced a system called Magnavox in 1997. This was due to the novel ways of marketing. The marketing research conducted by Philips revealed that consumers were reluctant to embrace WebTV, because they did not understand the benefits it would offer them. It was also revealed that shop assistants did not put enough time and effort into informing their customers about it, because it was easier to focus on selling the TV-s and cameras that were already well-known. Philips, on the other hand, started out by informing consumers about their product. They had advertisements in which consumers talked about the advantages and benefits of Internet TV. Only then did they start focusing on promoting sales. Philips broke with traditional marketing and pursued a so-called concept marketing, which consists of making the potential market understand the value concept of the product.

Coming back to the innovative evolution of marketing, the marketing of revolutionary innovation is first attempted with several marketing initiatives. After the emergence of the dominant product design, it is very likely that a *dominant form of marketing develops* as well in relation to the product category. *Dominant from of marketing means the strong similarity of the marketing mix tools applied and the same or similar ways they are used.* The dominant form of marketing applies to all marketing tools.

> **Dominant form of marketing means the strong similarity of the marketing tools applied and the same or similar way they are used.**

It is obviously more difficult to prove than in the case of products, where the technical functions can easily be compared. The best way to confirm the dominant form of marketing is to study the everyday practice of marketing. Let's take a few examples in the order of the marketing tools.

Product policy refers to the marketing tools closely related to the product, for example, packaging and form (design), colour, guarantee, etc. The dominant functional benefits of the product can materialize in a variety of forms and packaging. Looking at the historical development of a given product category, it can be noticed that the appearance possibilities include some dominant packaging designs.

Let's consider the example of milk and beverages within the food products. Milk was first sold in jugs, then in bottles, later in plastic bags and nowadays in special paper cartons. This latter has become dominant by now. But there were some interim developments: the differently shaped cartons (e.g. round shape) were gradually replaced with sqare ones, which allowed more efficient use of space in the fridge.

Similar development trends can be observed in the case of beverages; dominant packaging designs emerged that fit the intended use, such as glass bottles, cans and plastic bottles. A few dominant solutions can be noticed in the dispensing technology of containers too (compare for example the way beverage cans were opened ten years ago and today). However, the emergence of dominant colours can also be witnessed in the case of product design.

The dominant form of supply has emerged with the services as well. Let's think of the petrol stations, where the dominant fuel is supplied via dominant service systems. Should you happen to stop by an AGIP, BP or Shell, you will have the same facilities (self-service coupled with washing, shopping services).

A dominant design emerged for the interior equipment of hotel rooms of the same category; no matter where you stay, you can use exactly the same services, usually in the same form. Numerous other examples could be enumerated. Let's have a look at, for example, the terms of warranty used in the sale of passenger cars. Japanese companies came up with the marketing type innovation of offering a warranty for either three years or for 100.0000 km, which is becoming more and more dominant. South-Koreans have reacted by offering a five-year warranty.

As regards marketing tools used by product policy, the dominant design is none other than the standardization of the expected or in other words objectified product from Levitt's product levels (core product - expected product - extended product).

The packaging, design, colour, warranty etc. of the product remains dominant until a new marketing innovation does not create a new norm. As practical observation has revealed, there is continuous development and modernization between the two stages of innovations.

The price of products and services - The reader may have a detailed explanation of pricing from the book of Rekettye and Liu (2018). It seems enough to conclude that although the price of the product is the most difficult to standardize, the price levels are getting closer as a result of the increasing and more global competition. A dominant price emerges within a product category of the same value, while the prices of other products are dispersed around this price to a lesser degree due to the increasing transparency of the "new economy". Price forms can become dominant; in the communication and information business sectors, which are characterized by a high share of fixed costs, *bundled prices and dynamic prices* are becoming more and more dominant.

Distribution - marketing channels - Getting the products and services to the final consumers is a key area of marketing. A review of the practice confirms that dominant product related patterns emerge within the forms of distribution and selling techniques. The question is whether these dominant patterns evolve according to the expectations of the producer, or is it forced on the producer by the intensifying trade. Producers in a strong position seek to have maximum control over the distribution channel and to market their products through their own channels of distribution or through a franchise network in a controlled fashion. But the emergence of a dominant form can be observed in this area too. The innovations related to the distribution channels are copied by the others making the given from dominant. For example, Suzuki was the first to develop a specialized (exclusive) dealer network in the United States, when they launched the Suzuki Samurai. Almost every car manufacturer has launched their products in this way since then. In the market of fast moving consumer goods, especially in oligopolistic markets, a merchandising innovation introduced by a producer is immediately replicated by the others, which will then become dominant this way.

The other reason for the emergence of dominant designs in marketing is mass-market retail, which is becoming more and more oligopolistic too. It can be noticed that product groups are marketed almost in the same ways from the purchasing conditions, through product display to the forms of sale, or even including the special offers on the product group.

Marketing communication - The rise of a dominant design can also be witnessed in this area. Products within a product group are supported with very similar advertising messages, styles and even similar campaigns. It is even more prevalent in the other areas of market-making, e.g. the similarities of special offers, discounts, POS materials etc.

To sum it up, it is believed that shortly after the product design has become dominant, the marketing mix used during the launching of the product becomes rigid and dominant too. Those who cannot adapt to the dominant form of marketing cannot expect major successes in the market. This obviously does not rule out the possibility of continuous development or modernization in this field, which can lead to changes and improvements in the dominant marketing mix.

CHAPTER 14

THE UPDATED MODEL OF PRODUCT DEVELOPMENT

The previous chapter has discussed the patterns of the innovation development cycle and has pointed out that new product development is one of the most important areas of innovation in Creating new products is a key strategic issue for corporate management. It is also true, however, that this task requires the most creative ways of thinking and an interdisciplinary approach, and despite the need for formalizing the processes to make the development successful, this is the area that can be the least formalized and consequently is the function that everybody 'does differently' in practice. This chapter aims to introduce a new model for the planning, developing and launching of new products that may help practitioners to avoid the pitfalls lurking in new product policy and decrease the number of new product failures. The review of the relevant literature (Wheelwright - Sasser 1989, Topfer 1995, Hart 1996, Stein 1996, Clark – Fujimoto 1996, Crawford 1997, Cooper 1998, Iványi – Hoffer 1999, Samli – Weber 2000, Zhang – Doll 2001, Thomke 2001, Weber and Rohracher, 2012; Guzzini and Iacobucci, 2017) confirms that the majority of researchers draw their conclusions from making generalizations about the successful and non-successful product development practices, pointing out the critical factors and mistakes that may lead to failure.

14.1. SOME BASIC PRINCIPLES OF THE NEW PRODUCT DEVELOPMENT

As a summary of the secondary research conducted by the author, the following conclusions can be drawn with regard to determining the success of new product development:

- The development and commercialization of new products constitute strategically important areas for company practice. Only companies that attach a great significance to this field can *gain sustainable competitive advantage*. The nature of competitive advantage has significantly changed as a result of digitalization described in the first part of the book. Earlier, the *masterworks* of small workshop producers guaranteed success in a relatively narrow market. Then, during the period of *mass production*, success lied in *economies of scale* of the products launched into a broader market. Not long ago, *product differentiation* came to the foreground as a result of the globalization of competition. Then came the practice of *mass customization* (anything, for anyone, any time, in any quantity), the extreme manifestation of which is the personalization, which is a sort of return to the basics on a higher level. It includes personal contact with the customers, customization to meet their needs, involving the customer in product development and production. These changes in paradigms also affect the process of product development and marketing.

- *Time to market* is a vital element of today's product development. Analyses provide evidence that the development and market cycles both shorten, so those investments for growth offer a faster return where the time between the birth of the idea and the launch in the market is the shortest. This requirement inevitably has an impact on the process of product development and commercialization.

- New product development is a key strategic issue of corporate management, as has been pointed out. It will most likely yield success if the top management of the company and all the employees are *committed* to innovation. The task of the top management is not only to be the advocates of innovation, but also to create an internal environment, to introduce a *corporate culture,* which is susceptible to modernization and promotes the success of new product development. (Although it is not directly related to the topic, it should be emphasized that the external environment, e.g. state incentives, the amount of money spent on basic research etc., also plays an important role in the success of this activity.)

- The human factor is vital in new product development: only people who have both scientific (technical) and non-scientific (e.g., artistic) *creativity* can achieve success. These people, however, are not easy to manage. The management of the company should, therefore, adopt a form of governance, an incentive scheme or *organizational structure*, or corporate culture (Vágási, 1998) which contributes to attracting creative people to the company and makes them stay by allowing them to meet their expectations. It highlights *the organizational and human resources side* of new product development.

- New product development is feasible only in a processing system. There is a consensus in the literature that the process can be effective if it is *formalized,* but it is also generally true that the more sub-activities the process is made up of, the more likely the result will be wrong. The success of new product development does not solely depend on the number of constituents in a process, but rather on how successfully these sub-activities are carried out.

- It has already been pointed out in the second part of the book that the author considers the *product line* as the focal element of value management. This principle should apply in new product development too. There is no time in today's fast-moving world for companies to finish developing *one* product first, then start developing the second, third and n member of the product line. The development should be managed right from the beginning in a way, using the so-called platform strategy, that the company should be able to launch the other members of the product line immediately or shortly after the completion of the new product.

- Last but not least, new product development needs the input of the market from the beginning of the process until the end. Innovation, as it has been pointed out earlier, can be of a so-called "technological push" or „demand pull" nature. This is true for product development as well. In both cases, especially in the case of technological push, the incorporation of the feedback of the market into the process is of particular importance. Otherwise, the situation of "technophobia" could occur. It means that no matter what a technically and technologically remarkable product is created if it simply does not meet the demand of the target customers.

14.2. PRODUCT LINE EXTENSION OR BREAKTHROUGH NEW PRODUCT

During the discussion of new product classification and referring to the BAH study it was concluded that two types of new products can be distinguished from a market point of view: *revolutionary new products* (breakthrough) and *the extension of the product line with a new member.* This latter one has a different level of newness. The review of the relevant literature confirms that neither the literature nor practice makes any distinction between the development or the launch of these two types of new products. Product line extension is a very popular practice (Samli és Weber, 2000) because it

1. seems less risky in the eyes of the management,

2. usually involves routine development,

3. doesn't require the purchase of new production equipment or capacities,

4. can be launched faster into the market,

5. requires fewer new technical competences,

6. requires shorter planning, and

7. promises faster market expansion, consequently faster return.

By contrast, a truly new product (Olson, 1996):

1. offers unique benefits,

2. can extend and redefine the product category,

3. is distinct from the existing portfolio,

4. requires new marketing practices,

5. entails high risks and

6. is closely related to newly emerging consumer trends.

It follows from the above that the development and launch of revolutionary new products require more time and capital. At the same time, research also confirms that a genuinely new product promises higher profits in the long term. Samli and Weber (Op. cit.) explain that 90% of the new products launched between 1989 and 1993 were product line extensions, and only 10% were genuinely new products. This 10% accounted for 24% of the profit.

14.3. THE PROCESS OF NEW PRODUCT DEVELOPMENT AND LAUNCH IN THE LITERATURE

New product development is depicted as a process starting with the collection of ideas and ending with the launch of the product into the market by the literature on marketing, operational and production management. Considering the number of ideas and the projects launched, the process can be illustrated as a "funnel". Stein (1996) for example presents the process as follows (Figure 14.1.).

Figure 14.1. The funnel of innovation

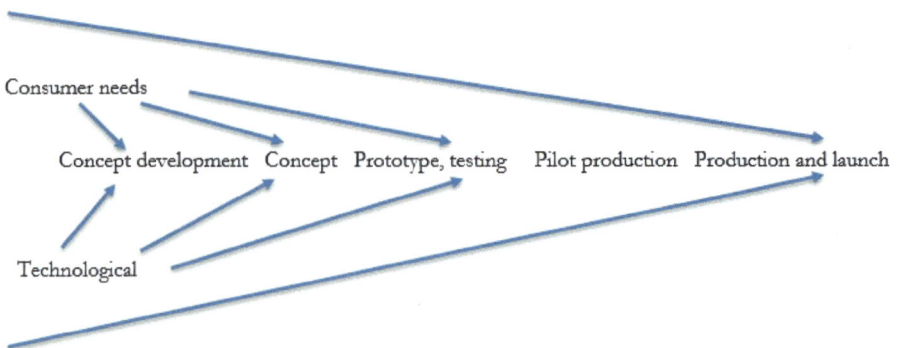

Different authors propose different models; and these models differ with regard to the number of activities, their connections and the decisions points. To illustrate the variation in the number of activities, let's have two authors. Kotler (1997) specifies eight actions, or decision points: (1) idea generation, (2) idea screening, (3) concept development and screening, (4) development of marketing strategy, (5) viability study, (6) product development, (7) market testing and (8) market launch. Poolton and Ismail (2000), referring to Cooper distinguish 13 phases: (1) first screening, (2) preliminary market analysis, (3) preliminary technical analysis, (4) detailed market study, (5) preliminary economic and financial analysis, (6) product development, (7) in-house testing, (8) testing with the customer, (9) pilot production, (10) test marketing, (11) pre-launch business analysis, (12) start of production and (13) launch into the market.

Citing Birman (1987) Iványi and Hoffer (1999) list the following models:

- the linear model of innovation,

- the closed innovation chain,

- the phase review model,

- the stage-gate model,

- the process-based innovation model,

- Landvater's spiral,

- the portfolio life-cycle model (value perception — value creation — value launch — value management cycle),

- chain-linked model.

The problems concerning new product development models described by the literature can be attributed to two interrelated factors.

- On the one hand, many of the models presented describe the process as a *sequence*, that is, as a series of consecutive activities. It would suggest that a given phase of the activity could only start if the previous one has already been completed successfully. This succession slows down the process and increases the time needed to get the product into the market.

- On the other hand, although all the models include the aspects of the market into the analysis, these remain separated due to the succession. The technical-technological aspects and the consumers' points of view constitute two different groups of arguments, and they only coincide at the decision points.

With the aim of rectifying these shortcomings, a model was created which knits these two important areas in a parallel way and in conjunction with each other. The concept of parallel development appears in the literature too, but parallelism primarily refers to the technical planning process. Maylor (1997) for

217

example says that "The critical factor in the parallel model of new product development is to schedule the production and development activities in parallel and to implement the whole process in a project-oriented structure and strong cross-functional coordination".

14.4. THE PROPOSED MODEL OF NEW PRODUCT DEVELOPMENT

The process of new product development is divided into four main stages in the proposed model. The division into stages provides better clarity and decreases the number of decisions points.

The first stage is *the exploration of options*, which includes (1) the analysis and research of the 'options', (2) the setting of the directions of corporate policies with regard to the new products, (3) the creation and collection of ideas relative to the new products, and (4) the screening of the ideas. These four activities can be broken down into two process phases:

- the phase of exploring innovation possibilities and setting new product policy objectives, and

- the phase of collecting and assessing (screening) new product ideas.

Exploring the innovation possibilities and determining the new product policy

The exploration of innovation possibilities is very strongly related to the company's strategic planning process, as is illustrated in Figure 14.2. The company's strategic plan sets the directions of new product policy by specifying the market and financial objectives of the company, and its visions for growth. Linda Rochfort (1991) describes two functions of corporate strategic planning which are intended to set the direction for brainstorming, idea collection and screening. They are the following:

Identification of the company's innovation needs - The innovation needs can be determined with the help of situation analysis and market research. The company needs to analyse the environment, the market and technological trends that characterize its product groups, as well as the strengths and weaknesses of the company. The determination of the innovation needs will serve as a basis for the objectives relating to the new products and will help allocate the necessary resources for implementing the new product policy.

Identification of the research areas - To make the search for new product ideas efficient, the company should select the potential product-market groups and technological areas on which to focus the search. The analysis of the situation, the mission of the company, the analysis of the strengths and weaknesses of the company, the study of the product and product line related objectives can already designate most of the research areas. The methods of portfolio planning known form the literature can also play a significant role in identifying the research areas.

Figure 14.2. The first stage of product development: the exploration of options

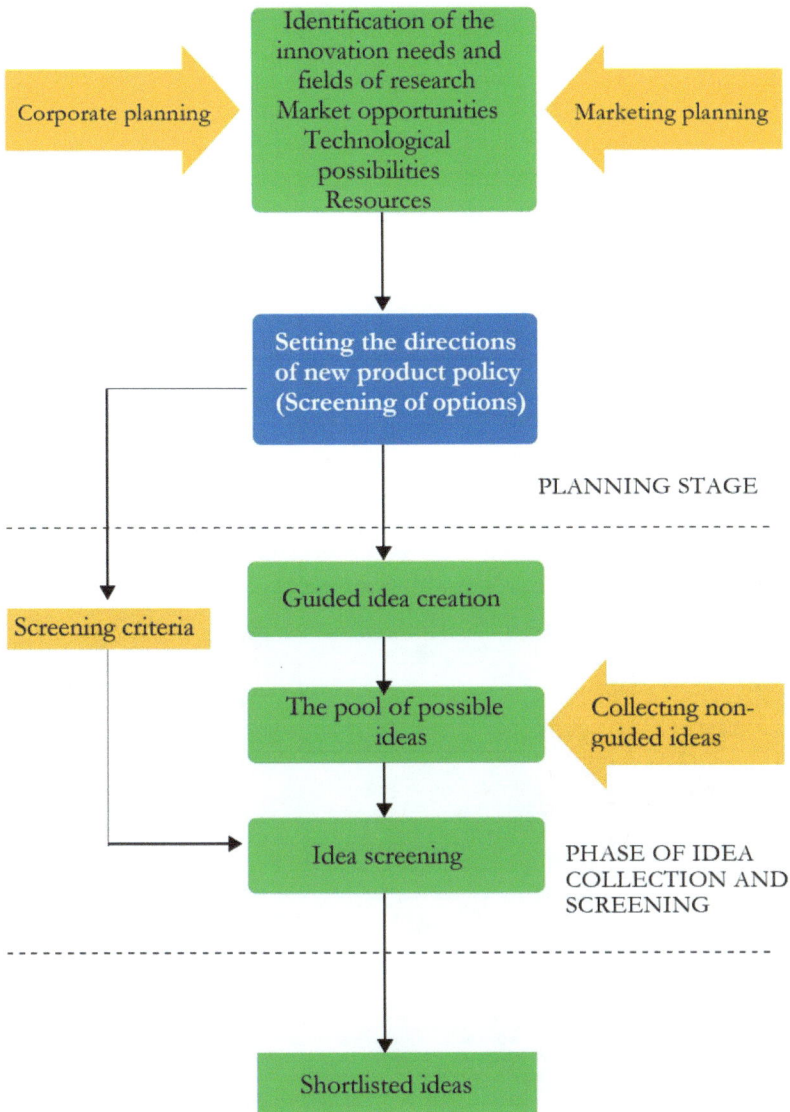

The so-called first stage outlined in Figure 14.2. can be interpreted as a general planning activity, which is not yet connected to the development of specific new products. The activities of this stage should be carried out continuously by the company to have an up-do-date view of the prevailing possibilities.

Figures 14.2. and 14.3. show that the first stage called exploration of options has been separated from the other three. It has been done because the literature strongly holds the view that the potential failure of new products can be traced back to the beginning of the process in most cases. The beginning stage of product development involves a series of uncertainties. The literature refers to these uncertainties as „front end fuzziness". Most of these uncertainties are related to knowing the needs of customers and translating these needs into value elements of the product, especially in the case of discontinuous innovation. The marketing costs incurred in the beginning stage can be recovered manifold if only minor modifications are necessary during the phases of implementation. The next exhibit illustrates the development model of Generation 10 of the Japanese Honda Civic 10.

EXHIBIT 14.1. THE DEVELOPMENT OF THE 10TH GENERATION HONDA CIVIC

First Generation: 1972-1979

Second Generation: 1979-1983

Third Generation: 1983-1987

Fourth Generation: 1987-1991

Fifth Generation: 1991-1995

Gary Evert feels like he's gone full-circle. One of his early jobs with Honda, following obtaining a mechanical engineering degree from the University of Washington, was in Japan, working on the Civic. He says that he "designed a little bracket on the suspension."

Now Evert is the North American Development Leader for the 10th generation Civic. And there's an interesting aspect of the development of this Civic. Historically, Honda and other companies that were once referred to as "transplants" in the U.S. worked hard to develop their own local design and engineering capabilities. Sure, they built plants in places like Marysville, Georgetown and Smyrna, but by and large the products produced in those factories were developed in places like Tochigi, Toyota City and Yokosuka.

With time, there has been more design and development transferred to places like Raymond, Ohio, and Ann Arbor and Farmington Hills, Michigan.

But Evert admits that in the case of Honda vehicles, the development responsibilities have pretty much been focused on work for vehicles that are North American-centric, vehicles like the Pilot crossover and the Odyssey minivan. As these are vehicles that are predominantly for the North American market, it makes sense to have development work done there.

The Civic is a global vehicle. A vehicle that has been purchased more than 35-million times since the first car went on sale in 1972. Of that number, U.S. sales have accounted for about a third.

Sixth Generation: 1995-2000

Seventh Generation: 2000-2005

Eighth Generation, USA: 2005-2011

Eighth Generation, Europe: 2005-11

So when they set about to develop the 10th generation platform for the two body styles that are fundamental for the car in the U.S. market — the sedan and the coupe — a platform that has global use the decision was made to base the development program in the U.S.

Said plainly: the global development for the global car is being done by a team that is not located anywhere near global HQ. The global leader for the Civic is

Mitsuru Kariya. Evert reports to him. Kariya relocated to Ohio for the program.

Ninth Generation, USA: 2011-16   *Ninth Generation, Europe: 2011-2016*

For those familiar with the Honda engineering position nomenclature, the person in charge is designated the LPL, or "large project leader." For the first-generation Acura RDX crossover, Evert was the LPL. He points out that the RDX was primarily focused on the U.S. market, and the first-gen vehicle was built from 2006 to 2012 in the Marysville plant in Ohio. So that, in large part, explains that.

LPLs have people working for them on various subsystems, like body and chassis. These people are designated "ALPLs"—with the "A" signifying "assistant." Evert says that in this case he's really the ALPL, as Kariya is the person who has primary responsibility for Civic the world over.

But given the fact that Honda has had a non-trivial presence in the U.S. for more than a quarter century, one might well wonder why it has taken so long for design and engineering responsibility of this magnitude to be given to the U.S.

And Evert answers, "There needs to be a maturing of an organization. And now it is time for R&D [as in the U.S. team in Ohio and California] to take that step. The level of difficulty when you take something from a North American product to a global product is unbelievable. You have so many variations coming off of it. It is phenomenal. You have to understand the different features and requirements from around the world - and the factories around the world. So it was felt that now it's time for U.S. R&D to take the next step in developing a global vehicle."

The ninth-generation Civic, model year 2012, was roundly criticized, so much so that the company did a non-trivial refresh for model year 2013.

Evert recalls of what had happened, "Somewhere along the line, we lost those exciting names and the character of some of those vehicles. We began to focus on the North American mass market competitors like the Corolla." Whereas the Corolla was arguably a car for young families and thrifty transportation, the Civic had come to develop a reputation for sportiness and had great appeal to driving enthusiasts. But that reputation was dented.

He goes on to say, "We wanted to make something truly special. So we started the development differently. We started with the goal to simply make the very best compact class car in the world. We were going to do this by going back to the roots of a sporty, fun-to-drive car that is still affordable, spacious and efficient." But they wanted to do a little more.

Rather than checking out the standard suspects in the compact segment in the U.S. market, "We started by benchmarking the best C-class vehicles in the world. This means that we went to Europe and drove not just our competitive set, but C-segment luxury vehicles from BMW, Mercedes and Audi." Evert and his team wanted to make sure that the vehicle they were developing would be up to the comparison. Yes, an Epic Civic.

"The Europeans are very good in terms of sporty handling and excellent road manners, including confidence-inspiring, high-speed stability. That's what we wanted of this Civic," he says.

Remember: Not only is this Civic meant for U.S. highways, but it is intended for other places, including the autobahn.

"To get buy-in on our new direction"—remember, the ninth-generation Civic, fundamentally, was developed with something less-lofty than an A3 in mind, and certainly not high-speed motorways, "we took an early development prototype and had our top global executive drive it and its European competitors at autobahn speeds. We created one truly world-class Civic platform that would satisfy global customers and underpin all Civics—the two-door, four-door and five-door versions."

To put into context what they did to achieve the 10th-generation car: "What did we need to change?" Evert asks, rhetorically, then answers with great understatement, "Besides the chassis, body, interior, and two new powertrains, not too much."

Full disclosure: Not everything in the 10th-generation Civic was developed in Ohio or California. Yes, the engines - a 1.5-liter direct-injected turbo and a 2.0-liter naturally aspirated four - are being manufactured at Honda's engine plant in Anna, Ohio (which, incidentally, is the largest engine plant that Honda has anywhere in the world). But the engines were developed in Japan. They had the resources. They have the expertise.

But the engine that provides what Evert considers to help provide a "leap-frog over the competition" is the 1.5-liter turbo, the first turbo that Honda has had in a car in the U.S. The engine provides 174 hp @ 5,500 rpm and 162 lb-ft of torque @ 1,800 to 5,500 rpm. Evert says that because they wanted the 2016 Civic to be a sporty, dynamic car, "We wanted that power. We needed that power." But, he adds, "Honestly, fuel economy is a huge focus for our company, so in order to get power and fuel economy, we needed the turbo."

The Civic is available with continuously variable transmissions (CTVs); the Civic CVTs are engineered so that power is immediately sent to the drive wheels.

The exterior styling of the sedan was done by Jarad Hall. The two-door was done by Guy Melville-Brown. In both cases, Evert says that the objective was to create a car that is low and wide. The car is 2.9 inches longer, 1.9 inch wider and 0.8 inch lower.

Gary Evert and of the car he developed

As for the interior, Evert says that when it came to the exterior design review in Japan, there was agreement across the board. But for the instrument panel design, things weren't quite as smooth. There were two approaches presented. One that Evert describes as "traditional sporty" the other "more of an elegant style". Evert admits that compared to the "traditional sporty" IP that had been presented, the "elegant" variation wasn't as fully developed for the presentation. So the designers and engineers went "underground" for a few weeks, and refined the IP property. Chief engineer Kariya agreed that it was better. Then he had to make the case for that IP. Which is what he did and which is in the car.

Safety was also an important question. Safety, of course, is not all about steel and structures. Sensors play an ever-increasing role. According to Evert, the 2016 Civic is available with "the most-robust version of the Honda Sensing yet." That's as in safety and driver-assist technology. The system makes use of both millimeter-wave radar and a monocular camera. The suite includes collision mitigation braking, lane departure warning, lane keeping assist, road departure mitigation, and adaptive cruise control with low-speed follow (with low speed going all the way down to zero).

Clearly, the development team worked to go above and beyond, to create something that is truly world class, given their charter.

Source of the text and photos: Excerpts from the article of Vasilash G. Developing the 10th-Generation Honda 28.01. 2016, https://www.adandp.media/articles/developing-the-10th-generation-honda-civic, With the permission of *Gardner Business Media, Inc.*

The other stages of new product development

The real project-based phase of the product development stage begins with the improvement of the ideas selected. The next part of the process has been divided into three main phases:

(I.) The phase of generating and testing the new product concept, which includes

    (1) creation and testing of the product concept,

    (2) the development of the marketing concept and the business plan.

(II.) The phase of product development, which includes

    (1) the actual development and testing of the product,

    (2) the development of the marketing program related to the product.

(III.) The phase of market launch, which includes

    (1) the implementation of the product's mass production,

    (2) the testing the market before launch,

    (3) the finalization of the marketing program for the product launch,

    (4) the launch of the product into the market

The process which is well presented in Figure 14.3. takes two main directions during the parallel activities of development and marketing planning. The continuous feedback about the implementation and evaluation of the tests ensures the relationship between the two. The model presents the process of new product development using a multidisciplinary view and builds on the premise that the success of product innovations has been shown to depend largely on the extent the process can integrate operations management and marketing (Prabhaker, 2001). The study of 120 development projects conducted by Tatikonda and Montoya-Weiss (2001) has confirmed that the integration of these two areas can significantly contribute to the success of innovation, particularly under conditions of the technological, market and environmental uncertainties. The use of this parallel model can help develop the customer-oriented value elements of products, speed up its launch into the market, and reduce the costs of development at the same time.

The present book does not cover the sub-activities of this model, their definition or the conditions of their use.

Figure 14.3. The other phases of new product development

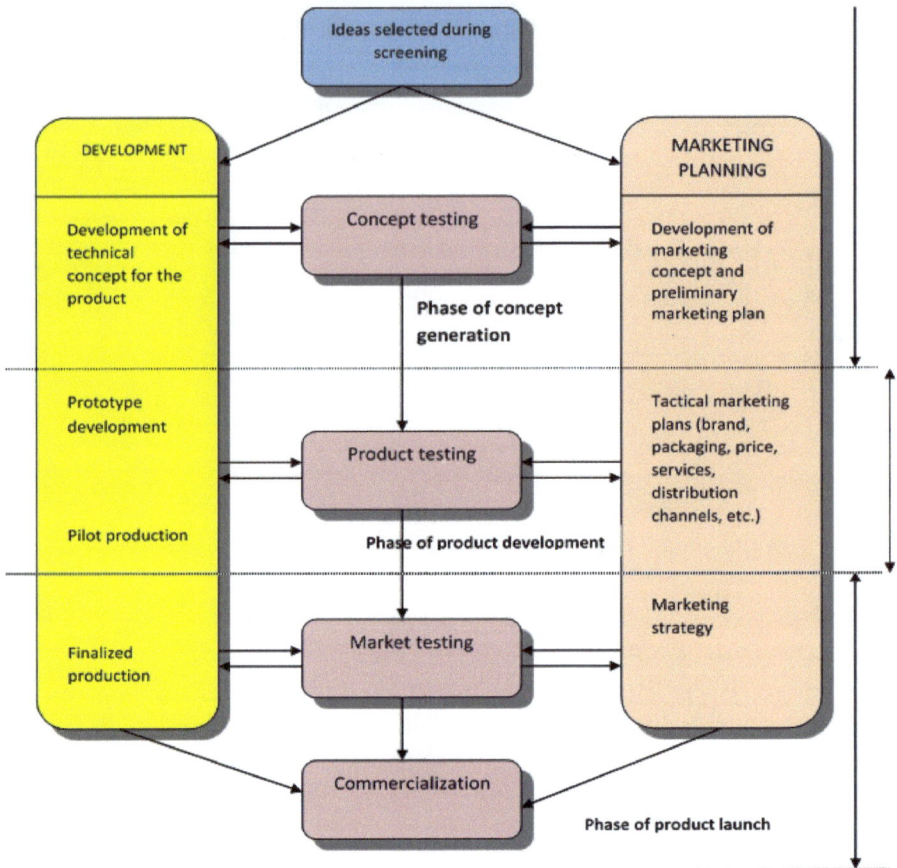

CONCLUSION

Value orientation presented in the first part of the book requires companies that are striving for long term competitive advantage to break free of the conventional way of thinking only in terms of products and services. Value orientation requires the management of the company to:

- Have a good understanding of what value means for the target customers.

- Consciously plan and manage value (translate it into functions and characteristics) by having full awareness of the expectations of the customers and the values offered by competitors, and by taking into account that today's markets require the development and marketing of consistently designed product lines, rather than that of a single product or service.

- Embrace more the possibilities of innovation at a time when customer needs and technology are continuallychanging, and the competition is getting more intensive. Accept that not every innovation becomes the dominant product form. Turn their attention to the additional improvements as soon as the dominant product form emerges.

- Realize that similarly to the dominant product design, the dominant combination of marketing tools emerges too.

- Realize how important it is to market products fast when introducing innovations, especially in the case of new product developments. A so-called parallel development model is proposed, in which the market and technological processes are connected by the different forms of testing, and which allow to fully satisfying customers' needs through the cooperation of marketing and development.

CASE IV-1. RISE AND FALL OF THE 'ROAD KING'

Vasanthi Reena Williams

Everybody worth their salt, living in Mysuru city identify with the Jawa Motorcycles Factory that was once the pride of our country. The company that created uproar between the 1960s and the late 1980s is a name to reckon with. Owning a Jawa was in itself a status symbol and the bikes still have a very sincere cult following to this day. This is true, even when the company is defunct and stopped production way back in 1998. All that remains today is the history and glorious days of its presence in Mysuru. Today, in its place stands a huge residential complex with the new generation living in its premises, oblivious to the fact that there stood in that very place, a well-reputed company that almost rocked the world. The collapse of such a successful venture is a lesson for other companies to set right their strategic management to ensure sustained triumph.

Company background

IDEAL JAWA (INDIA) LIMITED[1] popularly known as **JAWA** started operations with technical collaborations with JAVA Limited of Czechoslovakia in the year 1960-61 with the main objective to manufacture motorcycles among other things. The idea was to deliver to the consumers a product that defined value for money. The logo *"For Ever Bike For Ever Value"* very aptly signifies the ideology behind the product. Ideal Jawa (India) Ltd. was located in Mysuru, a small town in the erstwhile Mysore State (now Karnataka State), situated in the southern part of India. Presently, after Bangalore, the city of Mysuru is the next most prominent and advanced city in the State of Karnataka. Leading IT companies, Textile and manufacturing companies are situated in Mysuru-Infosys, WIPRO, L&T, TVS Bikes , Reid & Taylor, AT&S, Nestle, Software Paradigm, JK Radial Tyre Plant, Wuerth Elektronik, etc., to name a few. Mysuru is also famous for its landmark heritage buildings and therefore, also called the Cultural Capital of the State.

Mysuru is well connected to other cities by direct routes connecting trains and by air via Bangalore. In fact as the story goes, Ideal Jawa (India) Limited[2] would have been established in the Bombay (now Mumbai)- Pune region, had it not been at the instance of the late Sri Jayachamaraja Wadeyar, the last King of the princely state of Mysuru to set up the unit as he was very keen on opening an engineering industry in Mysuru. Mr. Farrokh K Irani and his uncle Rustom accepted the invitation of Sri Jayachamaraja Wadeyar and in 1961, the commercial production of Yezdi bikes started with a technical collaboration with Jawa Limited of Czechoslovakia.

---

[1] Source: http://www.yezdi.com

[2] Source: Deccan Herald, 'Yezdi, a 'beat' from the past'. Available online at: http://www.deccanherald. com/ content/171359/yezdi-beat-past.html

Before this, Jawa bikes were imported to India from Czechoslovakia in 1949. Sri Jayachamaraja Wadeyar provided 26 acres for setting up of the factory and provided all the necessary facilities and support for its inception. The company was granted a licence to manufacture 36,000 bikes a year, though most of the materials required for the manufacture of the motorbikes had to be imported. Mr. Irani looked after the promotion of the motorbikes and the business perspective while his uncle Mr. Rustom was the engineering brain of the company. During the time when Yezdi motorbikes hit the road, there were three other motorbikes in the market, namely Rajdoot, Royal Enfield and Yezdi (imported). It was also a time when scooters had a higher demand in the Indian Market as it was termed a family vehicle. A common grouse during the 1950s – 70s was that the customer had to wait for a long period to get a motor vehicle. However, due to the demand for scooters, the delivery time for the scooter would be fifteen[3] months, something that is unbelievable in today's terms.

The rise of Jawa

Yes, the **Jawa** and **Yezdi** are definitely two among India's best–known motorcycles of the yesteryears. The name Jawa was derived from the first two letters of the partners Janeck, an arms manufacturer and Wanderer[4] in the year 1929. The bikes that rolled out of the factory had 500cc, 18BHP engines. The going was good until World War II in 1946, which forced the temporary stoppage of production. The factory was later taken over by the Germans and later by the Soviets who merged the Jawa trademark with CZ which was another Eastern European motorcycle brand. The 1935 model 250 cc Kyrvaka was the forerunner of the Indian model while the 1954 version known as the type 353, was what first came to India in a knocked down state to be assembled and later enitrely manufactured here. The first bike rolled out of the Mysuru plant on 5th March 1961 and once production started in full swing, there was no looking back over the next thirty - five years. Most of its variants were a phenomenal success mainly because of their extremely simple and yet rugged design that literally made them workhorses sans cumbersome maintenance.

In 1985, the production went up by 85% of installed capacity. They produced 36,000 bikes of 20 models. The employees were paid 57% of the cost of production which was the highest when compared to normal wage bills. The bikes had wide popularity and brand loyalty which was more in the western and northern regions of India. In the mid1980s, it faced stiff competition due to the entry of Japanese 100 CC bikes in India. These bikes were easy to ride and were fuel-efficient when compared to the existing models manufactured in India. However, the Yezdi bikes still held their heads high. Initially, it was available only against the payment of 150 US Dollars in foreign exchange and therefore became

---

[3] Source: http://www.deccanherald.com/content/171359/yezdi-beat-past.html
[4] Source: JAWA: Vintage Heart-Throbs of Mysore. Available online at: http://www.ourkarnataka.com/ Articles/ starofmysore/jawa08.htm

a status symbol and a very prestigious possession.

Manufactured to last a lifetime, many Jawa and Yezdi bikes regularly outlived their owners. Their reliability saw them exported to Afghanistan, Turkey, Egypt and Sri Lanka and also to Nigeria where they were inducted for use by the Police force. This explains why Jawa was the most sought-after bike by many Nigerian students who used to come to India for studies.

The Downfall

The manufacture of Yezdi motorbikes was stopped totally in 1998, with many reasons being cited for its discontinuation. Prominent among them was that the two-stroke motorcycles were less fuel-efficient and the vehicles were not able to adhere to the pollution control norms set by the pollution control board and added to this were the prevailing and ever-increasing labour problems. The setup of the unit was not flexible and hence making major changes in the bike was not feasible. Instituting major changes meant huge capital investment. At that time the company had on its rolls, 2000 employees for manufacturing the sanctioned 36,000 units (per year). When the present day statistics are taken into consideration, a similar company would need to employ around 600 employees for manufacturing a couple of million units.

To ensure that the company would not go defunct, the model of Roadking was modified but that did not create many ripples in the market hence, the management tried to have a tie-up with Japanese companies this was because the Japanese models were lighter, more fuel efficient and had better technology, moreover the Japanese companies were looking not at profitability but were focused on market share. Java(India) Ltd., lost 28% of market share due to the entry of Japanese bikes on India roads. However, both these factors were not feasible for Yezdi.

Salaries paid to the employees were way too high when compared to the salary being paid in the similar sector in the country. The ratio of employees too was disproportionate to the required number which meant that there was over employment. In addition, Bharathiya Mazdoor Sangah played a major role in influencing the employees which further led to disharmony between the management and employees.

Shortcomings of the strategies that could have been corrected

Having set a trend in the automobile industry, as observed from available literature, the company could have adopted a few strategies that could have ensured its presence to this day, making it the most popular bike on the road today.

Every business enterprise is set up with the primary objective of earning goodwill and profits. Therefore, it is important for them to stay agile and proactive by analysing the business environment with reference to the political/legal environment, the economic environment, the social environment and the technological environment.

Of course, we observe from the available literature that the company nearly satisfied the social environment requirements of bringing out the most popular models in bikes for the masses, however the bikes were not fuel-efficient. But in terms of the legal environment, it could not fulfil the regulatory requirements pertaining to pollution control norms. In terms of the economic environment, the company was paying higher than required salary to the employees without having the required funds through the sale of motor vehicles and which was not feasible for the company at that time. In terms of the technological environment, the company could not meet the requirement of fuel efficiency and upgradation like the Japanese bikes which were both fuel efficient, light to handle and economical as well.

It is important for every company to keep in mind the factor forces mentioned through the Porters Industry Analysis: Five Forces Model, which states that every company needs to stay alert reflecting on; threat of new entrants, bargaining power of buyers, bargaining power of suppliers, rivalry among existing players and threat of substitute product.

Further, the company could have periodically conducted an internal analysis to evaluate the individual departments and their respective functioning, conduct a financial audit and focus on its research and development activities. This could have helped the company to a very great extent and could probably have ensured a stiff competition to the Japanese bikes that were making their presence felt in the country. By having completed the company's vulnerability analysis, proper initiatives could be put in place to ease out challenges at the company level and business level. All these strategies could effectively help the company to a great extent, keeping in view various business factors to ensure the fulfilment of objectives.

New beams of hope

However, there is good news for the fans of the motorcycle. **JAWA Forty-Two**[5] is the new incarnation of the legendary JAWA bike and is now being manufactured by Classic Legends Private Ltd, which is a subsidiary of the Mahindra Group and was launched in the second half of 2018. The company is reviving the bike with the New Mahindra Yezdi-350 as well.

Questions and tasks:

1. Discuss the reasons for the downfall. How could it have been avoided?

2. Explain the role of disruptive innovation with reference to this case.

3. How would you describe the financial and marketing activity of the company?

References

Deccan Herald, 'Yezdi, a 'beat' from the past'. Available online at: http://www.deccanherald.com/content/171359/yezdi-beat-past.html

http://www.deccanherald.com/content/171359/yezdi-beat-past.html

http://www.mathrubhumi.com/travel/article/travel_special/when_yezdi_was_the_king/124735/

JAWA: Vintage Heart-Throbs of Mysore. Available online at: http://www.ourkarnataka.com/Articles/starofmysore/jawa08.htm

The Hindu. 'Chaos forces adjournment of hearing on housing project'. Available online at : http://www.hindu.com/2006/05/23/stories/2006052304890300.htm.

Yezdi. http://www.yezdi.com

For racers and enthusiast, the Jawa legacy lives on. Available online at https://www.deccanherald.com/specials/racers-and-enthusiasts-jawa-716037.html

Phadnis, Vive, DH News Service, Bengaluru. Feb 01, 2019. IST. Available online at: https://www.deccanherald.com/specials/racers-and-enthusiasts-jawa.

---

[5] Source: https://auto.ndtv.com

CASE IV-2. VALUE MANAGEMENT AND INNOVATION - THE CASE OF PICK SZEGED ZRT[6]

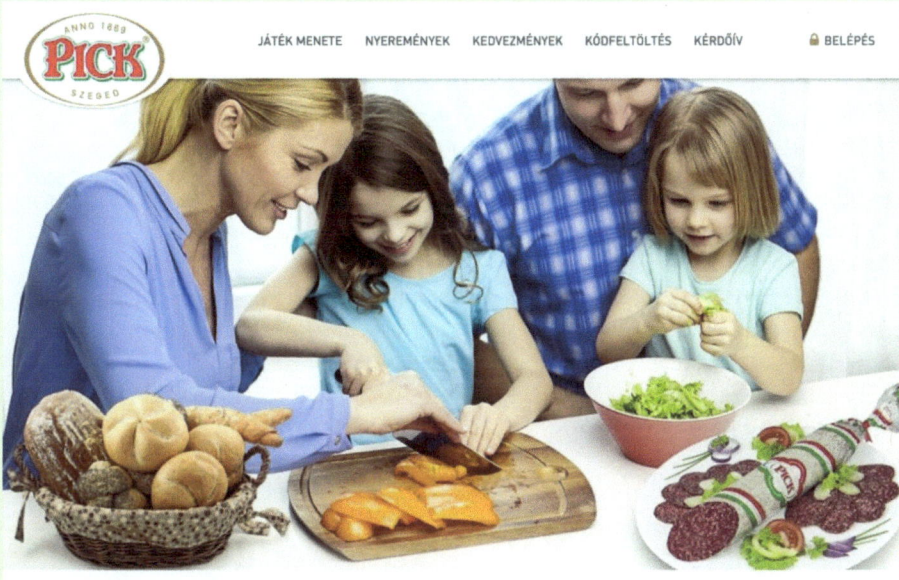

Pick Szeged Zrt is the best-known member of a vertically integrated Hungarian supply chain and it can be described with two phrases: traditional value and innovation.

Pick Szeged Zrt has kept its traditions with unbroken success ever since it was established in 1869. The company's history is interwoven with the history of its best-known product, PICK Wintersalami, which is produced according to the original recipe even today. The experience gained for one and a half centuries has led to Pick's dry products becoming the most popular Hungarian salami at its home market and in several countries abroad, too. The company aims to offer superior products in all categories by being thorough, focused and by striving for the highest quality.

Value management in the supply chain

In most of the cases, a company is only able to continuously deliver excellent customer value if it has a well-organised supply chain. It entails much more than just realising a well-organised co-operation with the suppliers and retailers. Nowadays, only those systems can be successful that can track the products' path all the way from raw material to the end user. Pick Szeged Zrt. happens to belong to such a supply chain - still a rarity in Hungary - which has all the characteristics

---

[6] Zrt is an abbreviation of a Hungarian version of companies, its best tranlation is Private Limited Company by Shares.

to be able to realise a successful value management both in the downstream and upstream stages of the chain.

The Bonafarm Group encompasses the members of the chain. This includes everything from sowing seed production through fodder production and animal husbandry to meat processing. As the Bonafarm website says:

"Each and every product at Bonafarm has its own story written by the company group from the foreword right through to the conclusion. The various chapters are added by our companies, from self-grown ingredients and high-quality production technology to the attentive care of our experienced employees. In addition to this modern approach, each and every letter of this story represents the centuries-old tradition of our predecessors. This is how every Bonafarm story has a happy ending, when top-quality food and drink is served at the table."

What Pick Szeged Zrt. has to offer?

In 2018, Pick Szeged Zrt.'s revenue exceeded HUF 60 billion, 27% of which had been generated by export. The company employs 2200 people and its products can be found in 35 countries, in over 200 supermarket chains. The company distributes its products under three main brands: PICK, HERZ, FAMÍLIA.

The company's best-known product is the PICK Wintersalami, which won the title of 'Hungaricum' in 2014 along with the HERZ Classic Winter salami. Its product offering includes processed meat products such as salamis, dry sausages, hams, cold cuts, liver pates, bacons, fulfilling the highest consumer requirements.

In all its communication and publications, the company places an emphasis on quality so it obviously targets top of the market. Considering, however, that the upper segment of the Hungarian processed meat industry is narrow due to the population's income levels, the product range has been widened downwards, toward the second third of the market. In such a case, the value management's task is to create a lower-positioned brand by proper brand and product differentiation, yet avoid product cannibalisation.

Based on its 2014 strategy, the company has been focusing on the PICK, HERZ and FAMÍLIA brands. The following figure shows the market position (price/quality perception) which clearly demonstrates that the FAMÍLIA brand targets the price-sensitive customers. While both PICK and HERZ are targeting the high quality and high price segment, they target different target segments - PICK focuses on main shopper housewives, HERZ targets young, urban customers-, with very different brand positioning.

The company's primary aim is to present its brand, price and communication policy in the higher market segments that increases brand attractiveness and market share.

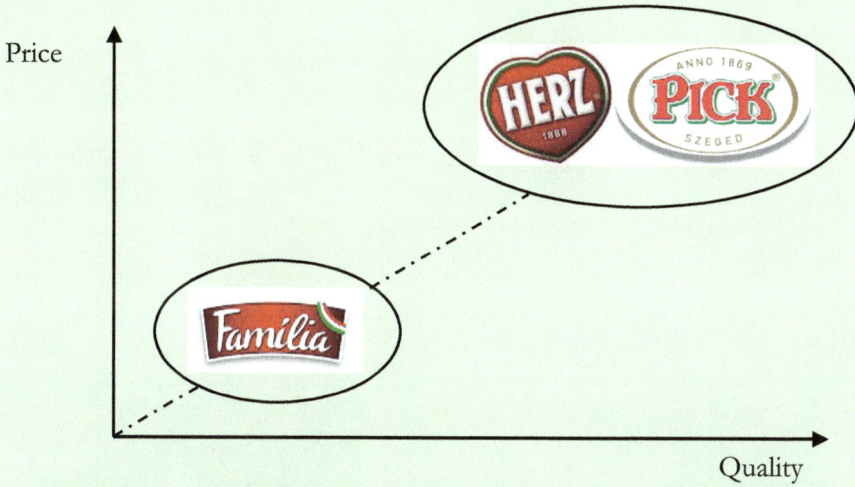

Introducing the PICKSTICK

One of the company's main priority is to increase the sales of dry meats by launching new products. Market research was carried out to explore the possibilities and to better understand the changes in consumer habits. The market research shows that outside-home consumption has a serious growth potential. Moreover, the findings reveal that life is getting faster, households have less and less time for cooking and shopping. Therefore, outside-home or on-the-go consumption is on the rise, which requires the foods which are not consumed at home to be transportable. Nowadays it is increasingly more common to skip a meal or two during the day and to have smaller portions in-between meals, which projects the growth of snack-like products substituting main meals.

Consequently, Pick has started to develop the new product. The company management considered the following criteria important when developing a snack-like product:

- a taste similar to that of the PICK Wintersalami but in the form of a thin dry sausage which can become the most popular Hungarian-type snack in the Hungarian and international market too,

- it should be one serving,

- it should be stored between 5-20 C,

235

- it should be transported easily and should be eaten between (or instead of) main meals,

- it should be consumable out of the packaging and should match on-the-go requirements.

Research and development has resulted in PICKSTICK which fulfils the requirements:

- 60 g product, suitable for single consumption,

- Can be stored and transported easily due to the 5-20 C storage temperature,

- Not requiring cooling makes it possible to also place it somewhere other than the display refrigerator, which ensures easier accessibility,

- The flowpack packaging ensures easy transportability and opening, while it is also possible to take the product out of it with ease as you walk and to eat it right away (without preparation).

PICKSTICK is produced using an innovative technology with co-extrusion alginate casing, which enables efficient production compared to the product in the market which are filled into natural casing, such as intestines.

Thanks to the alginate casing, there is no leftover after chewing which has turned out to be the most common consumer complaint concerning typical sausage products..

The name PICKSTICK, made up of the brand PICK and the stick-like shape of the snack, has been trademarked by the company.

PICKSTICK was introduced in 2015 in Hungary and Germany simultaneously at a targeted retail price of HUF299 and €1,49, respectively.

The Hungarian launch was accompanied by an integrated marketing campaign, making PICKSTICK not only the leading product of the snack category, but also increasing the size of the category. The campaign won the company the "best promotion" award of the Trade Magazin. The Hungarian Association for Innovation greatly appreciated and recognised the introduction of the alginate casing technology with co-extrusion procedure as an important innovation at the 24th Innovation Grand Prize contest.

PICKSTICK, therefore, combines the company's two main values: tradition and innovation.

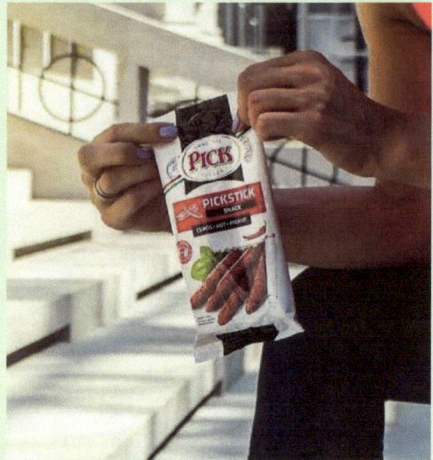

Questions and tasks:

1. Evaluate the product line of Pick Szeged Zrt. and enlist which characteristics constitute value for the customers.

2. Do you agree with the introduction of PICKSTICK? Is there any competition in the product category in Hungary and abroad?

3. How do you evaluate the price of the product?

4. Assuming the continued growth of the snack market, try to find new opportunities for Pick Szeged Zrt. in this segment.

CASE IV-3. THE 'JUGAAD' INNOVATION IN INDIA

S. Gayathri

Kumar, a farmer aged 40, leaves from his farm at Alandurai, a small village in the south Indian district of Coimbatore, every other morning. He travels on his bike along the lush fields of the Siruvani road to nearby markets in order to supply his farm's produce to rural traders.

Shanthi who runs a petty shop has two daughters and owns a two-wheeler from 2010. After sending her daughters to schools, she travels along the length and breadth of the small towns in Erode district to supply her special "Murukku" (a south Indian snack) to the bakeries and teashops. These are common scenes in any agrarian community where farmers and small traders travel to sell their produce. The surprising fact here is that they use electric vehicles and make a difference. Their sense of freedom and convenience come in a sustainable way. The examples given here refer to the widespread use of Ampere vehicles in the rural regions of India. Ampere Vehicles, a humble start-up from Coimbatore had enabled this sustainable revolution through their motto of affordable personal mobility through electric two-wheelers.

The depletion of fossil fuels and the awareness towards sustainability made many countries opt for cleaner fuels. The Government of India, in this regard, set the target to switch entirely to electric vehicles by 2030. There are many questions about the feasibility of this target and the available supporting eco system for this transition. The passenger vehicle segment lacks suitable technology, except for a few players like Mahindra& Mahindra, that manufactures and sells electric cars. While it will take some time before electric cars can be sold to the masses electric two wheelers had already made a good start. "Hero electric" leads the market with its brand recognition and wide distribution. The other players include Avon, Ather energy, Electro Therm, Eco motors, Tork Motors, Tunwal E bike and Lohia Auto. Apart from this, there are small companies like Ampere vehicles that have made a big difference preparing the nation for the giant leap.

In 2008, while the two wheeler market was flooded by conventional vehicles, Ampere vehicles entered the blue ocean of electric vehicles where there was no competition and immense opportunity. A blue ocean refers to the unknown or undeveloped market space which remains unexplored by the competitors. Hemalatha Annamalai, the CEO and founder of Ampere vehicles made up her mind to create a completely new manufacturing sector that had not existed before and which benefits the society in the long run. Her initial customers were farmers and rural traders who were able to save much on their fuel costs. It is worth mentioning that Ratan Tata had invested an undisclosed amount in Ampere in mid 2015. Ampere is the first automobile start-up investment for Mr. Tata, who conceived Nano, one of the world's cheapest cars. Mr.Tata is believed to have earned more than twice in this investment and in September 2018, had sold his entire equity holding in Ampere Vehicles to the Mumbai-based small engine manufacturer Greaves Cotton.

Benefits of Electric Two wheelers

Coimbatore city, called the Manchester of Tamilnadu for its cotton production, is unique in its own way with a rich blend of agriculture, technology and tradition. The people of this area are very industrious and frugal in nature, with their simple ways of life. When Ampere Vehicles marketed the electric bikes among the farmers, it was not an easy job for them. They worked with the farmers and small traders at the grass root level to make them understand the value created and the savings offered by their products.

Eco friendly	Licence not required	Registration not required	Zero maintenance	Affordable charging and no fuel cost

The farmers and the local people were worried about the durability of the vehicle, its suitability to all seasons, the charging options and availability of spare parts. Hemalatha, being a patient and determined player took the task of educating them on all aspects. She made them understand the concepts of zero maintenance, savings on fuel costs, need for non-registration, licence free and other associated benefits. Ampere had been successful in fulfilling the unmet basic need of the farmers, namely "affordable transportation".

The company has now 150 dealers across ten states with an annual production of 60,000 vehicles. The company plans to scale up to a production of 100,000 vehicles in the next 3 to 4 years. Ampere Vehicles has emerged triumphantly in identifying the untapped market demand, created its own market space and pioneered the widespread manufacturing and sales of electric two-wheelers.

Value innovation of Blue Ocean strategy

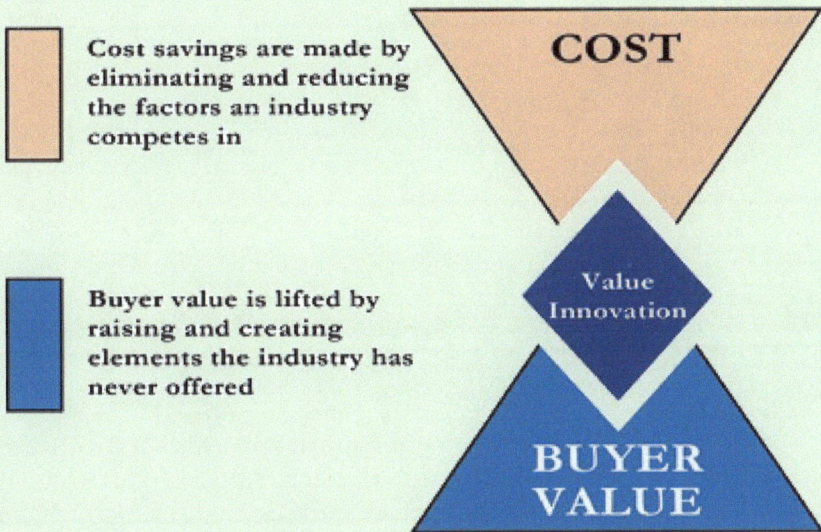

Cost savings are made by eliminating and reducing the factors an industry competes in

Buyer value is lifted by raising and creating elements the industry has never offered

COST

Value Innovation

BUYER VALUE

Source : https://www.blueoceanstrategy.com/tools/value-innovation/

The buyer value for Ampere Vehicles comes in the form of savings on the fuel and maintenance cost for the customers. When it comes to achieving a reduction in cost for the company, the company has defied the fossil fuel technology and adopted the battery technology. The company is engaged in designing, developing, manufacturing and marketing of battery operated electric cycles, two wheelers, three wheelers and custom-built vehicles. They manufacture their own chargers; AC-DC convertors and Intelligent chip integrated lead acid batteries that provide double the life of regular batteries and requires low maintenance.

The rural population of India, supported by the developmental policies of the Government is a viable and promising market with the potential to spend on new categories like education, health care and transportation. Ampere vehicles started their journey of innovation from the villages and had now attained a systematic level of progress through dedicated research and development on consumer needs, design, manufacturing and scalability. For an emerging economy like India, innovation should benefit the people across all levels of social strata. The rural market here is strongly poised offering space for many players.

Jugaad had been the traditional way of referring to innovation in India. Jugaad innovation is a frugal way of innovation involving improvisation of the existing resources. Jugaad when made systematic would become the ultimate solution to develop products for emerging markets. Ampere Vehicles had disrupted the two-wheeler market with their technological innovation and the sustainable aspect here is that their growth is clean and inclusive. It is clean because of the battery technology and inclusive because it has successfully served the farmers and disabled people with its affordable transportation solutions.

However, Corsi and Di Minin (2014) suggest that research in the western world cannot be directly transplanted to emerging economies. In the case of Ampere vehicles, they had managed to disrupt the market and yet the mainstream customers are yet to adopt the new technology. A small analysis on this line, based on secondary data had been made. As Pandit et al (2017), argue, the disruptive innovation success needs to be linked to the disruptive innovation capability of the firm. The multidimensional construct of dynamic capabilities of the organization includes sensing, learning, integrating, and reconfiguring inclusive coordination. (Pavlou and El Sawy, 2011). The methodology adopted by Pandit D (2017) had been used here to study Ampere vehicles based on observations and secondary data sources.

The CEO of the company has a keen sense of the market and is aware that the industry relies to a great extent on the regulation policies of the Government. A look into the timeline of Ampere Vehicles reveals the dynamic evolution of capabilities of sensing, learning, integrating, and reconfiguring inclusive coordination. New product introduction, indigenization Push, Investments, factory expansion and the final merger depict the strong capabilities. Effective leadership of the founder and the value driven organisational culture are additional merits. The company employs a young dynamic workforce more than thirty percent of which are women.

Timeline of Ampere vehicles:

2008   Foundation of Ampere Vehicles; Launch of 3 models of e-scooters

2009   Scooters for differently abled: the Government selects Ampere to supply vehicles for differently abled people

2010   E-Cycle launched : Launch of 3 models of e-cycle

2011   New product : Launch of V60

2012   Indigenization Push : Ampere gets R & D recognition from DSIR, Delhi; Ampere gets selected for a soft loan from TDB, Delhi.

2013   Innovation Galore : Introduction of indigenized charger and IQ battery

2014   Waste Management : Design and supply of battery operated waste management vehicles for Panchayat, First of its kind implementation in India

2015   Tata Joins The Ride :Shri Ratan Tata invests in Ampere

2016   Factory expansion :Ampere inaugurates its second factory

2017   New product: The launch of Reo and expansion of distribution footprint.

2018   New product: The Reo Lithium and Magnus 60V EScooter are launched.

Greaves Invests In Ampere : Greaves Cotton Ltd invests in Ampere and acquires a majority stake

Source : https://amperevehicles.com

The scalability challenges, as pointed out by the CEO, are awareness and finance. The company aims for global operations in the near future. The recent merger with Greaves Cotton is expected to bring intellectual synergies between the two companies. Ampere vehicles had shed the myths and emerged triumphant amidst a turbulent ecosystem in an emerging economy, thus exhibiting the true spirit of innovation.

Questions and tasks:

1. Please explain the essence of 'jugaad' innovation!

2. Please determine the target market of the Ampere vehicles and describe the customer value these products are offering.

3. How do you evaluate the Greaves' investment into Ampere?

References

Christensen, Clayton M. (1997). *The Innovator's Dilemma: When New Technologies Cause Great Firms to Fail.* Boston: Harvard Business School Press.

Corsi, S., & Di Minin, A. (2014). Disruptive innovation… in reverse: Adding a geographical dimension to disruptive innovation theory. *Creativity and Innovation Management*, 23(1), 76-90.

Pandit, D., Joshi, M. P., Sahay, A., & Gupta, R. K. (2018). Disruptive innovation and dynamic capabilities in emerging economies: Evidence from the Indian automotive sector. *Technological Forecasting and Social Change*, 129, 323-329.

Pandit, D., Joshi, M.P., Gupta, R.K. and Sahay, A. (2017). Disruptive innovation through a dynamic capabilities lens: an exploration of the auto component sector in India. *International Journal of Indian Culture and Business Management*, 14(1), 109-130.

Pavlou, P. A., & El Sawy, O. A. (2011). Understanding the elusive black box of dynamic capabilities. *Decision sciences*, 42(1), 239-273.

Websites

https://amperevehicles.com/about/

https://www.moneycontrol.com/news/technology/auto/ratan-tata-exits-ampere-vehicles-earns-2-times-on-investment-2923401.html accessed on 28/01/19

https://www.thehindu.com/business/Industry/ratan-tata-bets-big-on-electric-vehicle-company-ampere-in-coimbatore/article7396545.ece accessed on 28/01/19.

BIBLIOGRAPHY

Abernathy, C.A. – Utterback, M.J. (1978) Patterns of Industrial Innovations, *Technology Review,* 80, pp. 41-47

Acquia (2018) *Closing the Gap: Customer Experience Trends Report 2019,* https://www.acquia.com/resources/ebooks/closing-cx-gap-customer-experience-trends-report

Agárdi I. (2011) Kereskedelmi kontra gyártói márkák, *Marketing-megtakarítás, mérés, média,* III. 3. sz. pp 6-9

Almquist, E., Senior, J. and Blosh, N. (2016) The Elements of Value — Measuring - and delivering - what customers really want, *Harvard Business Review,* September, 2016, Reprint R1609C

Andreasen A. R. and Kotler P. (2008) *Strategic Marketing for Nonprofit Organisations,* Pearson

Anthony, Scott (2016) Kodak's Downfall Wasn't About Technology, *Harvard Business Review,* https://hbr.org/2016/07/kodaks-downfall-wasnt-about-technology

Armstrong G, Kotler, P, Opresnik, M.,O. (2017) *Marketing – An Introduction,* Pearson, Boston

Arrunada, B.–Vazquéz, X. H., (2006), When Your Contract Manufacturer Becomes Your Competitor. *Harvard Business Review,* September, Reprint R0609J, 1–10.

Bagozzi, R.P., Gopinath, M., Nyer, P.U. (1999) The role of emotions in marketing, *Journal of the Academy of Marketing Science,* Spring 1999; 27, 2; 184-206 pp.

Baker, K. (2018) *Key Trends in the Global Beer Market,* Presentation at the International Beer Strategies Conference, London, May 2018, GlobalData

Baldwin, R. – Ito, T. – Sato, H. (2014*): The smile curve: Evolving sources of value added in manufacturing.* Working paper (http://www.uniba.it/ricerca/dipartimenti/ dse/e.g.i/egi2014-papers/ito, downloadwed at June 22, 2015)

Bhattacharjee, D. Moreno, J. and Ortega F. (2016) The secret of customer experience: Putting employees first, *McKinsey & Company,* March, 2016

Bitcoin (2009-2019), *How does Bitcoin work? This is a question often surrounded by confusion, so here's a quick explanation!* Accessed online [*https://bitcoin.org/en/how-it-works*], Access date [24/01/2019].

Bitcoin Wiki (2018), Address, Accessed online [*https://en.bitcoin.it/wiki/Address#A_Bitcoin_address_ is_ a_single-use_token*], Access date [23/01/2019].

Bitcoin Wiki (2018), *How does Bitcoin work?* Accessed online [*https://en.bitcoin.it/wiki/Main_Page*], Access date [24/01/2019].

Bloch, P. H. (1995) Seeking the Ideal Form: Product Design and Consumer Response, *Journal of Marketing,* Vol. 59, 16-29 pp.

Bloch, P. H. (2011) Product Design and Marketing: Reflections After Fifteen Years, *Journal of product Innovation Management,* Vol. 28, Issue 3, pp 378-380

Bloem J, Van Doorn, M, Duivestein, S, Wxcoffier D, Maas, R., Van Ommeren, E. (2014) *The Fourth Industrial Revolution,* Sogeti VINT, Groningen

Booz, Allen and Hamilton (1982) *New Product Management for the 1980s,* Booz, Allen & Hamilton, Chicago, IL.

Bower, J.L. and Christensen C.,M, (1995) Disruptive Technologies: Catching the Wave, *Harvard Business Review,* January-February Issue, 1995

Boxer, I and Rekettye G. (2010) The influence of perceived emotional intelligence on the perceived service value and customer loyalty *ACTA OECONOMICA* 60: (3) pp. 275-293. (2010)

Bradley, J., Loucks, J. Macaulay J. Noronha, A. Wade, M. (2015a) *Digital Vortex – How Digital Disruption is Redefining Industries,* Global Center for Digital Business Transformation, IMD

Bradley, J., Loucks, J. Macaulay J. Noronha, A. Wade, M. (2015b) *New Path to Customer Value,* Global Center for Digital Business Transformation. IMD

Brown, J. (2017) *7 Ways to Outperform your Competitors* in NPD, http://tech-clarity.com/7-npdi/6123

Buday, T. (1989) Capitalizing on brand extension, *Journal of Consumer Marketing*, Vol. 6., No. 4., pp. 27-30

Buffoni, A., de Angelis, A., Grüntges, V. and Krieg, A., (2017) How to make sure your next product or service launch drives growth, *The McKinsey Company* October, 2017

Cecere, G., Corrocher, N., Battaglia, R., D. (2014) Innovation and competition in the smartphone industry: Is there a dominant design? *Telecommunications Policy* http://dx.doi.org/10.1016/j.telpol.2014.07.002i

Chandrupatla, T. R. (2009) *Quality and Reliability in Engineering*, Cambridge University Press, Cambridge, New York, Melbourne, Madrid, Cape Town, Singapore, Sao Paulo, Delhi

Chesbrough, H., W. (2006) *Open Innovation: The New Imperative for Creating and Profiting from Technology*, Harvard Business School Press, Boston, Massachusetts

Chiesa, V., & Frattini, F. (2011). Commercializing technological innovation: Learning from failures in high-tech markets. *Journal of Product Innovation Management*, *28*(4), 437–454. https://doi.org/10.1111/j.1540-5885.2011.00818.x

Chikán Attila – Demeter Krisztina (1999*) Az értékteremtő folyamatok menedzselése (Managing Value Creation Processes)*, Aula, Budapest

Christensen, C., M., Raynor, M.E. and McDonald, R (2015) What Is Disruptive Innovation? *HBR* December

Chryssochoidis, G. (2000) Repercussions of consumer confusion for late introduced differentiated products, *European Journal of Marketing*, Vol. 34 Issue 5/6

Clark-Fujimoto (1996) *The Product Development Imperative: Competition in the New Industrial Marathon*, In: The Relevance of a Decade, Harvard Business School Press, Boston, 278-323 pp.

Cocco, L. and Marchesi, M. (2016), Modeling and Simulation of the Economics of Mining in the Bitcoin Market, *PLoS ONE* 11(10): e0164603. *https://doi.org/10.1371/journal.pone.0164603*

Coleman D. (1997) *Emotional Intelligence*, Bantam Books, New York

Constantinos C. Markides and Paul A. Geroski, (2008) Fast Second, *Harvard Management Update* February 26, 2008 (https://hbr.org/2008/02/fast-second)

Cooper, Juett R. (1998) A multidimensional approach to the adoption of innovation, *Management Decision*, Vol. 36, No. 8. pp. 493-502

Copeland, Melvil T. (1923)   The Relation of Consumers' Buying Habits to Marketing Methods, *Harvard Business Review* 1. April, 282-289 pp.

Court D, Elzinga, D., Mulder, S. and Vetvik O., J. (2009) The consumer decision journey, *McKinsey Quarterly*, June 2009

Crawford, C. Merle (1997) *New Products Management*, Fifth Edition, Irwin, Homewood

Crosby, P. B. (1979)   *Quality is Free: The Art of Making Quality Certain*, McGraw-Hill, New York

Cumming, Brian S. (1998) Innovation overview and future challenges, *European Journal of Innovation Management*, Vol. 1., No. 1., pp 21-29

DeVries, P. D. (2016), An Analysis of Cryptocurrency, Bitcoin, and the Future, *International Journal of Business Management and Commerce, Vol. 1, No. 2, pp.1-9*.

Dhebar, Anirudh (1994) *Complementarity, Compatibility, and Product Change: Braking with the Past?* Harvard Business School, 9-593-120

DHL Global Engineering & Manufacturing Summit October 7, 2015 Amsterdam

Drucker P.F. (2006) *Managing the Non-profit Organisations: Principles and Practices*, HarperCollins, Inc. New York

Drucker, P.F. (1985) *Innovation and Entrepreneurship: Practice and Principles*, HarperBusiness, NY.

Dumond, E.J. (2000) Value management: an underlying framework, International *Journal of Operations and Production Management*, Vol. 20, No. 9, pp. 1062-1077

Eppinger, S. (2011). The fundamental challenge of product design. *Journal of Product Innovation Management*, 28(3), 399–400. https://doi.org/10.1111/j.1540-5885.2011.00810.x

European Commission (2014), The 2015 *Ageing Report*, European Economy 8/2014

Fernandez-Stark, K., Frederick S. and Gereffi G. (2011) *The Apparel Global Value Chain: Economic Upgrading and Workforce Development.* Durham, NC: Duke University Center on Globalization, Governance and Competitiveness, November 2011. http://www.cggc.duke.edu/pdfs/2011-11-11_CGGC_Ex.Summary_Apparel-Global-Value-Chain.pdf

Gandhi, P., Gordon, J., Perrey, J. and Serra, S. (2017) Five questions brands need to answer to be customer first in the digital age, *McKinsey & Company*, July 2017,

Garda, R.A. and Marn M.V. (1993) Price wars, *The McKinsey Quarterly*, No. 3., pp. 87-100

Golub, H and Henry J. (2000) Market Strategy and the price – value model, *www.mckinseyquarterly*.com/strategy/deva00.asp

Grönroos, C. (2011): Value co-creation in service logic: A critical analysis, *Marketing Theory*, 11 (3), 279-301.

Grönroos, Ch. (2007) *Service Management and Marketing: Customer Management in Service Competition*, 3rd Edition, Wiley

Guzzini, E., & Iacobucci, D. (2017). Project failures and innovation performance in university–firm collaborations. *Journal of Technology Transfer*, *42*(4), 865–883. https://doi.org/10.1007/s10961-016-9554-8

Gyöngyössy Z. – Lissák Gy., (2005) *Stratégia, termékpolitika, termékdesign (Strategy, product policy design)*. Akadémiai Kiadó, Budapest

Hart, S. (1996) *New Product Development*, A Reader, The Dryden Press, London.

Hetesi E. és Veres Z. (2013) *Nonbusiness marketing*, Akadémiai Kiadó, Budapest

Hillmann (1971) *Grundlagen einer Warensystematik*, Verlag Neue Wirtschafts-Briefe, Herne/Berlin

Hooley and Sauders (1993) *Competitive Positioning*, Prentice Hall, New York

Hoványi Gábor (2000) Párhuzamos versenyelőnyök a 21. század küszöbén (Parallel competitive advantages in the 21st century) . In: *Új kihívások és vállalati válaszok az ezredfordulón*, Tudományos emlékülés, PTE, KTK, pp. 4-21

How Digital Disruption is Redefining Industries, Global Center for Digital Business Transformation. IMD

https://www.mckinsey.com/business-functions/mckinsey-design/our-insights/more-than-a-feeling-ten-design-practices-to-deliver-business-value

Imai, Masaaki (1991) *Kaizen: The key to Japanese success*, McGraw-Hill, New York

Iványi A.Sz. – Hoffer I. (1999) *Innováció a gazdálkodásban (Innovation in management)*, Aula, Budapest

Jaruzelski, B., Holman, R. and MacDonald, I. (2013) Product Management Gets Stronger, *strategy+business*, February 26, 2013 / Spring 2013 / Issue 7

Johannessen, J-A., Olsen, B. and Lumpkin, G.T. (2001) Innovation as newness: what is new, how is new, and new to whom?, *European Journal of Innovation Management*, Vol. 4., No. 1., pp 20-31

Kenesei Zsófia – Kolos Krisztina (2017) Szolgáltatásmarketing: múlt vagy jövő? (Services marketing: past or future?) http://docplayer.hu/33511745-Kenesei-zsofia-kolos-krisztina-szolgaltatasmarketing-mult-vagy-jovo.html

Kim, W.C. and Mauborgne, R. (1999) Creating New Market Space*, Harvard Business Review*, January – February, pp. 83-95

Knudsen, T., R., Randel, A., Rugholm, J. (2005) The vanishing middle, The *Mckisey Quarterly*, 2005. Nov., 4: 6-9

Kotler, P, Keller, K.L. (2006) *Marketing Management*, Pearson

Kotler, P., Keller, K.L. (2012) *Marketingmenedzsment*, Akadémiai Kiadó, Budapest

Krajewski - Ritzman (1996)   *Operations Management*, Fourth Edition, Addison-Wesley, Reading, Mass.

Krajewski, L.J. and Ritzman, L.P. (2004) *Operations Management: Strategy and Analysis*, 7th ed., Prentice Hall, Inc., Upper Saddle River, New Jersey

Krajewski, L.J., Malhotra, M.K. and Ritzman, L.P (2018) *Operations Management: Processes and Supply Chains,* 11th Edition, Pearson

Kriss, P. (2014) The Value of Customer Experience, Quantified, *Harvard Business Review*, 2014, August.

Kuhnert F., Stürmer C. and Koster A. (2018) *Five trends transforming the Automotive Industry*, Published by PricewaterhouseCoopers https://www.pwc.com/gx/en/industries/automotive/publications/eascy.html.

Lapierre, Jozéé (2000) Customer-perceived value in industrial contexts, *Journal of Business & Industrial Marketing*, Vol. 15 No. 2/3 2000, pp. 122-140,

Levitt, Theodor (1973) "What's Your Product and What's Your Business" in: *Marketing for Business Growth*, McGraw-Hill, New York

Lilien, G., L. and Rangaswamy, A. (2004) *Marketing Engineering: Computer-Assisted Marketing Analysis and Planning*, Revised Second Edition, Traffort Publishing, International

Loeb, W., (2017) These 21 Retailers Are Closing 3,591 Stores -- Who Is Next?, *The Forbes*, Mar 20, 2017 (https://www.forbes.com/sites/walterloeb/2017/03/20/these-21-retailers-are-closing-3591-stores-who-is-next/#5bc4f9c64854)

Loucks, J., Macaulay, J., Noronha, A., Wade, M. (2016) *Digital Vortex*, IMD, Lausanne, Switzerland

Lovelock, Ch., J. Wirtz (2011) *Services Marketing*: Global Edition, 7th Edition, Pearson

Lovelock, Christopher H. (1983) Classifying Services to Gain Strategic Marketing Insights, *Journal of Marketing*, Vol 47, Summer, 9-20 pp.

Lovelock, Christopher H. (1984) *Services Marketing*, Prentice-Hall, Englewood Cliffs

Lovelock, Christopher H. (1992) *Managing Services*, Prentice Hall, Englewood Cliffs

Maechler, N., Neher, K. and Park, R. (2016) From touchpoints to journeys: seeing the world as customers do, *The McKinsey Co.*, March, 2016

Maylor, Harvey (1997) Concurrent new product development: an empirical assessment, *International Journal of Operations & Production Management*, Vol. 17 No. 12, 1997, pp. 1196-1214.

McCarthy-Perreault (1987) *Basic Marketing*, Ninth Edition, Irwin, Homewood

McLuhan, M. and Powers, B., R. (1989) *The Global Village*, Oxford University Press, New York

Meyer and Utterbach (1993) Product Family and the Dynamics of Core Capability, *Sloan Management Review*, Spring pp 29-47

Miller, W.L. and Morris, L. (1999) *4th Generation R and D — Managing Knowledge, Technology, and Innovation*, John Wiley and Sons, Inc.

Mitchell, V. W - Papavassiliou, V. (1999) Marketing causes and implications of consumer confusion, *The Journal of Product & Brand Management,* Vol. 08 Issue 4

Moavenzadeh, j., (2015) The 4th Industrial Revolution: Reshaping the Future of Production

Moore – Pessemier (1993) *Product Planning and Management*, McGraw-Hill Inc., New York

Naware, A. M. (2016), Bitcoins, Its Advantages and Security Threats, *International Journal of Advanced Research in Computer Engineering & Technology (IJARCET), Vol. 5, Iss. 6, pp.1732-1735.*

Nielsen (2015) The sustainability imperative —New insights on consumer expectations October 2015, Nielsen

Nijssen, E.J. (1999) Success factors of line extensions of fast-moving consumer goods, *European Journal of Marketing*, Vol. 33., No. 5/6, pp. 450-469

Nilson, Torsten H (1992) *Value Added Marketing*, McGraw-Hill, London

OECD, 2005, *"The Measurement of Scientific and Technological Activities: Guidelines for Collecting and Interpreting Innovation Data: Oslo Manual,* Third Edition" prepared by the Working Party of National Experts on Science and Technology Indicators, OECD, Paris

Peterson, H. (2017) A German grocery chain with the power to cripple Aldi, Whole Foods, and Trader Joe's is about to invade America, *Business Insider*, May 17, 2017. (http://www.businessinsider.com/lidl-is-opening-stores-in-the-us-2017-5)

Poolton, J. and Ismail, H. (2000) New developments in innovation, *Journal of Managerial Psychology,* Vol. 15 No. 8, pp. 795-811

Prabhaker, Paul (2001) Integrated marketing-manufacturing strategies, *Journal of Business & Industrial Marketing*, Vol. 16 No. 2, pp. 113-128,

Pride-Ferrel (1989) *Marketing - Concepts and Strategies*, Sixth Edition, Houghton Mifflin Co., Boston

Quelch J.A. – Kenny, D. (1994) Extend Profits, Not Product Lines, *Harvard Business Review*, Sept-Oct, pp. 153-160

Radjou N, and Prabhu, J (2014) What Frugal Innovators Do, *HBR*, December, 2014

Rekettye G (2018*) Értékteremtés 4.0 (Value Creation 4.0)* Akadémiai Kiadó, Budapest

Rekettye G and Liu, J. (2018) *Pricing – The New Frontier*, Transnational Press, London

Rekettye G and Rekettye, G., Jr. (2013) Global trends and their influence on future business, performance*, Int. J. Business Performance Management*, Vol. 14, No. 1, pp 95-100

Rekettye G. (1994) *Nemzetközi marketing (International Marketing)* JPTE, KTK, Pécs

Rekettye G. (1997) *Értékteremtés a marketingben, (Value Creation in Marketing)*, KJK, Budapest

Rekettye G., Tóth t. and Malota E. (2015) *Nemzetközi marketing (International Marketing)* Akadémiai Kiadó, Budapest

Rekettye, G., Jr (2017) The future performance of marketing communication – a comparative study *International Journal of Business Performance Management* (IJBPM) 18:(3) pp. 293-306.

Rekettye, G., Jr. (2016) *A marketingkommunikáció jövőjét befolyásoló globális trendek — nemzetközi kitekintés, (Global trends influencing marketing communication – an intenational perspective)* PhD thesis, Győr

Richardson, A. (2010) Touchpoints Bring the Customer Experience to Life, *HBR*, December 02, 2010

Richardson, A. (2010) Understanding Customer Experience, *HBR*, 2010/10

Rochfort, Linda (1991) Generating and Screening New Product Ideas, *Industrial Marketing Management*, Vol. 20, pp. 287-296.

Rogers, E. M. (1962) *Diffusion of Innovations*, The Free Press, New York

Samli, A.C. and Weber, J.A.E. (2000) A theory of successful product breakthrough management: learning from success, *Journal of Product & Brand Management*, Vol. 9 No. 1, pp. 35-55.

Schwabe, K. (2016) *The Fourth Industrial Revolution*, World Economic Forum,

Shan, J., Wade, M., and Noronha, A. (2017) *Life in the Digital Vortex — The State of Digital Disruption:* 2017, IMD International Institute for Management Development

Shapiro B. – Dolan, R.J. (1989) *Performance Curves: Costs, Prices, and Values*, Harvard Business School Publishing, MA, TN 9-590-010, 1-37 pp.

Shapiro B. (2002) *Commodities, Specialties and the Great In-Between*, Harvard Business School Publishing, MA, TN 9-999-005

Sheppard, B., Edson, J. and Kouyoumjian, G. (2017) More than a feeling: Ten design practices to deliver business value, *The McKinsey Quarterly*, December 2017

Sheppard,B., Kouyoumjian, G., Sarrazin, H. and Dore, F. (2018) The Business Value of Design, *McKinsey Quarterly*, October 2018

Stágel Imréné (2008*) Milyen adatokat, információkat kell ellenőrizni a termékeken, a csomagoláson, a termékcímkéken? (What date, information you have to check on the product, packaging and labels?) Working paper*, Nemzeti Szakképzési és Felnőttképzési Intézet

Stein, E. (1996*) Product Development: A Customer-Driven Approach*, Harvard Business School, 9-695-016

Szintay I., Berényi, L., Tóthné Kiss A. (2011) *Minőségügy alapjai (The Basics of Quality)*, Miskolci Egyetem Vezetéstudományi Intézet

Tapscott, D. and Tapscott a. (2018) *Blockchain Revolution*, Portfolio/Penguin, New York

Tatikonda, M.V. and Montoya-Weiss, M.M. (2001) Integrating Operations and Marketing Perspectives of Product Innovation: The Influence of Organizational Process Factors and Capabilities on Development Performance, *Management Science*, Vol. 47, No. 1. pp. 151-172

Thiry, M. (2014). *Strategic value management.* Paper presented at PMI® Global Congress 2014— EMEA, Dubai, United Arab Emirates. Newtown Square, PA: Project Management Institute.

Thomke, Stefan (2001) Enlightened Experimentation: The New Imperative for Innovation, *Harvard Business Review*, February, pp. 67 – 75.

Tolonen, A., Harkonen, J., Haapasalo, H. (2014) Product Portfolio Management—Governance for Commercial and Technical Portfolios over Life Cycle, *Technology and Investment*, 2014, 5, 173-183

Topfer, A. (1995) New Products – Cutting the Time to Market, *Long Range Planning*, Vol. 28, April, 61-77

Törőcsik M. (1996) *Ipari marketing, (Industrial Marketing)* Nemzeti Tankönyvkiadó, Budapest

Törőcsik M. (2016) *Fogyasztói magatartás, (Consumer Behaviour)* Akadémiai Kiadó, Budapest

Utterback,J.M.(1994*). Mastering the dynamics of innovation: How companies can seize opportunities in theface of technological change*. Boston:Harvard Business School Press, Boston

Vargo, S. L., - Lusch, R. F. (2004). Evolving to a new dominant logic for marketing. *Journal of Marketing*, 68, (January), 1–17.

Veres, Z. (2009) *A szolgáltatásmarketing alapkönyve*, Akadémiai Kiadó, Budapest

Waite, T.J., Cohen, A.L. and Buday, R. (1999) Marketing Breakthrough Products, *Harvard Business Review*, Reprint F99606

Wan, T. and Hoblitzell, M. (2014), *Bitcoin: Fact. Fiction. Future. Deloitte University Press.*

Wan, X., Evers, P.T. & Dresner, M.E. (2012). Too much of a good thing: The impact of product variety on operations and sales performance. *Journal of Operations Management,* Vol. 30, No. 4, pp. 316–324.

Weber, K. M., & Rohracher, H. (2012). Legitimizing research, technology and innovation policies for transformative change: Combining insights from innovation systems and multi-level perspective in a comprehensive "failures" framework. *Research Policy*, *41*(6), 1037–1047. https://doi.org/10.1016/j.respol.2011.10.015

Wellington, P., (1995) *Kaizen Strategies for Customer Care*, Pitman Publishing

Wheelwright, S.C. and Sasser Jr., W.E. (1989) The New Product Development Map, *Harvard Business Review*, May-June 1989, pp. 1-14.

Willman, J. (1999) Brands on the run, *The Financial Times*, Friday, 29 October, p. 18

World Bank, 2015, *Data—World Development Indicators*. Washington, D

Yumusak, T., Yilmaz, K. Gungordu, A. (2016) Perceptual Maps of Smart Phones with Multi-Dimensional Scaling Analysis, International *Journal of Research In: Social Sciences* Vol. 6, No.5 pp. 40-45

Zairi, Mohamed (1995) Moving from continuous to discontinuous innovation in FMCG: a re-engineering perspective, *World Class Design to Manufacture*, Vol. 2., No. 5., pp. 32-37

Zalthalm, G., Duncan,R. and Holbeck, J. (1973) *Innovations and Organizations*, Wiley, New York

Zerényi, K. (2016) A Likert-skála adta lehetőségek és korlátok (Possibilities and limits of the Likert scale). *Opus et Educatio,* [S.l.], v. 3, n. 4, aug. 2016. Available at: <http://opuseteducatio.hu/index.php/opusHU/article/view/39/29>. Date accessed: 26 July 2017

Zhang, Q. and Doll, W.J. (2001) The fuzzy front end and success of new product development: a causal model, *European Journal of Innovation Management*, Volume 4 . Number 2., pp. 95 – 112

INDEX